SUPPLY CHAIN
Excellence

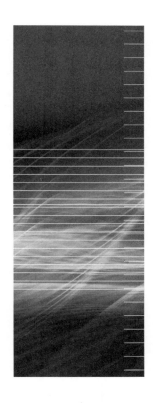

SUPPLY CHAIN
Excellence

A Handbook for

Dramatic

Improvement

Using the

SCOR Model

Peter Bolstorff
Robert Rosenbaum

AMACOM
American Management Association

New York • Atlanta • Brussels • Buenos Aires • Chicago • London • Mexico City
San Francisco • Shanghai • Tokyo • Toronto • Washington, D.C.

Special discounts on bulk quantities of AMACOM books are available to corporations, professional associations, and other organizations. For details, contact Special Sales Department, AMACOM, a division of American Management Association, 1601 Broadway, New York, NY 10019.
Tel.: 212-903-8316.   Fax: 212-903-8083.
Web site: www.amacombooks.org

This publication is designed to provide accurate and authoritative information in regard to the subject matter covered. It is sold with the understanding that the publisher is not engaged in rendering legal, accounting, or other professional service. If legal advice or other expert assistance is required, the services of a competent professional person should be sought.

Library of Congress Cataloging-in-Publication Data

Bolstorff, Peter.
    Supply chain excellence : a handbook for dramatic improvement using the SCOR model / Peter Bolstorff, Robert Rosenbaum.
        p.   cm.
    Includes index.
    ISBN 0-8144-0730-7
    1. Business logistics—Management.   I. Rosenbaum, Robert (Robert G.)
    II. Title.

HD38.5 .B64   2003
658.7—dc21

2002013787

Printing number

10 9 8 7 6 5 4 3 2

To our own supply chain gangs:
Cary, Kristi, and Jenni and
Barb, Nicky, Kelly, and Adam

Contents

List of Tables and Figures

Tables

Figures

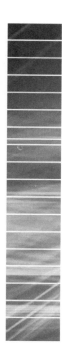

Introduction

Once, at a seminar on the supply chain operations reference model, an executive in attendance opened the Q&A portion with this request: "Most of us don't have good control of our supply chains—inside the company or with trading partners. What two or three things would you say to motivate us to address the supply chain?"

"If you can *define* your supply chain—which isn't hard to do—then you can *measure* it," Peter answered. "Once you've measured it, you'll find the opportunities are so big that you won't need any more motivation. You'll want to *drive continuous improvement* in your supply chain."

This book is not a manifesto on the power of supply chain management. In fact, the two paragraphs that you've just read are the only argument you're going to get in this book about why supply chain management is important.

The rest of this book is about the how—how to achieve these two fundamental principles of supply chain management: Define/measure and drive performance improvement.

Defining Supply Chains

Like most bandwagons, supply chain management (SCM) has been defined and redefined in many ways over the past ten years. To a large degree, the definition depends on your motivation and interest.

A technology provider trying to sell software might align SCM with using advanced planning functionality; a third-party logistics provider (3PL) trying to sell its outsourcing capabilities will align SCM with distribution practices; and a consulting firm selling services will align SCM with its intellectual property. But there really is an objective, unbiased way to define supply chain management; it's a cross-industry standardized model called the Supply Chain Operations Reference—or SCOR—which is the foundation of this book.

Supply Chain Performance Improvement: Eleven Common Themes

Supply chain performance issues can show up in a variety of places including:

- ❑ Profit-and-loss statements
- ❑ Balance sheets
- ❑ Corporate key performance indicators
- ❑ Employee satisfaction surveys
- ❑ Customer report cards
- ❑ Market competitive reports
- ❑ Analyst ratings and commentary

Ultimately, supply chain performance issues reach a point that pushes an enterprise to take action. The next question becomes: How do you take action?

Leading companies in every industry have teams of skilled and motivated business managers working to build integrated supply chains. But many of these managers run into trouble; projects stall and valuable initiatives get scrapped. That doesn't have to be the case. SCOR offers a step-by-step engineering approach that can help you to analyze, design, and improve supply chain performance. Its framework is both rigorous and flexible, allowing it to work in any industry and for any supply chain issue.

In more than thirty projects I've done with SCOR, eleven general business issues have been identified, which seem to cover just about any circumstance. Some of these issues are rare, while others are present in almost every company. Because you have come far enough in your thinking about supply chain management to be reading this book, you'll see yourself and your company in at least a few of the following scenarios.

Scenario One: Building a Technology Investment Plan

A chief information officer deflected pressure to install an enterprise resource planning (ERP) system before 2000—making the case that simply being Y2K compliant was not a good enough reason to put her entire company into the kind of upheaval that such implementations create. Even after Y2K, as she watched the rapid evolution of web-based applications and robust advanced planning systems, she found herself without a technology investment plan that supported the company's business strategy.

Scenario Two: In Search of Return on Investment (ROI)

A company bought its ERP package during the vendor's end-of-quarter push to meet sales goals. The deal included all the latest add-ons—things like customer relationship management, transactional processing, advanced supply chain planning, and web portals providing self-service for customers and suppliers. Now the executive team is looking for an answer to a deceptively difficult question: When will a return on investment start to show up in the earnings statement?

Scenario Three: Creating a Supply Chain Strategy

Three executive vice presidents—for sales, marketing, and operations—assembled their own well-articulated strategies for developing supply chain competence within their departments. Then they invested in application technology, manufacturing processes, and product development—all with measurable success. Now what's missing is a comprehensive blueprint that combines their individual efforts to drive profit and performance across the entire company.

Scenario Four: Implementing a Supply Chain Strategy

The company's top executive for supply chain management assembled a dozen of his brightest managers for a structured brainstorming process—resulting in a list of forty-five high-priority projects. But when the managers began implementation, the results were not encouraging. General managers were being asked to support multiple initiatives with many of the same financial, human, and technical resources. Goals seemed in conflict. They needed to align their objectives and prioritize projects to make good use of the available resources.

Scenario Five: Improving Sales and Operations Planning

The vice president of operations had serious cash-to-cash problems and declining customer satisfaction—all resulting from raw materials shortages, mismatched capacity, poor forecasting, and inventory build-up. The challenge was to address the planning and forecasting issues and put the balance sheet back in shape.

Scenario Six: Meeting Financial Commitments

The CEO promised the board of directors that he would improve earnings per share. An analysis of competitors' balance sheets and income statements indicated the company's direct and indirect costs were out of line, and that its cash-to-cash cycle was too long. The leadership was charged with identifying the right mix of improvements to obtain a predictable result that would satisfy shareholders. The CEO's credibility was now at stake.

Scenario Seven: Building Support and Competence

The director of a new supply chain solutions team needed a proven method for evaluating and implementing projects. That meant being able to show documented examples of its use and evidence that it was both scalable and repeatable. Then she would have to sell the method throughout the organization—which would require executive references and easy, low-cost access to the method itself. Finally, she would have to develop a team that could use the model to deliver early successes.

Scenario Eight: Optimizing Enterprise Resource Planning

As the ERP implementation wore on and business processes were increasingly automated, things suddenly started to go wrong at one organization. The project leader had a pretty good idea why: The company was organized in rigid, vertical functions that directed AS IS practices. But the ERP system was essentially horizontal, organized by transaction flow for purchase orders, sales orders, forecasts, master data, and so on. How could the corporate culture shift from functional management to process management?

Scenario Nine: Maximizing Use of Existing Technology

The vice president of administration was being pressured by her colleagues to replace a two-year-old transactional system with a new, name-brand system offering advanced supply chain planning. But the ROI analysis just wasn't adding up. A more detailed investigation revealed that not all of the business leaders were complaining. In fact, the vice president found a direct correlation between a business leader's satisfaction and the effort he or she had exerted to learn the system. Those who were least satisfied didn't handle implementation very well and as a consequence were utilizing few of the available modules. The challenge was to motivate business leaders to use existing functionality better.

Scenario Ten: Achieving Operational Excellence

The executive team achieved consensus that it would differentiate the company through a strategy of operational excellence. The other choices had been customer intimacy and product innovation. Now that the decision was made, the team had to define—at more tactical levels—the characteristics of an operationally excellent supply chain.

Scenario Eleven: Mergers and Acquisitions

The executive teams from the acquiring and purchased companies needed the acquisition to go smoothly and yield short-term synergies. The challenge was how to leverage efficiencies in material flow, technology platforms, work and information flow, and capacity in the due diligence, integration, and stabilization stages of the merger.

A common thread connects these situations. In every case, SCOR helped define supply chains, measure the size of the issues, and identify necessary changes to improve performance. But beyond the tactical focus, SCOR helped transform organizational behavior from event-driven reflexes to strategic, integrated team behaviors that put more focus on customers. It helped these companies to achieve a core competency in solving supply chain problems and achieving goals.

◼ Why This Book?

Of all the conferences, seminars, and individual coaching sessions in which the SCOR model is discussed, none has been more profoundly rewarding than a workshop for fifteen members of the Japanese chapter of the Supply-Chain Council. It was an intensive lecture and interactive discussion, conducted with simultaneous translation. I walked away from it with two major "a-ha's" about the SCOR model as a reliable roadmap for driving a world-class organization.

❑ *A-Ha Number One.* Education is essential to any successful supply chain project. It's a complex subject—more than just transportation and logistics. It demands a heightened understanding of the organizational benefits in terms of finance, customers, and employees. Executives who understand the payback of supply chain projects will more likely fund and sponsor them.

❑ *A-Ha Number Two.* The SCOR model is a global methodology, understandable in any language. No matter what your company produces, executives everywhere are asking the same basic questions about SCOR: What is it? What is its value? How is it used? Who is using it? How can my organization get started? The answers are the same in any language, as my Japanese friends concurred.

Supply Chain Excellence is a handbook for anybody who is motivated to improve and wants to rely on a rigorous, proven methodology to make sure supply chain improvement is done right. This book tells how one company, Fowlers Inc., started its journey toward supply chain excellence using SCOR.

Specifically, *Supply Chain Excellence* tells how Fowlers navigated through the eight steps of the SCOR project lifecycle:

1. Educating the enterprise about supply chain improvement to gain support
2. Building consensus on where to begin the improvement effort
3. Organizing the effort for success
4. Conducting the proper competitive analysis to define business opportunity
5. Building the burning platform for change
6. Aligning strategy, material flow, work flow, and information flow to focus on the right changes
7. Putting hard numbers to the financial value of change
8. Implementing those changes to achieve sustainable competitive advantage

So this book is a working guide for using SCOR as a tool to help senior managers at every step as they undertake supply chain initiatives. To that end, *Supply Chain Excellence* is structured on a week-by-week project timetable, providing achievable action plans to navigate through the eight steps listed above.

Each chapter focuses on a week's worth of work conducted in two days of meetings with follow-up assignments. Included are sample deliverables, summaries of tasks, tables, and figures to illustrate the step-by-step processes. An important note about Fowlers, Inc.: It is not a real company, and the Fowlers employees are not real people. Fowlers is a compilation of circumstances found in a variety of projects. The purpose was to provide a textbook case study that addresses the broadest range of issues, while maintaining continuity to help readers follow the logic of the SCOR approach from beginning to end.

Peter Bolstorff

Acknowledgments

We would like to acknowledge those individuals who have directly (and indirectly) contributed to this book. The supply chain colleagues at Pragmatek helped drive the spirit of continuous improvement in applying the SCOR framework—hatching a new set of ideas and refinements with each new project. These are manifest in many of the templates included in this book, and they have helped to improve the effectiveness of our clients' supply chains. Specifically, thanks are in order to Tim Allen, Chris Anderson, Doug Bley, Steve Bloom, Joe Comerford, Ron Evans, Chaz Hanisch, David Hendrickson, Bob Jones, Cathy Kuklinski, Sandy Leverentz, Michelle Lohse, Jane Mallin, Steve Manske, Bernie Pieper, Elaine Reichardt, David Strachan, Dan Swartwood, Mike Welch, and Janet Wilson.

The editorial team at Penton Media's *Supply Chain Technology News* and *Transportation & Distribution* also lent an invisible hand in this book by offering a wealth of insights and perspectives from the fast-changing world of supply chain management. It includes Dave Blanchard, Jennifer Kuhel, Dan Jacobs, Perry Trunick, Mary Aichlmayr, and Roger Morton.

Gratitude is in order to the Supply-Chain Council and its organization—specifically Scott Stephens and Michihiko Kitakaze-san for their expertise, feedback, and encouragement. Since 1996, many nights have been spent translating supply chain theory into reliable practice. We are also grateful to Dr. Richard Swanson for his research work in the theory and practice of performance improvement, as well as his mentorship in applying this knowledge through the eras of total quality management, Six Sigma, business process reengineering, lean manufacturing, and now, supply chain. Last, and most important, thanks to the design teams for which it has been such a privilege to serve as their coach. In all cases, we learned more about supply chain performance improvement—saving a lot of money, improving customer satisfaction, and having fun in the process.

1

About the Supply Chain Operations Reference Model

Peter was introduced to the Supply Chain Operations Reference model (SCOR) in the fall of 1996 as part of a newly formed corporate "internal consulting" team for Imation, which had just been spun off from 3M. He'd been using it in supply chain project work ever since. He has also been active in the Supply-Chain Council, involved in the process of improving SCOR, and teaching others how to use it.

So he's heard all the questions. Among those most frequently asked are: What is the Supply-Chain Council? What is SCOR? How do I use SCOR? What is the value to my organization? How do I learn more about SCOR?

The Supply-Chain Council

The Supply-Chain Council (supply-chain.org) is an independent not-for-profit corporation formed in 1996 as a grassroots initiative to develop a supply chain implementation model. Among those involved at the start were individuals from such organizations as Bayer, Compaq, Procter & Gamble, Lockheed Martin, Nortel, Rockwell Semiconductor, Texas Instruments, 3M, Cargill, Pittiglio, Rabin, Todd, & McGrath (PRTM), and AMR Research, Inc. In all, sixty-nine of the world's leading companies participated in the council's founding. Its mission today is to perpetuate use of the SCOR model through technical development, research, education, and conference events. By the end of 2001, the council's technical community had released five subsequent versions of SCOR, providing updates to process elements, metrics, practices, and technology.

The council has attracted about 750 members worldwide, with chapters in Europe, Japan, Korea, Latin America, Australia, New Zealand, and Southeast Asia. Membership is open to any organization interested in applying and advancing principles of supply chain management. There are five special-interest industry groups within the council: aerospace and defense, automotive, electronics, retail and consumer packaged goods, and pharmaceuticals. Members work in private-sector companies, academics, government, consulting firms, and technology service providers. In 2002, a corporate membership cost $2,000 a year and the educator's fee was under $300. With permission, attached as Appendix A is the SCOR overview available in PDF form from the Supply Chain Council's Web site.

The SCOR Framework

SCOR combines elements of business process engineering, benchmarking, and leading practices into a single framework. Under SCOR, supply chain management is defined as these integrated processes: PLAN, SOURCE, MAKE, DELIVER, and RETURN—from the suppliers' supplier to the customers' customer, and all aligned with a company's operational strategy, material, work, and information flows. (See Figure 1-1.)

Here's what's included in each of these process elements:

❑ *PLAN.* Assess supply resources; aggregate and prioritize demand requirements; plan inventory for distribution, produc-

Figure 1-1. SCOR framework.

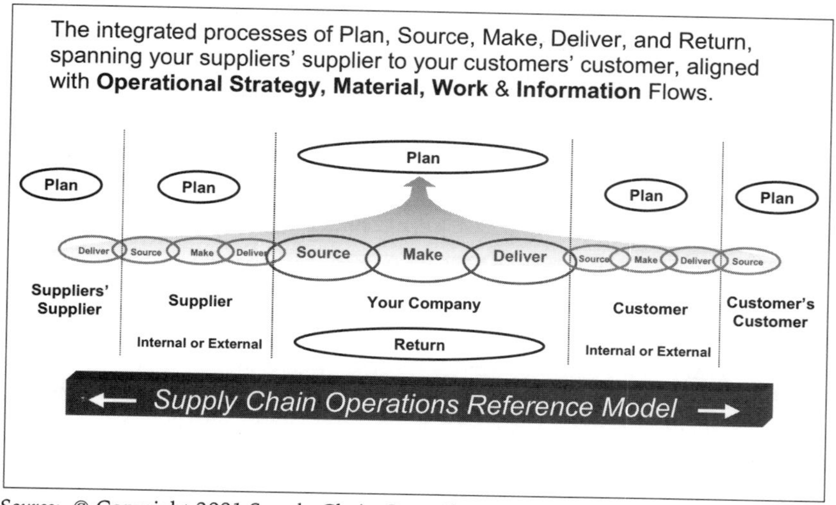

The integrated processes of Plan, Source, Make, Deliver, and Return, spanning your suppliers' supplier to your customers' customer, aligned with **Operational Strategy, Material, Work** & **Information** Flows.

		Plan			
Plan	Plan			Plan	Plan

Deliver Source Make Deliver | Source | Make | Deliver | Source Make Deliver Source

Suppliers' Supplier | Supplier | Your Company | Customer | Customer's Customer

Internal or External | Return | Internal or External

← Supply Chain Operations Reference Model →

Source: © Copyright 2001 Supply-Chain Council, Inc. Used with permission.

tion, and material requirements; and plan rough-cut capacity for all products and all channels.

❏ *SOURCE.* Obtain, receive, inspect, hold, issue, and authorize payment for raw materials and purchased finished goods.

❏ *MAKE.* Request and receive material; manufacture and test product; package, hold, and/or release product.

❏ *DELIVER.* Execute order management processes; generate quotations; configure product; create and maintain customer database; maintain product/price database; manage accounts receivable, credits, collections, and invoicing; execute warehouse processes including pick, pack, and configure; create customer-specific packaging/labeling; consolidate orders; ship products; manage transportation processes and import/export; and verify performance.

❏ *RETURN.* Defective, warranty, and excess return processing, including authorization, scheduling, inspection, transfer, warranty administration, receiving and verifying defective products, disposition, and replacement.

In addition, SCOR version 5.0 includes a series of enable elements for each of the processes. Enable elements focus on information policy and relationships to enable the planning and execution of supply chain activities.

SCOR spans all customer, product, and market interactions surrounding sales orders, purchase orders, work orders, return authorizations, forecasts, and replenishment orders. It also encompasses material movements of raw material, work-in-process, finished goods, and return goods. In version 5.0, SCOR specifically does not address sales processes, product development, and customer relationship management processes.

The SCOR model includes three levels of process detail. In practice, Level One defines the number of supply chains and how their performance is measured. Level Two defines the configuration of planning and execution processes in material flow, using standard categories like stock, to-order, and engineer-to-order. Level Three defines the business process used to transact sales orders, purchase orders, work orders, return authorizations, replenishment orders, and forecasts.

The SCOR Project Roadmap

While the framework seems simple, there are multiple levels of detail integrating more than sixty process steps, 200 metrics, fifty leading practices, and a hundred potential material flow configurations.

Simply having the dictionary does nothing to save money. You need to do something with it. That's what the SCOR Project Roadmap is about. (See Figure 1-2.) In four distinct segments, the roadmap addresses operational strategy, material flow, and work and information flow. The segments are:

1. Analyze your basis of competition, which focuses on supply chain metrics and operations strategy.
2. Configure supply chain material flow.
3. Align performance levels, practices, and systems—the information and work flow.
4. Implement the supply chain changes to improve performance.

Each segment is comprised of deliverables that help a company understand and improve a specific dimension of supply

Are we following this. It's hard to see if we are.

Figure 1-2. SCOR project roadmap.

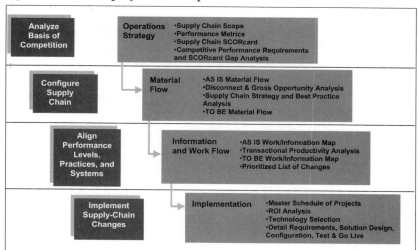

are we doing this?

Source: © Copyright 2001 Supply-Chain Council, Inc. Used with permission.

chain performance. The first segment helps to understand how many supply chains a company has and how they are performing compared to the competition. The second segment helps to optimize material flow inefficiency. The third helps to optimize transactional productivity. And the fourth helps to plan and implement supply chain improvements.

The SCOR Project Roadmap can be applied to projects of narrow scope, or broad-based initiatives that integrate many supply chains across multiple trading partners. It can work for manufacturers, distributors, retailers, value-added resellers, wholesalers, dealers, franchises, and service providers. It does well in a subordinate role within Six Sigma and Lean Enterprise infrastructures. And with a little creativity, the model can even be used to assemble sophisticated Internet-based trading networks, exchanges, and portals.

Applying the SCOR Project Roadmap

For all its power and flexibility, however, there are some essential success factors that are between the lines of the project roadmap—things like change management, problem-solving techniques, project management discipline, and business process engineering techniques. These are essential to a successful project and are not explicitly discussed. In other words, the roadmap can tell you where to go, but it can't teach you how to drive the car. This book attempts to fill in the lines and provide a comprehensive guide to using SCOR. (See Figure 1-3.)

The phases of a SCOR project as detailed in this book are:

- ❏ Educate for support — *Are we doing enough of this at higher levels?*
- ❏ Discover the opportunity
- ❏ Analyze
- ❏ Design
- ❏ Develop and implement

Who is our evangelist?

Educate for Support

Chapter 2 examines this phase of a SCOR project. Find an "evangelist" in the company who has the passion to lead a supply chain project and an executive to actively sponsor it. Both must be willing to invest personal time to learn SCOR. If an

Figure 1-3. SCOR project approach.

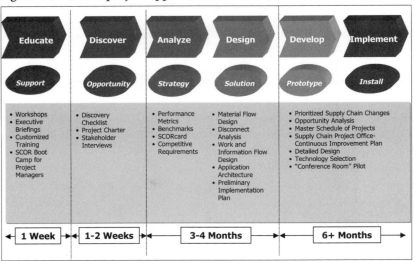

Source: © Copyright 2000 Pragmatek Consulting Group, Ltd. Used with permission.

Times seem short relative to our pace.

executive delegates this initial learning, the organization will probably fail to sustain change over time.

With an evangelist and sponsor in place, the next step of educating for support is to establish a core business team to buy into the approach and commit to supporting a project with words and deeds.

Even as these steps are taking places, there is a larger learning curve that every company must follow. It begins with general education about SCOR—how it works, the language in which it's written, and the available tools to support it. This chapter provides a basic introduction, but is not enough to be considered a general education like the curriculum provided by the Supply-Chain Council.

The next educational step is conceptual application of SCOR to your own company. At this stage, a real supply chain in the company is researched and summarized as a business case. Then, in a classroom environment, a trip with the project road-map is simulated. *Did we do this?*

The third educational stage is to apply the roadmap to a real project, setting expectations and results. Using a formal SCOR coach helps to expand the learning process from individuals to the organizations by including necessary teams.

Finally comes implementation of the supply chain improvement projects.

Discover the Opportunity

Discovery (Chapter 3) helps to form the business case that justifies spending money on a supply chain project. It's where the business team sorts out performance opportunities. The complexity of supply chain discovery can be visualized as a three-dimensional box of questions. The first dimension asks: At what performance level is your supply chain operating? The second dimension asks: Do we have the right strategy as well as the right work, information, and material flows to support the desired performance level? The third dimension asks: What other performance factors will impact the supply chain? These include organizational, process, and technology issues, in addition to understanding people-related factors such as skill, knowledge, and ability.

One of the key outcomes from the discovery step is a project charter, which organizes the supply chain opportunity into the approach, budget, organization, clear measures of successes, and communication plan.

The Analysis Stage

The analysis stage (Chapters 4 through 7) is where the value proposition is articulated in terms that the financial management of a company requires: cash-to-cash cycle time, inventory days, order fulfillment, and other performance factors. SCOR helps the team to prioritize and balance customer metrics with internal-facing metrics: delivery, reliability, flexibility/responsiveness, cost, and assets. The resulting SCORcard provides a direct connection to the balance sheet.

Performance requirements are established with respect to your competition and are prioritized by both definitions of a supply chain—product and channel. These priorities will help in the design phase of a SCOR project. The SCORcard also summarizes actual performance against benchmark performance with a gap analysis that defines the value of improvements.

The Design Phase

The design phase is divided into material flow (Chapters 8 through 13) and work and information flow (Chapters 14 through 18).

Material flow and work/information flow are the two key components for defining AS IS flows, uncovering disconnects in your processes, and mapping out TO BE flows that eliminate these gaps. The basic questions addressed are: What are my material flow problems and what's it worth to solve them? How efficient is my work and information flow and what's it worth to change them?

Is this how way future improvement projects will be identified rather than current sources? Essentially, we currently jump to this step.

Develop and Implement

This book leads to development of a portfolio of projects (Chapter 19) with a projected return on investment. Developing and implementing each project follows industry standard practices of initiating, planning, executing, and formal closing. The detailed development, planning, and rollout of individual projects is the subject of another book.

▋ The Value of a SCOR Initiative

Using the SCOR approach is reliable and predictable with respect to project duration, cost, and benefits. SCOR projects have been carried out with such base metrics as stock price improvement, income statement and balance sheet improvement, purchase of technology through cash-flow improvements, cost reduction, and ERP optimization.

Implementation results include:

❑ An average of 3 percent as a percentage to total sales operating income improvement for the initial SCOR project portfolio derived from cost reduction and service improvement

❑ Two- to six-times return-on-investment (ROI) within twelve months, often with cost-neutral quick-hit projects underway on a six-month timeframe

❑ Full leverage of capital investment in systems improving return on assets (ROA) for fixed-asset technology investments

❑ Reduced information technology (IT) operating expenses through minimized customization and better use of standard system functions

❑ Ongoing updates to a project portfolio, using continuous supply chain improvement to drive profit improvement at 1 percent to 1-to-3 percent per year

2

Building Organizational Support for Supply Chain Improvement

Project planning: Educate for support.

Brian Dowell called out of the blue after getting my name from the Supply-Chain Council—which he had located through a web search on the topic. He was looking for some direction for his company, Fowlers Inc., and described enough motivation within the company to justify making a visit.

We showed up a week later, and Brian, the company's chief operating officer, gave us a warm greeting and a quick overview that demonstrated Fowlers to be a well-run manufacturing conglomerate with the seeds of a supply chain strategy already in place.

The strategy had been developed at the division level by David Able, vice president of operations in the technology products group—one of the three operating units. He had pieced it together with just a little background in supply chain management and a whole lot of operating pain. His efforts had been encouraged by his boss, the division president, who had brought the strategy to the attention of other executives in the company.

They had become an informal "gang" with a common feeling

that, while David's ideas would solve some short-term issues, there had to be a way to solve the company's supply chain problems at a more strategic level. It didn't take much prodding to get this gang to start sharing their thoughts.

"Our products are good for a week, maybe ten days, in the store," said Doris Early, president of the food products group. "We've got to move a lot of inventory around with a lot of speed. And if the FDA were to bring in the label from something we processed six months ago, we need to be able to identify the plant, the line, the day, and the names of everyone on the shift that produced it."

"Our shelf life is short, but not that short," added Martha Tekitch, president of the technology products group. "We also have some other things in common with the food group; we buy a lot of commodities. The prices we pay change day-to-day, but our customers won't let us be quite that flexible."

Brian took over. "There's some seasonality in our sales—and spikes that are harder to forecast."

It all came together as they spoke: many products that have short shelf life and short life cycles; price-sensitive customers sold through various and sophisticated channels with volatility on both ends—demand and supply.

"The demands of our business tear us in every direction all the time," offered Joe Farelong, president of the durable products group. "And even at that, we're a pretty good company. If we had a supply chain that was really good and really strong, nobody would be able to touch us in our markets."

The executives described how a chosen manager, David Able, had outlined the strategy and its main components. They then assigned the strategy to their direct reports in other divisions to make it happen.

Brian wasn't quite ready to admit this at our first meeting, but it was clear what happened: The managers at the next level down thought they'd just been briefed on the latest program-of-the-month and did very little with the strategy. They did take some small steps, identifying a few projects and improving a metric here or there—at the expense of others. But after three months, Brian pushed Joe, Martha, and Doris to join him in looking for outside help.

Without realizing it, Brian had already taken a few important steps to ensure a successful approach. Selling supply chain management into an organization is tough. It's an educational sell to everyone involved. Not only is the reality of an integrated supply chain complex; everyone has his or her own preexisting ideas of what supply chains are all about and how they fit in with operational strategy.

SCOR, as an industry standard, makes the sell easier because it has gained credibility from a long list of successful case studies. But the model can't sell itself, and it can't teach people who aren't ready to learn. That's why any SCOR project will depend on three key roles in the education process. These are the evangelist, an active executive sponsor, and the core members of an executive steering team. Without these, you can't hope for a project's success.

The Evangelist

As is the case with any successful SCOR application, the people who brought SCOR to Fowlers started by educating the organization to support the effort. Their first step was to develop an evangelist. This is the person who is best able to learn the SCOR model; who can sell it to upper management; who has the experience to pilot a project and gain early results; who can become the executive-level project manager for spreading it throughout the business. If nobody steps up to this role, then a SCOR-based project probably cannot succeed.

The evangelist may be self-selected or appointed from above, and his or her first role in this position is typically as project manager of the first SCOR project.

At Fowlers, David Able, vice president of operations in the technology products group, placed himself into the role of evangelist based on his interest in supply chain integration, his diverse background, and his reputation as an effective, influential manager. He was readily confirmed by Brian Dowell, the company's chief operating officer and the man who would quickly assume another important role as the executive sponsor. (See Figure 2-1.)

Figure 2-1. Fowlers' organization chart.

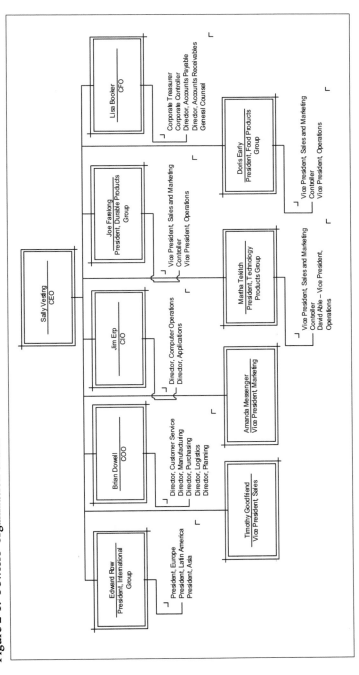

The Evangelist's Resume   Craig?

As the appointed evangelist, David Able had a portfolio of experiences that would help create general understanding of the relationship between financial performance and the central factors of organization, process, people, and technology. Over the course of fifteen years at the company, he had demonstrated a knowledge of "how things work" and built a strong foundation of leadership roles. He had participated on a large-scale reengineering effort a few years before, so he had seen the way an enterprise project works. Those who worked for him also confirmed such important qualities as the ability to teach, communicate, resolve conflict, and add humor at just the right time.

Experience

The right evangelist candidate will have the following experience on his or her resume:

❑ *Financial Responsibility and Accountability.* The former means understanding the details of how cost, revenue, and assets are assembled on a P&L statement and balance sheet—and all the financial impacts in real time. The latter means being able tell the business story behind the numbers. Accountability also means defending executive critique, explaining bad news with confidence, preparing for operations reviews, and having the ability to focus and effectively motivate an entire organization to "hit" a common set of financial goals and objectives.

❑ *Aligning Business Goals with Appropriate Strategy.* Cascading goals is the art of organizing objectives in such a way that every employee understands the higher levels of success and how their day-to-day goals support that success.

❑ *Setting the Organizational Learning Pace.* This means developing an atmosphere that supports team learning and fosters dialogue among individuals, teams, and departments. In managing the performance of individuals and departments, evangelists understand the day-to-day effort that is required to achieve success.

❑ *Multiple Worker Roles.* The evangelist will have first-hand experience in a variety of business functions that map to the SCOR Level One elements PLAN, SOURCE, MAKE, DELIVER, and RETURN. Leading practices in PLAN—such as sales and operations planning, materials requirements planning, and promotional event forecasting—can come from experiences as a demand planner, forecast analyst, supply planner, and inventory analyst. Leading practices in SOURCE and MAKE—such as Kanban, vendor managed inventory, rapid replenishment, cellular manufacturing, Six Sigma, total quality management, ISO 9002, to name a few—can come from experiences as a buyer, production superintendent, master production scheduler, and engineer. Leading practices in DELIVER and RETURN—such as available-to-promise, Cross-Docking, Cellular Kitting and Packaging, and so on—can come from experiences as a customer service representative, transportation analyst, and supervisor for shipping and receiving.

At Fowlers, as vice president of operations for one of the operating divisions, David Able had experience at a number of the above areas. In addition, his previous participation in a well-run reengineering effort had exposed him to disciplines in four important areas necessary to a supply chain improvement: process mapping, recommendations, justification, and project management.

❑ *Natural Talent.* The right evangelist candidate will demonstrate the following five talents in his or her daily work:

1. *A Talent for Teaching.* This is part skill and part art. The skill is showing employees how to perform a task, modeling the appropriate skill, guiding them to understanding, and finally letting them try it on their own. The art is a sixth sense that seems to monitor everyone's level of understanding and automatically adjusts the lesson for each individual. The ability to generate examples or anecdotes in the context of each individual can separate the great teachers from the average ones. Good evangelists are effective storytellers.

2. *A Talent for Listening.* It's important to know when to ask clarifying questions and when not to interrupt, further building an understanding of the speaker's point of view. For a suc-

cessful evangelist, listening and clarifying are more valuable than preaching.

3. *A Talent for Communicating with Executives and Peers.* There are four prerequisites for effective executive communication. The evangelist must:
   ❑ Have earned personal and professional credibility with members of the executive team.
   ❑ Be a subject matter expert.
   ❑ Be able to assemble effective executive presentations.
   ❑ Balance formal group communications (presentations, proposals, meetings) with informal one-on-one communications (lunch, golf, hallway, in private).

4. *A Talent for Using Humor Appropriately.* Every good evangelist has a great sense of humor and can introduce comic relief at just the right moment—whether planned or unplanned. The evangelist doesn't have to be the funniest person in the room; on a team of fifteen people, there will be at least two or three others who can be counted on to help at any time.

5. *A Talent for Conflict Management Among Groups and Peers.* The constraint to successful supply chain projects does not always lie in the technical challenges of material flow and application architecture; it's often in the conflicts that occur between people. Successful evangelists can handle large-group conflicts and individual conflicts—not by squashing them, but by constructively helping one side or both to move toward common ground.

Ward ?

▇ The Active Executive Sponsor

The active executive represents the leaders in the organization who will sign off on resources needed to make the changes happen. This person has the most to gain or lose based on the success of the project, and therefore takes on responsibility to review and approve recommended changes as proposed by the project design team. Behind the scenes, the executive sponsor needs to sell the changes up to the chiefs and down to their managers, eliminate barriers to progress, take ownership of the financial opportunity that comes through improvement, and prepare the organization for implementation.

As with the evangelist, picking the right person is critical. At Fowlers, the obvious choice was Brian Dowell, the chief operating officer and the executive with supervisory responsibility over the directors of planning (PLAN), purchasing (SOURCE), manufacturing (MAKE), logistics (DELIVER and RETURN), and customer service. But organizational role is just one factor.

One of the most simple measures of the right executive sponsor is a simple scale: "more faster" (MF) versus "less later" (LL). It sounds intuitive, but there are a lot of LL executives in the world; they behave in a manner that slows the rate of improvement and lengthens timeframes. The nature of a project lifecycle demands different behaviors at different times from the active executive sponsor. In all cases, the sponsor will be better served by MF behaviors.

Educate-for-Support Behaviors

At the beginning of a project, the focus is to get things moving effectively through process management in the right direction by understanding the strategic value of supply chain management and with increasing influence by encouraging public learning.

MF executives can look at their organizations from a process perspective as opposed to a collection of individuals grouped by a functional silo. They have experienced the power of process improvement and understand key roles in process management. MF executives have invested personal time learning about the strategic value of supply chain in their respective marketplace. That's why they are comfortable learning new things in a public forum regardless of rank—sometimes setting the capacity for change of the entire organization.

MF executives accelerate the educate-for-support step of a project (from six months to a year) by encouraging the progress of the evangelist as a SCOR subject matter expert and by facilitating core team buy-in.

LL executives, when in public, seem to know everything—

whether they do or not. They depend on individual heroics to make things better. Thus, LL executives need to be sold on the merits of supply chain improvement.

Discover the Opportunity: Behaviors of the Executive Sponsor

In this second step of the project lifecycle, the focus is on three essential areas: an understanding of how organizational change occurs, a respect for supply chain complexity, and effective integration business resources. The critical output of this step is a project charter that defines project scope, objectives, organization, benefits, and approach. MF executives understand their sponsor role and can articulate a burning platform for change. They learn to look at supply chain performance needs from various perspectives such as organization, process, people, technology, and strategy. MF executives can accelerate the discovery stage by effectively involving business leaders and participating directly in early steps of the project design.

LL executives, on the other hand, short-circuit the discovery work by directing efforts to focus on one or two prescribed metrics, rather than actively engaging business teams to define scope and opportunity. LLs delegate learning about SCOR to subordinates rather than understanding the basic steps of the SCOR Project Roadmap and associated deliverables themselves.

Analyze Strategy: Behaviors of the Executive Sponsor

At this stage of the project life cycle, important behaviors are respect for the schedule and fueling the fire on the platform for change.

MF executives commit themselves, their evangelists, and their design teams to the detailed, seventeen-week analyze-and-design process. This process involves two days a week for seventeen weeks plus homework for design team members; and half a day two times a month plus homework for executive members of the steering team. The project manager will work on the effort full time, and the MF executive sponsor will spend part of each week in oversight and review.

MF executives spend time understanding how actual, benchmark, and other comparative data were gathered, and they accept the completed analysis at face value as a defined opportunity. MF executives begin laying the groundwork for organizational change by initiating regular communication regarding the relative opportunity, the expected changes, and the approximate timing of the project.

LLs don't attend design team sessions, miss some executive sponsor reviews, and don't put in any personal time. They discount the validity of the data because they don't understand how it was gathered, and they view the analysis as the end of the project—not the beginning.

Design Solution: Behaviors of the Executive Sponsor

At this stage of the project life cycle, the focus is on understanding the integrated nature of material, work, and information flow; sparring with the difficulties of designing improvement; and prioritizing change.

To this end, an MF executive sponsor will spend time each week with the design team learning about the basic steps of producing desired material, work, and information and then leverage this knowledge to educate his or her other C-level peers and prepare them for anticipated supply chain changes.

MF executives constructively challenge the design team on assumptions and results, and invest time to understand the scope and sequence of recommended changes. LL executives are only concerned with the "what," not with how key milestone deliverables were built. LLs use a shotgun approach to savings by initiating all projects at the same time and letting the strong survive.

Who's on our Core Team?

■ Establishing Core Team Buy-In

With Brian Dowell established as the active executive sponsor and David Able in the role of evangelist and project manager, the two were solely responsible for picking the right people as the core of the executive steering team.

This group would bear responsibility to review and approve the project as it progressed. The challenge was to build the right mix of leaders who ultimately will determine the supply chain changes that happen.

It's a reality in any corporation that an executive steering team will contain some members who are not going to be helpful and forward thinking. That's why it was so important for Brian and David to hand-select the core of this team—an elite group that would actively power the steering team to provide constructive oversight and help keep the project moving. Leveraging momentum and knowledge gained in David's earlier supply chain strategy discussions, David and Brian picked the core team to include Doris, Martha, and Amanda Messenger, vice president of corporate marketing and a long-time proponent of organizational alignment.

There are four important criteria for the evangelist and executive sponsor to consider as they begin assembling this core group: collective experience, attitude, effective communication skills, and ability to cope well in chaos.

1. *Collective Experience.* Experience is measured individually and as a team. In either case, important considerations when forming this group include:

❑ *Level of Authority.* Effective steering teams have members at similar levels of authority within the organization who are willing to assign resources from their own teams to the project design effort and who have earned confidence from the senior executive team.

❑ *Cross-Functional Relationships.* An effective steering team member has built relationships over time instead of leaving a trail of "my way or the highway" casualties. The best contributors have a sense of how the whole business works and have developed cooperative relationships with other functional leaders.

❑ *Knowledge Contribution.* Depth of historical perspective is important—not only of business process evolution, but also of the organizational response to change. This perspective can be both good and bad; the right steering team members can balance their addition of knowledge with the occasionally unavoidable attitude of "we've tried that before."

2. *Attitude.* Steering team members don't have to go through a battery of psychological tests to determine whether they have the right attitude. But they should pass three simple ones. First, they should be immune to the "not invented here" syndrome. Second, they should have a controlled and adaptable style of communication. Third, they should be effective learners.

3. *Effective Communication Skills.* An effective steering team sets the learning pace of a SCOR project by dictating the effectiveness of the learning environment. It is deliberate about expectations and spells out exactly the type and frequency of feedback it needs to help keep the project moving. The most valued feedback can be categorized as either critique, opinion, or clarifying dialogue (team learning). Effective critique assumes that the steering team members understand the material under review, have assembled a list of checking questions for the design team, and are comfortable exploring the logic to check the integrity of the work. Opinion is reserved for forks in the road where decisions must be made to go forward with the project. It's rendered only after dialogue and critique. Clarifying dialogue is as simple as asking questions and discussing work both spontaneously and at planned reviews. The objective is simply to understand the design team's point of view with an open mind.

4. *Ability to Cope Well in Chaos.* Many leaders in industry suggest that the closer an organization can get to the edge of chaos without going over, the more it will thrive in today's business environment. Let's not kid ourselves; moving toward the edge of chaos is stressful, so steering team members need an intuitive feel for how close is too close. Process thinking helps set the appropriate distance from the edge. Process

Are we anywhere near chaos? How would we know?

thinkers look at performance as the result of the interaction of process steps. They look at an organization from a systems point of view. They can articulate the basic relationships between supplier inputs (capital, human resources, raw materials), the organization (business processes and functions), the customer (who buys products and services), competitors (who compete for supplies and customers), and other factors that touch the system. The alternative to a process thinker is a functional thinker who stakes out some territory, builds a big wall, and shuts out the rest of the world. This silo behavior is, at some level, an attempt to avoid chaos, and it is one of the first big changes to be addressed in a SCOR project.

The Fowlers core team rounded out the short list for an executive steering team to include Lisa Booker, chief financial officer; Tim Goodfriend, vice president of sales; and Jim Erp, chief information officer.

Do the D&L need a SCOR project?

Phase I

Discover the Opportunity

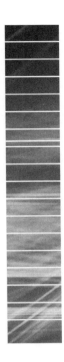

3

Week One: Planning and Organizing

Decide what to work on and how to get started.

Understanding the business reasons for a project and then properly defining the project's scope are critical steps to a successful launch. There are three primary deliverables for this phase. They are 1) the business context summary, 2) a supply chain definition matrix, and 3) an approved project charter. A third deliverable in the first week of active project planning is a complete package of information to be used in the project kickoff meeting.

![] The Business Context Summary

You'll start with a checklist, which outlines information that needs to be reviewed and summarized to gain a full understanding of the business context for supply chain improvement. This information eventually helps to set the direction for supply chain focus.

Just as important, though, are the soft benefits of working through the checklist. By involving the business leaders in this process, they will help set the agenda for the company's supply chain. Getting these important people engaged in the earliest stages of a project has untold value in the change management challenge that all companies face. Understanding their problems, asking for their point of view, and acknowledging their good work goes a long way toward positioning the supply chain as "our thing" versus "a corporate thing."

Assembling the business context summary involves several techniques, including interviewing key stakeholders; scouring the company's website and 10K earnings reports; reviewing existing business plans as found in the annual report or any other big-picture document; locating and reviewing competitive analyses that have been conducted internally or by any external entity; and checking out the reviews of financial analysts readily available on such websites as hoovers.com, forbes.com, market-guide.com, and reuters.com.

Why all the emphasis on public documents and financial statements? Because the important step you're taking is to create the often-overlooked connection between the company's operations and the real-world business goals as defined by the people who hold the purse strings. There's always a temptation to dismiss investors and bean counters as being out-of-touch and unrealistic in their demands. But by understanding their goals and creating a bridge to operations, you can establish the basis for high performance at all levels over the long term.

There are four categories of information that make up a business context summary: 1) strategic background, 2) financial performance, 3) internal profile, and 4) external profile.

Strategic Background

Strategic background summarizes the business and its status in a competitive environment with respect to meeting customer needs and compared to competitors.

A business description is the first component of the strategic background. It describes the enterprise, its businesses, and a high-level view of the competitive landscape. It's the kind of information that managers should be able to develop off the top of their heads, or by drawing from the dozens of such descriptions that probably reside in brochures, memos, and written documents throughout the organization.

A SWOT analysis (strengths/weaknesses/opportunities/threats) is another source of information that describes the relationship between the enterprise and its marketplace. First it outlines where the company surpasses direct competitors and where it falls short. Then it projects ways in which it might grow and ways in which it is most likely to be overtaken by competition. On its surface, the SWOT analysis is a simple, four-point document. But for large or diversified organizations, this can become an intricate document with information on each major product or served market.

Another piece of the strategic background is a value proposition statement, which describes the competitive value of a business from the customer's point of view. Inherent in a good value proposition is an intimate understanding of the business requirements of each major customer or customer segment.

For example, a company such as Procter & Gamble—with a broad range of consumer products sold primarily through large retailers—might view its relationship with Wal-Mart as deserving its own value proposition, owing to Wal-Mart's particular requirements of suppliers. At another level, it might include Wal-Mart in a "large retailer" value proposition, while developing a separate value proposition for its network of distributors that serve grocery chains and small retailers.

Common requirements in a value proposition statement are price, product quality, technical innovation, customized packaging, delivery reliability, order lead-time, strategic relationship, and value-added services like inventory management. Customer value propositions are most frequently found in a market segment analysis; in some cases they are explicitly referred to as customer value propositions; in other cases, they need to be interpreted.

The last important components of the strategic background document are critical success factors and critical business issues.

Critical success factors describe three to five variables most central to an organization's success. (Success is defined as thriving—not merely surviving.)

SCOR defines the following as critical success factors in supply chain performance: delivery reliability, order flexibility and responsiveness, supply chain cost, and effective asset management.

Critical business issues describe how well an organization stacks up against the competition for each of these factors. In each category, the comparative performance level will be rated as disadvantage, parity, advantage, or superior. Sources for these perspectives are not standardized. Good places to look for ratings include annual business plans, quarterly business reviews, annual reports, analyst webcasts, and regular company communications.

■ Fowlers Inc. Strategic Background

Here are highlights of the strategic background for Fowlers, from the business context summary developed by the core team. (For a complete version of the Fowlers business context summary, see Appendix B.)

Business Description

Fowlers Inc., is a billion-dollar conglomerate with worldwide leadership in three businesses: food processing (food products group), optical technology products (technology products group), and business services (durable products group).

Fowlers' food products group is a leading North American supplier of premium fresh and frozen meat products and management services to the food service, retail, on-line retail, and government sectors. Customers include SuperValu, Wal-Mart, Aramark, Simon Delivers, and thousands of independent grocers and specialty restaurants.

Fowlers' technology products group is one of the world's largest independent suppliers of optical storage products and services such as CD-ROM replication, CD-read and CD-write media, title fulfillment and distribution services, and optical drives. Customers include retail leaders like Wal-Mart and Target as well category leaders such as Best Buy, Circuit City, Office Depot, and CompUSA. Fowlers is also a major supplier to the North American original equipment manufacturers (OEMs) for the personal computer market. Customers include Compaq, Dell, and Apple Computer.

Fowlers' durable products group was formed by acquiring one of the fastest-growing suppliers of business services, providing personalized apparel, office supplies, and promotional products to more than 14,000 companies and a million individual wearers. Using a dealer franchise as the route delivery mechanism, Fowlers' durable products group has gained a competitive edge by being both knowledgeable and responsive to individual customers in the markets it serves.

SWOT Analysis

Key points in the SWOT analysis include:

Strengths

❑ The company has superior product quality in the food products group and technology products group.

❑ Low-cost manufacturer status in the technology products group existed prior to outsourcing several key items in the product line.

❑ The durable products group is perceived as the most responsive group in its chosen geographic markets, often delivering products and services on the same day as ordered.

❑ The food products group has a reputation of having superior delivery performance, mitigating criticism of its premium prices in a commodity marketplace.

❑ The company's growth in durable goods exceeded expectations.

Weaknesses

❑ There is a lack of organization-wide assimilation of the new Tier One Enterprise Resource Planning (ERP) system, due to acquisitions and the diversified nature of the company.

❑ Delivery performance is inconsistent, especially in the technology products group. Customer complaints in this market are especially high. Because the market visibility is so high, Fowlers is developing a reputation in customers' eyes as being tough to do business with (hard to place an order with, having incomplete and incorrect product shipments, inaccurate pricing, poor order status capability, and so on). This is negatively impacting overall satisfaction ratings.

❏ Operating income of the food and technical product groups is eroding due to price pressure and too flat of a cost reduction slope.

❏ The company has high, indirect purchasing costs, despite lower cost of sales.

❏ The company's rate of cost increase for customer service is significantly higher than the rate of sales growth.

❏ In spite of sales growth, Fowlers' stock price has taken a hit due to five quarters of poor profit-after-taxes and a bloating cash-to-cash cycle. Analyst criticism focuses on the inability of Fowlers to effectively manage return on assets and integrate profit potential of the business services acquisition.

Opportunities

❏ Leverage commodity buys across all product groups to improve gross profit.

❏ Improve effectiveness and efficiency of order fulfillment to improve customer satisfaction and reduce rate of spending on indirect goods and services (those that don't add value to the product being produced).

❏ Develop more advanced knowledge management capability to add financial value to customers beyond simple price-cutting.

❏ Accelerate market share in the durable products group by introducing an online catalogue for its end customers.

❏ Leverage cost-to-manufacture leadership in the technology products group to increase profits.

Threats

❑ Key competitors in the food products group are buying their way into the marketplace with a "lowest list price" strategy.

❑ While the overall market for the technology products group has been in a period of decline, the group's market share is declining even faster; customer satisfaction scores put this group in the lowest quartile of performance.

❑ Price point in the technology products group is getting too low to meet profit targets with the current cost structure.

❑ Established catalogue apparel companies are potential competitors to the online sales channel being introduced this quarter.

Fowlers' Value Proposition

The Fowlers Inc. corporate value proposition is summarized by profitable growth as the preferred supplier of customers in targeted markets, driven by exceeding customer requirements.

Fowlers' Critical Success Factors

The critical success factors for Fowlers include:

❑ Maintaining revenue contribution by increasing the share of the food products group in existing markets

❑ Driving revenue growth by introducing durable products in the direct-to-consumer market and capturing targeted share

❑ Achieving overall revenue growth for current year, targeted at 10 percent, and achieving targeted after-tax profit of 7 percent

❑ Maintaining an image as technical leader in the technology products group and food products group, while improving overall return on assets and aggressively driving costs out of operations

❑ Improving overall cash-to-cash position

❑ Optimizing the newly implemented Tier One Enterprise Resource Planning system

❑ Effectively integrating assets of the new durable products acquisition

Fowlers' Critical Business Issues

Fowlers' critical business issues are:

❑ Customer satisfaction from all channels in the technology products group is negatively impacting sales.

❑ Profits are disappearing from the technology and food products groups due to higher direct and indirect costs.

❑ Revenue is targeted to grow to $1.02 billion, but actual projection after nine months is $1 billion.

❑ The durable products group integration of online capability is behind schedule.

❑ Inventory and receivables are expanding, seemingly uncontrollably.

❑ Key customers in the food products group are leaving based on price-only criteria.

Financial Performance

Finding information about a publicly traded company's financial health is as easy as knowing the stock symbol and logging on to hoovers.com. There you can find all the ratio statistics, share price analyses, profit reports, and cash flow data necessary to paint the relative financial picture of a company.

To complete a current-state summary, you'll need information about income and cash position. The income statement contains revenue, cost, and profit data. The balance sheet looks at the right-now cash position by documenting assets and liabilities, including inventory.

In the business context document, profit is considered three ways, and each will eventually have its place in planning a supply chain project. First is gross margin: revenue less the cost of goods sold. This picture of profit is usually stated as a percent of total revenue. The second picture of profit is the operating margin (also referred to as operating income), which is gross margin less the costs of sales and administration. In effect, it's the gross margin with all indirect costs removed. It, too, is usually represented as a percent of total revenue. The third picture of profit is economic profit, which is operating margin less taxes and interest expense. The interest expense is impacted by the amount of cash tied up in the business through inventory, receivables, and payables. By using these industry standards for developing your profit picture, you'll gain a better understanding of how your business fits into its competitive environment—an important piece of the business context summary.

In Fowlers' case, the business context summary contains consolidated income (Table 3-1) and balance sheet data (Table 3-2) from the 2000 and 2001 financial reports. In addition, because each operating unit of the company may have its own supply chain requirements, the business context summary contains product group revenue and operating income financial reports for 2000 and 2001 (Table 3-3). This kind of information can be harder to obtain, because not all companies report division financial reports separate from the parent company.

Internal Profile

The internal profile summarizes the physical aspects of the company and other performance measures that influence results. The first physical aspect is the organization chart. In a publicly held company, you can find this at the top level—usually down to the management of operating units or divisions—in the executive profile section of a corporate-reporting website like hoovers.com. Many companies also share this information, including names, titles, and brief biographies, on their own websites. Good starting places for this website hunt are the "inves-

Table 3-1. Fowlers' 2000, 2001 consolidated income statement
(in millions).

	2001	2000	Change
Revenue	1,000	925	8%
Cost of Revenue (Sales) Expense	860	750	15%
Gross Profit	140	175	−20%
%	14%	19%	
Selling, General, Administrative Expenses	70	65	8%
Research and Development Expense	0	0	0%
Total Operating Expenses	930	815	14%
Operating Income	70	110	−36%
%	7%	12%	
Interest Expense	(10)	(11)	−9%
Income Before Tax	60	99	−39%
%	6%	11%	
Income Tax Expense	23	38	−39%
Income After Tax	37	61	−39%
%	4%	7%	
Extra Item Expense	(2)	(3)	−33%
Net Income	35	58	−40%
%	4%	6%	

tor relations" section or "about the company" section of the
website.

The second physical aspect of the internal profile is identification of all locations where the company has operations, including manufacturing sites, warehouses, call centers, technical
service centers, return locations, headquarters, and all contract
locations in cases where these functions are outsourced. This
usually takes some work to collect; good sources for this information are the human resources department, the information
technology department, the purchasing department, and accounting.

The third physical aspect of the internal business context is
a picture of how the organization is set up to plan, manage, and
execute key performance measures or indicators. For example,

Table 3-2. Fowlers' 2000, 2001 consolidated balance sheet (in millions).

	2001	2000	Change
Cash and Short-Term Investments	20	15	26%
Total Receivables	371	370	0%
Total Inventory	215	175	19%
Other Current Assets	50	58	−17%
Total Current Assets	656	618	6%
Property/Plant Equipment Gross	269	248	8%
Accumulated Depreciation	(140)	(123)	12%
Goodwill	122	116	5%
Long-Term Investments	16	14	15%
Other Long-Term Assets	24	25	−4%
Total Net Assets	291	279	4%
Accounts Payables	72	62	14%
Accrued Expenses	31	32	−3%
Short-Term Debt	21	26	−24%
Leases	2	2	20%
Other Current Liabilities	62	60	4%
Total Current Liabilities	188	181	4%
Long-Term Debt	76	71	6%
Minority Interest	11	13	−14%
Other Liabilities	40	43	−6%
Total Liabilities	127	127	0%

Fowlers' organization chart (Figure 2-1) reflects that sales, operations, and finance are controlled at both the corporate level and the business unit level. Note that the chief operating officer is at the same hierarchical level as the product group presidents; corporate directors have potential for conflict with the vice presidents of operations in each product group.

Most companies have such intricacies built into their reporting structures, and it can lead to overly complicated supply chains and delays in making improvements, as politics of control get in the way.

Fowlers' physical locations contain similar quirks. Each product group manages its own manufacturing locations (see Appendix B). But the distribution locations are a mix—some are managed by a product group, and others are managed at the

Table 3-3. Fowlers' product group revenue and operating income performance.

	Food Products			Technology Products			Durable Products		
	2001	2000	Change	2001	2000	Change	2001	2000	Change
Revenue	250	278	-10%	450	463	-3%	300	185	62%
Cost of Revenue (Sales) Expense	215	225	-4%	390	375	4%	255	150	70%
Gross Profit	35	53	-33%	60	88	-31%	45	35	29%
%	14%	19%		13%	19%		10%	8%	
Selling, General, Administrative Expenses	18	20	-10%	35	33	8%	18	13	35%
Research and Development Expense	0	0		0	0		0	0	
Total Operating Expenses	233	245	-5%	425	408	4%	273	163	67%
Operating Income	18	33	-47%	25	55	-55%	28	22	25%
%	7%	12%		6%	12%		6%	5%	

corporate level, demonstrating previous efforts to manage efficiency.

A final element of the internal profile is how success is measured. At Fowlers, there are five key performance indicators, and the project team assessed how each was being managed overall—with a plus indicating meeting or exceeding expectations, and a minus representing performance below expectation.

1. Unit Cost −
2. Line Item Fill Rate −
3. Operating Income −
4. Revenue +
5. Backorders −

External Profile

The external profile categorizes customers and suppliers. To keep it simple, the customer is defined as the entire buying organization, rather than a collection of individual ship-to locations. Market is defined as a group of customers and potential customers who operate on similar business models, (i.e. direct-to-consumer, retail, distributor, and original equipment manufacturer). The external profile also summarizes basic characteristics and requirements of customers and markets. For customers, you can apply the 80/20 rule—those representing 80 percent of the revenue and those representing 80 percent of the profit. For the largest customers, performance criteria is most often found on some kind of report card, master agreement, or purchase order. Also seek to understand how much revenue and profit the company derives, as a percent of your total revenue and profit, from each major channel and market. Assess typical order methods, requirements, and most frequently used terms.

A supplier profile groups the supply base from three perspectives. First, use the 80/20 rule to identify the largest suppliers—the 20 percent that get 80 percent of your material spend. Second, identify the largest suppliers for each major commodity type, such as packaging; tooling; process materials; maintenance, repair, and operations (MRO); value-added service; and so on. This identifies the variety and complexity of the spend. Third, group the supply base in relation to strategic value in the product life cycle. Some suppliers provide the research and development expertise to launch new products quickly and effectively—best at the beginning of the product lifecycle. Others will provide the cost advantage that's important in the product's midlife commodity phase. Still others will provide end-of-life services, such as outsourced fulfillment, to maximize profit during the final decline of the product. This identifies potentially different supply chain requirements and perhaps uncovers some suppliers that are trying to do it all, whether or not they are succeeding.

In Fowlers' case, the customer profile summary yielded seven market/customer channels across all of the product groups:

1. Retail markets, including mass merchant and category killer
2. Distributor/wholesaler markets
3. Direct-to-consumer markets
4. OEM/key account customers
5. The U.S. government
6. Home delivery/route sales markets
7. International markets

Fowlers' key supplier profile included raw material commodity types of resins, packaging, electronic components, live produce, hard goods, and apparel. In addition, the supply base included several contract manufacturers that supply apparel, optical media, precooked food, and computer hardware.

How To Define a Supply Chain

Up to this point in the discovery process, the emphasis has been on gathering individual pieces of information. Now that work starts to show results as the team begins to develop a consensus on how, in the big picture, the company's supply chains are defined. That's an important piece in defining a project's scope—

how far it will reach throughout the organization and what functions and processes will be included.

In most cases, a supply chain is defined by a combination of product, customer, and geography. It can also include financial reporting and other factors. To create its definition, an executive team must take into account all points of view and prioritize the importance of each. Regardless of the outcome, all factors in your defined supply chains need to be aligned and organized together.

Using a matrix can help. To keep it simple, assume that each major geographic market should have its own matrix; for companies with lesser reliance on global business, each major geography might instead be included as a customer channel with its own column. (See Table 3-4 for an example of Fowlers' supply chain definition matrix.) Use the financial reporting perspective to help identify "major" geographies of the world. For example, if a company has profit-and-loss (P&L) reports for Europe, Latin America, the Far East, North America, and Japan, then start with five matrices. To start, choose the geography that either has the most sales, or that is the headquarters' location.

The columns of each matrix represent the customer's point of view, while the rows represent the product point of view. To build the columns on your first matrix, look at how sales regions are tracked, market channels are organized, and customers are segmented. For each customer type, know the delivery requirements (i.e., lead-time, on time–in full, etc.) and the product mix that the customer buys as stated on the purchase order. The goal is to group customers into similar requirements with similar product mix.

To build the rows, look at the highest level of product families or groups. Sometimes this lines up with how the business units are organized and managed, which would be the financial reporting perspective. More often, though, a complicated web of products is mapped to the financial reporting. So the goal is to identify meaningful groups of products or services and link them to financial reporting hierarchy. This is unique to each company and each project.

Most companies seem comfortable defining their supply chains solely by product and financial definitions, regardless of

Table 3-4. Fowlers' supply chain definition matrix.

Supply Chain Definition Matrix		Geography—Customer or Market Channel						
		U.S. Retail Markets	U.S. Distributor Markets	U.S. Direct-to-Consumer Markets	U.S. OEM—Key Accounts	U.S. Government	U.S. Home Delivery	International
Product	Food Products	X	X	X		X		X
	Technology Products	X			X			X
	Durable Products			X			X	

the customer. They worry about how the product is made, what suppliers are involved, and where the revenues and earnings are credited, but they don't build in concern for the customer. This can derail a supply chain's success. First, customer requirements are key factors that drive supply chain performance; while the gross margin may look good, the net profit might suffer due to high SGA (sales, general, and administration) costs of meeting customer requirements. Second, manufacturers are often indiscriminant about what items of the total product line should be available to a particular customer segment. Third, with a product-only view, supply chain costs can evolve to support the delivery requirements of the most aggressive customers—meaning the manufacturer provides superior delivery performance even where it is not needed or valued.

At Fowlers, supply chains could be defined in more than one way. If defined by product, the company would have three supply chains: food, technology, and durable products. If defined by market or customer channel, there would be seven supply chains: retail/mass merchant, distributor/wholesaler, direct-to-consumer, original equipment manufacturer (OEM), U.S. government, home delivery/route sales, and international. Fowlers could also define supply chain by geography, in which case there would be two: international and North America. Lastly, Fowlers could say there are ten supply chains defined by customer and product (count the X's in Table 3-4).

After some sparring, the Fowlers core team used the last approach to identify ten supply chains (Table 3-4). In narrowing the scope for its supply chain project, team members agreed to work with the six supply chains defined by the U.S. sales of technology products and food products (Table 3-5).

Now, with the four basic components of a business context summary complete—strategic background, financial performance, internal profile, and external profile—the team was able to complete their summary (see Appendix B for sample Fowlers' business context summary) and move ahead to the project charter.

◼ The Project Charter

The project charter is created during the planning-and-organization phase to establish a complete understanding of the project's

Table 3-5. Fowlers' supply chain project scope matrix.

Supply Chain Definition Matrix		Geography—Customer or Market Channel						
		U.S. Retail Markets	U.S. Distributor Markets	U.S. Direct-to-Consumer Markets	U.S. OEM—Key Accounts	U.S. Government	U.S. Home Delivery	International
Product	Food Products	X	X	X		X		
	Technology Products	X			X			
	Durable Products							

scope and objectives. The document helps to align assumptions and expectations among executive sponsors, stakeholders, and team members.

Components of the project charter are: scope, business and project objectives, methodology, schedule, deliverables, risks and dependencies, budget, organization chart, roles and responsibilities, stakeholder expectations, benchmarks, benefit analysis, critical success factors, communication plan, and control procedures. (See Appendix C for the Fowlers' supply chain project charter.)

■ Kickoff Preparation

Preparing for the kickoff is like preparing for any other well-organized meeting, with advanced notice, a crisp agenda, and clear and concise presentation materials.

The basic agenda focuses on SCOR, the project approach to be utilized, and the highlights of the project charter, the tasks to be undertaken. Prepare the active executive to incorporate some additional slides to put the project in a strategic business context. (See Figure 3-1 for Fowlers' project kickoff agenda.) Finally, it's a good idea to include some kind of social event. While the real big to-do should be reserved for later on, when you report results from the project, the purpose of the kickoff is to bring everyone into the team's understanding of the project and to make them feel good about the initiative.

Figure 3-1. Fowlers' project kickoff agenda.

Supply Chain Project
Kickoff Presentation

Kickoff Agenda
- Introductions
- Fowler's business case for supply chain improvement
- Supply chain FAQs and the SCOR approach
- Lunch
- Fowlers' project charter
- Social event

Fowlers Business Case
- Technology products group strategy, critical success factors, and critical business issues
- Food products group strategy, critical success factors, and critical business issues
- The case for supply chain improvement

SCOR—FAQs
- What is the Supply-Chain Council?
- What is SCOR?
- How do you use SCOR to achieve supply chain performance improvement?
- How can this apply to my company?
- How can I learn more about SCOR?

Resources
- www.supply-chain.org
- www.totalsupplychain.com
- www.hoovers.com
- www.pgmbenchmarking.com
- gravity.lmi.org/course
- sce.webex.com
- www.pragmatek.com

Project Charter Review
- Business objectives
- Project objectives
- Milestones
- Design team schedule
- Steering team schedule
- Organization chart
- Dependencies
- Communication plan

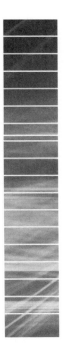

Phase II

Analyze Basis of Competition

4

Week Two: Project Kickoff and SCOR Metrics

Get a good start and begin to design supply chain metrics.

The objectives of this week are to kick off the project effectively and to initiate the design steps for assembling a balanced set of supply chain metrics and associated SCORcard. Two face-to-face days are required for this week. Typically, the project kickoff can be orchestrated in half a day; the remaining day-and-a-half are allocated to identifying and defining supply chain metrics and then initiating homework to collect actual supply chain performance data.

The Project Kickoff

There are two ingredients necessary for a great kickoff. First, all of the right people have to be there. The audience should include all resources participating on the project, including the steering team, executive sponsor, project manager, design team, and extended team. If in doubt about a particular person or group, invite them. Providing the big picture to anyone who might participate in the project makes their support in gathering details more productive.

At Fowlers Inc., executive sponsor Brian Dowell invited the eight-member steering team and ten-member design team as identified on the project charter (Appendix C). He also invited extended team resources from information technology, finance, and site operations in both the technology and food product groups. In all, there were thirty-six people present.

The second ingredient to a great project kickoff is having the right materials presented by the right person. The most popular and effective agenda organizes the content into three basic chunks: 1) setting the strategic context for supply chain improvement, delivered by the executive sponsor(s); 2) providing a high-level overview of how SCOR works, delivered by the coach; and 3) summarizing critical elements of the project charter, delivered by the project manager. (See Figure 3-1.)

To prepare for the kickoff, Brian Dowell, Martha Tekitch, and Doris Early prepared "state of the business" summaries highlighting the issues related to supply chain improvement. Their presentations summarized business plans, strategy, critical success factors, critical business issues, and expectations with regard to supply chain improvement.

The coach prepared the SCOR overview presentation. It provided the big picture of the SCOR framework, highlighted the project roadmap, and gave examples of the deliverables that individuals across the extended team would be asked to produce in the coming weeks.

Finally, David Able prepared key points from the approved project charter, emphasizing the thing most people were interested in—the schedule. He allowed time for everyone to synchronize their own calendars to the rhythm of the project set by the schedules of the design and steering teams, as outlined in the project charter. In addition to the schedule, the kickoff provided the opportunity to set remaining stakeholder interviews left over from Week One. These would be incorporated into a revised project charter, in the stakeholder expectations section.

Mixing the three ingredients—the business context for supply chain improvement, the SCOR education, and key points of the project charter—built a powerful shared vision of the pace of the project. It aligned expectations for deliverables and outlined the effort required for the various project roles.

◼ Reviewing a Balanced Set of Supply Chain Metrics

With the kickoff meeting complete, the real design work begins. Typically, the only people in the room at this point are the project manager, coach, and design team. The first order of business is to define the number of SCORcards to be assembled. In an ideal world, it would be simple: slice financial and customer data by product and by channel to come up with an infinite number of perfectly matched measures. In reality, the many variables in how financial reports and customer-order data are organized makes it difficult to have all three key metric sets—customer, internal, and shareholder—on every SCORcard. For example, a company may report the profitability measures at multiple layers of the organization and the balance sheet only at the corporate level. Or, a company may be able to track revenue by customer channel but costs by product group only. In almost all cases, compromises are necessary between the desire to measure all aspects of every supply chain and the ability to collect that data.

To help the Fowlers design team figure out what data to put on each SCORcard, the coach suggested creating another matrix. This time, the rows would be defined by available customer, internal, and shareholder data. The columns would represent the number of desired SCORcards, which in turn was influenced by the scope of the project.

Fowlers reported balance sheet data at the corporate level, while profits, customer revenue, and order data were all reported at the business group level. After some discussion, the design team agreed that it needed to build three SCORcards: Fowlers consolidated enterprise, food products group, and technology products group. The consolidated SCORcard would omit the customer-facing metrics because these metrics don't add value at the highest level. The product group SCORcards would

Figure 4-1. Fowlers' SCORcard matrix.

Fowlers SCORcard Matrix		Number of SCORcards		
		Fowlers Enterprise	Food Products	Technology Products
Data per SCORcard	Customer Facing	Omit	X	X
	Internal Facing	X	X	X
	Shareholder Facing	X	x Omit Return and Share	x Omit Return and Share

omit the return and per share categories of the shareholder-facing metrics, because such data simply wasn't available at the business group level.

The next order of business was to educate the team on definitions, benchmark sources, metric decomposition, and query strategies for supply chain metrics to be used in each SCORcard. The basis for education was the SCOR Metrics Template. (See Tables 4-1a—customer facing, 4-1b—internal facing, and 4-1c—shareholder facing.)

The education process of the template is conducted like a guided tour. First there is a discussion of the column and row headers with most of the time dedicated to a thorough review of each metric definition and how the data will be collected. The goal is to identify the Level One metrics that will comprise the company's balanced supply chain SCORcard. The best approach is to start with the template list as a default and look for excuses not to deviate from it. Additions and subtractions should only be made with strong reason and passionate argument from the design team.

For example, the director of logistics argued that line-item fill rate ought to be a SCOR metric, though it was not in the original template, and the corporate controller sparred on the necessity and definitions of some of the shareholder metrics. By day's end, the Fowlers design team had identified the following

(text continues on page 54)

Table 4.1a. SCOR metrics template—customer-facing metrics.

	Performance Attribute or Category	Level 1 Performance Metrics	Working Definition	Benchmark Sources	Main Level Two Components	Main Level Three Components	Typical Query
Customer Facing	**Supply Chain Delivery Reliability** The performance of the supply chain in delivering: the correct product, to the correct place, at the correct time, in the correct condition and packaging, in the correct quantity, with the correct documentation, to the correct customer.	Delivery Performance	Delivery Performance measures the percentage of orders delivered "on time and in full" to customer request date AND/OR to customer commit date.	**PMG** On time and in full delivery to customer request and customer commit.	Supplier on time and in full delivery, Manufacturing schedule attainment, Warehouse on time and in full shipment, and Transportation provider on time delivery.	**Not Hardwired Yet** These are departmental and/or diagnostic measures supporting delivery performance goals.	Customer Orders Delivered On Time and In Full / Total Number of Customer Orders; use the PMG survey as a guide.
		Fill Rates	Fill Rates measures the percentage of ship from stock orders shipped within 24 hours of order receipt. Many companies use Line Item Fill Rate as an alternative metric measured by the percentage of lines filled within "committed to" hours of order receipt.	**No Source Identified** Most companies have their own internal gauge as to their competitive rank for Line Item Fill Rate.	Forecast Accuracy has been assigned level 2 relationship to Fill Rate or Inventory Days of Supply	**Not Hardwired Yet** These are departmental and/or diagnostic measures supporting perfect order fulfillment performance goals.	Customer Lines Delivered On Time and In Full Quanitities.
		Perfect Order Fulfillment	Perfect Order Fulfillment measures the percentage of orders delivered "on time and in full" to customers request date AND flawless match of purchase order, invoice, and receipt.	**No Source Identified** This metric is important but difficult to get good statistical benchmark comparisons.	In addition to Delivery Performance components, Supplier Match % and Customer Match %	**Not Hardwired Yet** These are departmental and/or diagnostic measures supporting perfect order fulfillment performance goals.	Customer Orders Delivered On Time and In Full with 100% match of price, item, and quantity on the invoice, packing slip, and customer PO / Total Number of Customer Orders.
	Supply Chain Responsiveness The velocity at which a supply chain provides products to the customer.	Order Fulfillment Lead Time	Order Fulfillment Lead Time measures the number of days from order receipt in customer service to the delivery receipt at the customer's dock. Originally intended only for "Make-to-Order Items," it has been broadened to include stock and engineer-to-order items.	**PMG** Order Receipt to Order Entry, Order Entry to Order Shipment, Order Shipment to Order Receipt, and overall Order Fulfillment Lead Time.	**For Stock Items** Order Receipt to Order Entry, Order Entry to Order Shipment, Order Shipment to Order Receipt **For To Order Items** Order Receipt to Order Entry, Order Entry to Complete Manufacturing to Order Shipment, Order Shipment to Order Receipt. **Backorder Duration** Another frequently used level 2 decomposition is that of Back Order Duration.	**Not Hardwired Yet** These are departmental and/or diagnostic measures supporting cycle time within the order fulfillment processes.	Absolute Value (actual Delivery Date—Order Entry Date) for each line item AND/OR each Customer Order; use the PMG survey as a guide.
	Supply Chain Flexibility The agility of a supply chain in responding to marketplace changes to gain or maintain competitive advantage.	Supply Chain Response Time	Supply Chain Response Time measures the number of days it takes a supply chain to respond to (plan, source, make, and deliver orders) an unplanned significant increase or decrease in demand without cost penalty.	**No Source Identified** This metric is important but difficult to get good statistical benchmark comparisons.	Source Leadtime (often contractual), Order Fulfillment Lead Time for To Order items	**Not Hardwired Yet** These are departmental and/or diagnostic measures supporting cycle time or leadtime improvement in Purchasing, Manufacturing, and Order Management.	Source Leadtime for Contraint Item + Manufacturing Cycle Time for Make-to-Order + Order Fulfillment Leadtime for Stock Items.
		Production Flexibility	Production Flexibility measures the number of days to achieve an unplanned 20% increase or decrease in orders without cost penalty.	**PMG** Upside Production Flexibility.	Days to Increase or Decrease Production Labor, Material, and/or Capacity	**Not Hardwired Yet** None Identified.	Anecdotal Query based Utilization, Staffing Model, and Supplier Contracts; use the PMG survey as a guide.

Source: © Copyright 2001 Pragmatek Consulting Group, Ltd. Used with permission.

Table 4.1b. SCOR metrics template—internal-facing metrics.

Performance Attribute or Category	Level 1 Performance Metrics	Working Definition	Benchmark Sources	Main Level Two Components	Main Level Three Components	Typical Query
Supply Chain Cost The costs associated with operating the supply chain.	Cost of Goods	Cost of Goods measures the direct cost of material and labor to produce a product or service.	**PMG and www.hoovers.com** See COGS under Income Statement and calculate median (middle), superior (average of top 20%), and advantage (midpoint of median and superior) based on the industry or other designated competitors.	Material Cost, Direct Cost of Production, and Indirect Cost of Production.	**Not Hardwired Yet** These are departmental and/or diagnostic measures supporting unit cost goals.	Cost Centers for Material + Cost Centers for Direct Manufacturing Labor + Cost Centers for Indirect Manufacturing Labor.
	Total Supply Chain Management Cost	Total Supply Chain Management Cost measures the direct and indirect costs to plan, source, and deliver products and services. Make costs are often captured in COGS while Return costs are calculated in Warranty/Returns Processing Costs.	**PMG** Order Management Cost, Material Acquisition Cost, SC Related IT Cost, Inventory Carrying Cost, Finance and Planning Related Cost.	Order Management Cost, Material Acquisition Cost, Finance and Planning Related Costs, MIS Costs, and Inventory Carrying Costs.	Customer Service Cost, Outbound Transportation Cost, FG Warehouse Cost, Purchasing Cost, Inbound Transportation Cost, RM Warehouse Cost, Demand Planning, and Supply Planning Transactional Productivity is an alternative Level 3 measure; i.e., divide Material Acquisition Costs (people hours) divided by Purchase Orders.	Map the cost centers that support the supply chain activities listed at Level 3 then add them up; use the PMG survey as a guide.
	SG&A Cost	Sales, General, and Administration Costs measures the indirect cost of sales, administration, engineering, and lab to support a product or service.	**www.hoovers.com** See SG&A under Income Statement and calculate median (middle), superior (average of top 20%), and advantage (midpoint of median and superior) based on the industry or other designated competitors.	Revenue, Indirect Costs.	**Not Hardwired Yet** These are departmental and/or diagnostic measures supporting unit cost goals.	Cost Centers for Sales and Marketing + Cost Centers Administration + Cost Centers Lab and Engineering.
	Warranty / Returns Processing Costs	Warranty / Returns Processing Costs measures the direct and indirect costs associated with returns including defective, planned maintenance, and excess inventory. This includes the entire reverse logistics process.	**No Source Identified** This metric is important but difficult to get good statistical benchmark comparisons.	Returns Warehouse Cost, Returns Authorization Processing Cost, Returns Maintenance Cost, Returns Transportation Cost (inbound from customer, intercompany, and outbound to supplier).	**Not Hardwired Yet** These are departmental and/or diagnostic measures supporting warranty and return cost goals.	Map the cost centers that support the supply chain activities listed at Level 2 then add them up.
Supply Chain Asset Management Efficiency The effectiveness of an organization in managing assets to support demand satisfaction. This includes the management of all assets: fixed and working capital.	Cash-to-Cash Cycle Time	Cash-to-Cash Cycle Time measures the number of days that cash is tied up as working capital.	**PMG and www.hoovers.com** Days Payables Outstanding, Days of Inventory, and Days Sales (Receivables) Outstanding.	Days Payables Outstanding, Days of Inventory, and Days Sales (Receivables) Outstanding.	$ Payables, Cost of Materials, Accounts Payables Terms, Inventory $, Cost of Goods, $ Receivables, Revenue, Accounts Receivables Terms.	[$ Inventory / (COGS / 365)] + [$ Receivables / (Revenue / 365)] − [$ Payables / (Material Cost / 365)] Use PMG Survey as a guide.
	Inventory Days of Supply	Inventory Days of Supply measures the number of days that cash is tied up as inventory.	**PMG and www.hoovers.com** Days RM Inventory, Days WIP Inventory, and Days FG Inventory; for marketguide, calculate median (middle), superior (average of top 20%), and advantage (midpoint of median and superior) based on the industry or other designated competitors.	Days RM Inventory, Days WIP Inventory, and Days FG Inventory.	Within each Level 2 inventory type, inventory classifications differ by organization but often are based on volume and/or turns; classification language often is noted by A items, B items, C items, and D items as well as nonworking inventory.	$ Inventory by classification / (COGS by classification / 365).
	Asset Turns	Asset Turns is calculated by dividing revenue by total assets including both working capital and fixed assets.	**PMG and www.hoovers.com** Revenue, Total Net Assets; for marketguide, calculate median (middle), superior (average of top 20%), and advantage (midpoint of median and superior) based on the industry or other designated competitors.	Revenue, Working Capital, and Fixed Assets.	Use Level 2 metrics as source for Level 3 components.	Revenue $ / Total Net Asset $.

Internal Facing

Source: © Copyright 2001 Pragmatek Consulting Group, Ltd. Used with permission.

Table 4.1c. SCOR metrics template—shareholder-facing metrics.

Performance Attribute or Category	Level 1 Performance Metrics	Working Definition	Benchmark Sources	Main Level Two Components	Main Level Three Components	Typical Query
Profitability Income after cost.	Gross Margin	Gross Margin is calculated by subtracting *Cost of Goods* from Revenue and is most often expressed as a % of the remaining dollars to sales.	**www.hoovers.com** Revenue, Cost of Goods; for marketguide, calculate median (middle), superior (average of top 20%), and advantage (midpoint of median and superior) based on the industry or other designated competitors.	Revenue, Cost of Goods.	Use Level 2 metrics as source for Level 3 components.	(Revenue $ − Cost of Goods $) / Revenue $.
	Operating Income	Operating Income (or Margin) is calculated by subtracting *Cost of Goods AND Sales, General, and Administration (SG&A)* from Revenue and is most often expressed as a % of the remaining dollars to sales.	**PMG and www.hoovers.com** Revenue, Cost of Goods, and SG&A; for marketguide, calculate median (middle), superior (average of top 20%), and advantage (midpoint of median and superior) based on the industry or other designated competitors.	Revenue, Cost of Goods, SG&A.	Use Level 2 metrics as source for Level 3 components.	(Revenue $ − Cost of Goods $ − SG&A Costs) / Revenue $.
	Net Income	Net Operating Income (or Margin) is calculated by subtracting Cost of Goods AND Sales, General, and Administration (SG&A) AND Taxes from Revenue and is most often expressed as a % of the remaining dollars to sales.	**www.hoovers.com** Revenue, Cost of Goods, SG&A, and Taxes; for marketguide, calculate median (middle), superior (average of top 20%), and advantage (midpoint of median and superior) based on the industry or other designated competitors.	Revenue, Cost of Goods, SG&A, and Corporate Taxes.	Use Level 2 metrics as source for Level 3 components.	(Revenue $ − Cost of Goods $ − SG&A Costs − Tax $) / Revenue $.
Effectiveness of Return	Return on Assets	Return on Assets is calculated by dividing Net Operating Income by Total Net Assets.	**www.hoovers.com** Net Operating Income, Total Net Assets.	Revenue, Cost of Goods, SG&A, Corporate Taxes, Interest Expense, and Total Net Assets.	Use Level 2 metrics as source for Level 3 components.	Net Operating Income $ / Total Net Asset $.
Share	Earnings Per Share	Earnings Per Share is the adjusted income available to common shares divided by the diluted weighted average shares outstanding.	**www.hoovers.com** Adjusted income, Diluted weighted average shares outstanding.	**Not Hardwired Yet** None Identified.	**Not Hardwired Yet** None Identified.	Use company formula.

Shareholder Facing

metrics for its balanced supply chain SCORcard and created a
blank SCORcard template (Table 4-2):

- ❏ Delivery performance
- ❏ Line-item fill rate
- ❏ Perfect order fulfillment
- ❏ Order fulfillment lead time
- ❏ Supply chain response time
- ❏ Production flexibility
- ❏ Cost of goods
- ❏ Total supply chain cost
- ❏ Sales, general, and administrative cost (SGA)
- ❏ Warranty/returns processing costs
- ❏ Cash-to-cash cycle time
- ❏ Inventory days of supply
- ❏ Asset turns
- ❏ Gross margin
- ❏ Operating income
- ❏ Net income
- ❏ Return on assets

Building on the momentum of the first day and knowing that
relationships were critical to executing the schedule, Brian, Martha, and Doris sponsored a social event to finish up a day that
all agreed was one of the best project launches anyone at the
company could recall.

Defining Metrics and Benchmarks

The second working day of Week Two begins the process of fill-
ing the blank SCORcard with data. The main objective is to establish a plan to collect actual and appropriate benchmark data
for review during Week Three (Chapter 5). There are two main
sources for the benchmark data. First, statistically significant
supply chain data is available through the Supply-Chain Council's subscription contract with The Performance Measurement
Group (PMG). Second, publicly acquired 10K financial data is

Table 4-2. Fowlers' blank SCORcard template.

	Performance Attribute or Category	Level 1 Performance Metrics	Actual	Parity Median of statistical sample	Advantage Midpoint of parity and superior	Superior 90th percentile of population	Parity Gap Parity—actual
External	Supply Chain Delivery Reliability	Delivery Performance					
		Line Item Fill Rate					
		Perfect Order Fulfillment					
	Supply Chain Responsiveness	Order Fulfillment Lead Time					
	Supply Chain Flexibility	Supply Chain Response Time					
		Production Flexibility					
Internal	Supply Chain Cost	Cost of Goods					
		Total Supply Chain Cost					
		SGA Cost					
		Warranty / Returns Processing Costs					
	Supply Chain Asset Management Efficiency	Cash-to-Cash Cycle Time					
		Inventory Days of Supply					
		Asset Turns					
Shareholder	Profitability	Gross Margin					
		Operating Income					
		Net Income					
	Effectiveness of Return	Return on Assets					

Source: © Copyright 2001 Supply-Chain Council, Inc. Used with permission.

available from sources like Marketguide, Hoovers, *Forbes,* and so on.

PMG data is used to fill in the customer-facing and supply chain–specific internal metrics, while the 10K data fills in the standard internal and shareholder metrics. In addition to those standard sources, the company may have internal sources of benchmark data that may be relevant.

The most important rule of thumb is to calculate the actual data in the same way the benchmarks are calculated. With that in mind, the first part of the day is a guided line-by-line tour of the PMG benchmark survey questions. (See pmgbenchmarking.-com for a sample question.) Using SCOR metric definitions on the worksheets as the formula, the team develops the actual data query for each appropriate SCORcard metric, and then identifies the most appropriate individual on the design team to collect the actual data for a particular metric. The second part of the day focuses on planning the assembly of an industry comparison spreadsheet. This spreadsheet summarizes additional actual and benchmark data for the shareholder metrics of profitability, returns, and share performance at the enterprise level (Table 4-3). The first step in building the comparison is to search for the company name on hoovers.com. From the Search Results screen, click on Financials to access the company's quarterly financial income statement and balance sheet summaries. Under the Free section, choose Annual Financials. Now copy the appropriate shareholder data to the spreadsheet. To search other relevant companies, click on the highlight industry group at the top of the screen. Go through these steps for each publicly traded company to be included in the comparison. The industry comparison list should contain somewhere between fifteen and twenty-five companies and as many industries as necessary to compare relevant competition at the business group level. At Fowlers, the corporate controller, director of logistics, and director of customer service volunteered to collect the PMG data together because they had the easiest access to the financial and customer order information and had extended team resources who could help collect the data. The design team decided to aggregate the food and technology products data for a single submission to PMG. The corporate controller, vice president of sales

Table 4-3. Sample industry comparison spreadsheet and raw data.

Industry Comparison—Computer Network Industry—Hoovers.com	Revenue	SG&A	Cost of Goods	Cash-to-Cash Cycle Time	Inventory Days of Supply	Asset Turns	Gross Margin	Operating Income	Net Operating Income	Return on Assets
YOUR COMPANY—Q3	55.4	40%	60%	151	106	0.84	40%	0%	4%	−0.1%
YOUR COMPANY—2000	176.1	41%	47%	159	98	0.66	53%	12%	7%	7.8%
YOUR COMPANY—2001 Q3 YTD	126.3	49%	61%	205	137	0.64	39%	−11%	−4%	−5.1%
Network Appliance, Inc.	1006.0	29%	40%	58	20	1.58	60%	31%	7%	49.1%
Dassault Systemes S.A.	546.0	57%	14%	91	0	1.17	86%	28%	16%	33.0%
The Titan Corporation	1033.0	25%	73%	105	12	2.23	27%	1%	−2%	3.3%
RadiSys Corporation	340.7	24%	66%	130	87	1.30	34%	10%	10%	12.9%
Convergys Corporation	2320.6	30%	55%	35	0	5.91	45%	16%	9%	70.0%
3COM	2820.9	64%	81%	39	32	1.61	19%	−45%	−34%	−54.9%
Enterasys Networks, Inc.	1071.5	66%	52%	106	64	1.08	48%	−18%	−57%	−15.0%
Jack Henry and Associates	345.5	19%	56%	94	0	2.68	44%	25%	16%	49.8%
Novell, Inc.	1040.1	80%	32%	51	1	1.35	68%	−12%	−26%	−11.8%
Reynolds and Reynolds	1004.0	39%	44%	24	9	4.68	56%	17%	10%	60.0%
Cerner Corporation	404.5	71%	22%	149	9	1.87	78%	6%	26%	8.9%
The Black Box Corporation	827.0	26%	60%	79	38	4.13	40%	14%	8%	43.7%
Integraph Corporation	690.5	40%	63%	86	21	2.44	37%	−3%	1%	−6.3%
Entrada Networks, Inc.	25.7	66%	67%	130	98	1.56	33%	−33%	−82%	−38.6%
Inrange Technologies Corporation	233.6	35%	45%	197	102	1.03	55%	20%	6%	15.6%
Computer Networks Industry	100.0	35%	52%	58	20	1.23	48%	13%	2%	12.0%
Networking Solutions Q3	38.9	50%	47%	NA	NA	NA	53%	3%	NA	NA
Storage Solutions Q3	16.5	17%	91%	NA	NA	NA	9%	−8%	NA	NA
Industry Parity	618	40%	55%	99	27	1.57	45%	8%	6%	8%
Industry Advantage	970	33%	43%	69	13	2.90	57%	17%	11%	30%
Industry Superior—90th Percentile	1321	25%	30%	38	0	4.24	70%	25%	16%	52%

(continues)

Table 4-3. (Continued).

Raw Data (in millions)	Revenue $	SG&A $	Cost of Goods $	Inventory $	Receivable $	Total Assets $	Gross Margin $	Operating Income $	Net Operating Income $
YOUR COMPANY—Q3	55.4	22.3	33.3	38.6	45.5	262.3	22.1	-0.2	2.4
YOUR COMPANY—2000	176.1	72	83.2	22.4	43.6	268.6	92.9	20.9	12
YOUR COMPANY—2001 Q3 YTD	126.3	62.3	77.3	38.6	45.5	262.3	49	-13.3	-5
Network Appliance, Inc.	1006.0	292	402	22.5	187	636	604	312	75
Dassault Systems S.A.	546.0	313.5	78.3	0	181	467	467.7	154.2	90
The Titan Corporation	1033.0	260.7	757	25.4	347	463.3	276	15.3	-18.7
RadiSys Corporation	340.7	82.9	223.8	53.2	68.2	262.8	116.9	34	32.6
Convergys Corporation	2320.6	685.5	1268.7	0	413	523.1	1051.9	366.4	215.5
3COM	2820.9	1814.6	2287.3	200.1	286.8	2334.8	533.6	-1281	-965.4
Enterasys Networks, Inc.	1071.5	711.2	558.4	98.2	210.9	1322.2	513.1	-198.1	-606
Jack Henry and Associates	345.5	65.9	193.9	0	117.1	172.1	151.6	85.7	55.6
Novell, Inc.	1040.1	833	327.9	0.9	227	1027.4	712.2	-120.8	-272.9
Reynolds and Reynolds	1004.0	389.4	442.9	10.8	125	286.2	561.1	171.7	99.6
Cerner Corporation	404.5	288.8	90.1	2.2	188	288.5	314.4	25.6	105.3
The Black Box Corporation	827.0	216.2	493.9	51.1	160.9	267.3	333.1	116.9	64.2
Integraph Corporation	690.5	275.9	438.2	25.3	178.9	377.5	252.3	-23.6	10.1
Entrada Networks, Inc.	25.7	17	17.2	4.6	4.4	22	8.5	-8.5	-21.2
Inrange Technologies Corporation	233.6	81.5	105	29.3	80	301.1	128.6	47.1	14.3
Computer Networks Industry	100.0	35	52	2.8	18.8	108.7	48	13	2.4
Networking Solutions Q3	38.9	19.5	18.3	NA	NA	NA	20.6	1.1	NA
Storage Solutions Q3	16.5	2.8	15	NA	NA	NA	1.5	-1.3	NA

Source: © 2000 Pragmatek Consulting Group, Ltd. Used with permission.

and marketing in the food products group, and—in his capacity as vice president of operations for the technology products group—David Able took responsibility for assembling the industry comparison spreadsheet. Because the team knew that Fowlers' own data was listed in the "conglomerates industry" on hoovers.com, they requested that food and computer industries be added to the list for more specific comparisons to the operating groups. The director of applications planned to assign an extended team resource to help with actual data queries and collection.

The key deliverables that the team set out to produce (which will be needed for review during Week Three) include: a completed PMG benchmark survey form, a completed industry comparison spreadsheet, and updated SCORcards with actual query results.

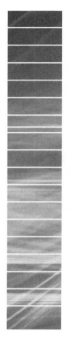

5

Week Three: Benchmarks, Competitive Requirements, and Steering Team Review Number One

Start to put data to work.

The objectives of the third week are to review the results of the data collected during Week Two, including industry comparisons, metric queries, and other information required for the PMG benchmark survey (Chapter 4). Also on the schedule is steering team review number one, conducted by the project manager and chosen members of the design team.

Data Review

The first agenda item on Day One is to review results of the detailed query data collection (far-right column of the SCORcard metric template, Tables 4-1a–c) assigned during Week Two. The owner of each metric should lead the review of data, making adjustments to the type or form of information being sought, assumptions, and estimates on the time required to finish collecting data for the SCORcards.

The second agenda item is to review the completed benchmark data results assigned during the previous week. For this, the team will use its industry comparison spreadsheet (Table 4-3). By now, all actual data, plus large portions of the internal and shareholder benchmark sections of the SCORcard, should be complete. After the data has been reviewed, submitting the completed PMG benchmark survey is the last step in completing the customer-facing and supply chain–specific benchmark data of the SCORcard.

When the Fowlers team reached this point, the corporate controller, the vice president of sales and marketing—food products group, and the vice president of operations—technology products group volunteered to present their findings. (See Table 5-1.)

They had assembled company data and industry summary data for conglomerates, but also added summary data for the "food/meat products" industry and "media/movie, television, and music production services and products" industries. These provided meaningful comparisons for the company's food and technology product groups, respectively. They used the most recent actual data and didn't bother with current-year data that was reported as preliminary. The team filled out the appropriate sections in the Fowlers enterprise SCORcard but had little time for analysis. (See Figure 5-1.)

Even on the first examination of the data, several things jumped out. First, the wide range of figures for cost of goods and SGA costs made it clear that there is no standard for reporting these numbers from one company to another. Operating income seemed to be a good comparison point for expenses. "But there's still no way to compare supply chain costs using the data we have so far," the coach pointed out. "You can't add cost of goods and SGA and supply chain costs to create a working SCORcard metric. Supply chain costs are activity based, and they borrow from the other two categories, so you'd be double-counting certain costs if you just added them. We'll have to wait for the results of the PMG survey to come back."

Second, the metrics of 197 days for the cash-to-cash cycle

(text continues on page 67)

Table 5-1. Fowlers' industry comparison spreadsheet and raw data.

Fowlers Industry Comparison

Conglomerate Industry	Revenue	SG&A	Cost of Goods	Cash-to-Cash Cycle Time	Inventory Days of Supply	Asset Turns	Gross Margin	Operating Income	Net Operating Income	Return on Assets
Fowlers—2001	1000.0	7%	86%	197	91	1.52	14%	7%	4%	10.7%
National Service Industries	563.3	32%	62%	48	20	0.63	38%	5%	5%	3.4%
Maxxam Inc.	2448.0	7%	82%	120	82	0.54	18%	11%	1%	6.2%
US Industries	3088.0	23%	66%	119	88	1.24	34%	11%	1%	13.1%
Pacific Dunlop Ltd.	2120.4	30%	66%	132	105	1.59	34%	4%	-3%	4.8%
Sequa Corporation	1773.1	14%	75%	127	102	1.37	25%	11%	1%	11.1%
GenCorp Inc.	1047.0	4%	82%	95	78	1.05	18%	15%	12%	11.5%
Olin Corporation	1549.0	9%	77%	82	66	1.84	23%	14%	5%	19.7%
Federal Signal Corporation	1106.1	20%	67%	103	78	1.49	33%	13%	5%	14.7%
Kawasaki Heavy Industries Ltd.	8394.8	12%	87%	253	137	1.13	13%	0%	-1%	0.4%
Valhi Inc.	1191.9	17%	63%	144	118	0.70	37%	20%	6%	10.5%
Pentair Inc.	2748.0	17%	71%	106	73	1.39	29%	12%	2%	12.3%
Tomkins PLC	5875.0	7%	81%	88	52	2.01	19%	12%	2%	17.5%
ITT Industries Inc.	4829.4	24%	62%	96	65	1.40	38%	14%	5%	15.1%
Six Continents PLC	5939.0	27%	49%	39	17	0.59	51%	24%	11%	10.7%
TRW Inc.	17321.0	9%	80%	42	23	1.40	20%	10%	3%	11.0%
Textron	13090.0	11%	73%	231	72	1.07	27%	16%	2%	12.7%
Johnson Controls Inc.	18427.0	9%	83%	42	14	2.48	17%	8%	3%	14.9%

Dover Corporation	5400.7	21%	60%	120	89	1.47	40%	19%	10%	21.4%
Ratheon Company	16895.0	10%	76%	123	54	0.84	24%	14%	1%	8.7%
ABB Ltd.	22967.0	19%	75%	170	68	0.99	25%	6%	6%	4.5%
RWE AG	48181.6	27%	68%	95	30	0.87	32%	6%	2%	3.6%
Emerson Electric	15479.6	20%	61%	104	74	1.37	39%	19%	7%	19.9%
Honeywell International	25652.0	12%	71%	111	75	1.36	29%	17%	6%	17.6%
United Technologies	26206.0	17%	69%	108	76	1.38	31%	14%	7%	14.3%
Koninklijke Philips Electronics NV	35658.0	17%	70%	106	73	1.31	30%	14%	25%	13.6%
Minnesota Mining and Manufacturing	16724.0	30%	46%	142	109	1.54	54%	23%	11%	26.8%
Vivendi Universal SA	40138.4	22%	62%	213	45	0.38	38%	16%	5%	4.5%
Siemens AG	86208.0	27%	66%	134	85	1.29	34%	7%	2%	6.6%
Tyco International Ltd.	34036.6	22%	53%	488	102	0.41	47%	25%	12%	7.7%
General Electric Company	129417.0	37%	34%	566	65	0.39	66%	29%	10%	8.7%
Conglomerate Industry	100.0	30%	54%	291	78	0.67	46%	16%	11%	7.8%
Food—Meat Products Industry	100.0	13%	83%	49	52	2.13	17%	4%	3%	6.7%
Media—Movie, Television, & Music Production Services and Products Industries	100.0	55%	46%	83	19	0.67	54%	0%	-4%	-0.1%
Diversified Services—Miscellaneous Business Services	100.0	35%	61%	48	17	1.33	39%	4%	0%	3.8%
Industry Parity	**8395**	**17%**	**69%**	**119**	**74**	**1.31**	**31%**	**14%**	**5%**	**11%**
Industry Advantage	**24267**	**12%**	**61%**	**84**	**48**	**1.45**	**39%**	**19%**	**8%**	**15%**
Industry Superior—90th	**40138**	**7%**	**53%**	**48**	**23**	**1.59**	**47%**	**23%**	**11%**	**20%**

(continues)

Table 5-1. (Continued).

									Net
	Revenue $	SG&A $	Cost of Goods $	Inventory $	Receivable $	Total Assets $	Gross Margin $	Operating Income $	Operating Income $
Fowlers—2001	1000.0	70	860	215	371	656	140	70.0	35
National Service Industries	563.3	182	351.2	19.2	89	898.4	212.1	30.1	27
Maxxam Inc.	2448.0	167.7	1999.3	451.3	453.9	4504	448.7	280	33.9
US Industries	3088.0	721	2040	494	517	2492	1048	327	36
Pacific Dunlop Ltd.	2120.4	629.5	1405.6	405.2	328.4	1773.2	714.8	85.3	−71.1
Sequa Corporation	1773.1	246.6	1334.7	373.7	266.8	1731.1	438.4	191.8	24
GenCorp Inc.	1047.0	40	855	182	135	1324	192	152	129
Olin Corporation	1549.0	132	1196	216	197	1123	353	221	81
Federal Signal Corporation	1106.1	220.7	739.7	157.6	168	991.1	366.4	145.7	57.6
Kawasaki Heavy Industries Ltd.	8394.8	1040.9	7318.5	2743.4	3371.7	9875	1076.3	35.4	−81.7
Valhi Inc.	1191.9	201.7	753.3	243	183.9	2256.8	438.6	236.9	76.6
Pentair Inc.	2748.0	469.7	1952.5	392.5	468.1	2644	795.5	325.8	55.9
Tomkins PLC	5875.0	412.4	4780.7	677.6	1060.5	3906.5	1094.3	681.9	95.8
Tomkins PLC	5875.0	412.4	4780.7	677.6	1060.5	3906.5	1094.3	681.9	95.8
ITT Industries Inc.	4829.4	1141	2993.5	531.3	814.9	4611.4	1835.9	694.9	264.5
Six Continents PLC	5939.0	1617	2895	133	850	13399	3044	1427	676
TRW Inc.	17231.0	1557	13869	870	2328	16467	3362	1805	438
Textron	13090.0	1482	9534	1871	6791	16370	3446	2074	218

Fowlers Industry Comparison—Raw Data (in millions)

Johnson Controls Inc.	18427	1642.9	15307.3	577.6	2928.3	9911.5	3119.7	1476.8	478.3
Dover Corporation	5400.7	1124	3230.1	783.2	903.2	4892.1	2170.6	1046.6	519.6
Ratheon Company	16895	1740	12836	1908	4566	26777	4059	2319	141
ABB Ltd.	22967	4360	17222	3192	8328	30962	5745	1385	1443
RWE AG	48181.6	12814	32684	2721	12502	74224.7	15497.6	2683.6	1073.1
Emerson Electric	15479.6	3081.9	9410	1896.8	2551.2	15046.4	6069.6	2987.7	1031.8
Honeywell International	25652	3134	18095	3734	4623	25175	7557	4423	1659
United Technologies	26206	4473	18111	3756	4445	25364	8095	3622	1808
Koninklijke Philips Electronics NV	35658	5894	24837	4972	6122	36298	10821	4927	9043
Minnesota Mining and Manufacturing	16724	5064	7762	2312	2891	14522	8962	3898	1782
Vivendi Universal SA	40138.4	8935.1	24802.5	3032.1	21802.4	141965	15335.9	6400.8	2165.2
Siemens AG	86208	23209	57107	13284	18756	89298	29101	5892	2069
Tyco International Ltd.	34036.6	7324.5	18180	5101.3	38759	111287.3	15856.6	8532.1	3970.6
General Electric Company	129417	47437	44087	7812	188317	437006	85330	37893	12735
Conglomerate Industry	100	30	54.32	11.56	66.67	200	45.68	15.68	11.22
Food—Meat Products Industry	100	13.1	82.74	11.82	7.46	62.5	17.26	4.16	2.93
Media—Movie, Television, & Music Production Services and Products Industries	100	54.57	45.62	2.4	25.64	200	54.38	-0.19	-4.22
Diversified Services—Miscellaneous Business Services	100	35.14	61.02	2.8	16.67	100	39.98	3.84	-0.36

Figure 5-1. Fowlers' enterprise SCORcard.

	Performance Attribute or Category	Level 1 Performance Metrics	Actual	Parity Median of statistical sample	Advantage Midpoint of parity and superior	Superior 90th percentile of population	Parity Gap Parity—actual
External	Supply Chain Delivery Reliability	Delivery Performance					
		Line Item Fill Rate					
		Perfect Order Fulfillment					
	Supply Chain Responsiveness	Order Fulfillment Lead Time					
	Supply Chain Flexibility	Supply Chain Response Time					
		Production Flexibility					
Internal	Supply Chain Cost	Cost of Goods	86%	69%	61%	53%	
		Total Supply Chain Cost	15.5%				
		SGA Cost	7%	17%	12%	7%	
		Warranty / Returns Processing Costs	0.7%				
	Supply Chain Asset Management Efficiency	Cash-to-Cash Cycle Time	197	119.0	84.0	48.0	
		Inventory Days of Supply	91	74	48	23	
		Asset Turns	1.5	1.3	1.5	1.6	
Shareholder	Profitability	Gross Margin	14%	31%	39%	47%	
		Operating Income	7%	14%	19%	23%	
		Net Income	4%	5%	8%	11%	
	Effectiveness of Return	Return on Assets	10.7%	11%	15%	20%	

Source: © Copyright 2001 Supply-Chain Council, Inc. Used with permission.

and 1.5 asset turns confirmed what many in the finance community seemed to feel about Fowlers: It utilized physical assets well and cash assets poorly.

Third, the 7 percent operating income in the food products group compared well against the food/meat products industry. It was a similar story for technology products. But sales were declining in each business, and profits were nearly half of what they had been the previous year. The strategy of charging a premium price for a premium product wasn't holding, and in fact was causing some customers to go elsewhere.

But as the team looked at the "parity opportunity" portion of the chart, their eyes got wide. As a conglomerate with a $1 billion in revenue, Fowlers' 7 percent operating income ($70 million) was only half the level of the conglomerate industry benchmark. To achieve parity in operating income, they would need to find another $70 million of additional supply chain performance.

Next, the corporate controller, director of logistics, and director of customer service took their turn. In addition to the review of enterprise supply chain and warranty/returns processing costs, they reviewed some data not included on the enterprise SCORcard. They learned that combined food and technology products delivery performance was 22 percent— meaning that just twenty-two orders out of one hundred were delivered on time and complete. Line-item fill rate was 80 percent, perfect order fill rate 5 percent, order fulfillment lead time 4.1 days, supply chain response time was 122 days, and production flexibility was sixty days. By the next week, they said they'd be ready to provide data for each product group SCORcard; enterprise delivery data was out of scope.

By this time, everyone was nearly speechless. Each measure in the customer-facing section was new, and it was the first time that the team had really thought about overall delivery performance through the customer's eyes. Especially disturbing to the team was the big picture about delivery performance.

The ensuing discussion sounded a bit like a classic session with a grief counselor; there was denial, bargaining, anger, and eventually acceptance of the data. Every member of the team wanted to bolt from the room and jump right into fixing the problem—like they had all done so many times before. Fortunately, it was the end of the day. Tomorrow's agenda would focus the team on something else. And a good night's sleep would put this information in perspective: The team had found an opportunity for the kind of improvement it needed to make.

■ Chip Exercise: Competitive Requirements Analysis

The agenda for Day Two is comprised of two tasks: conducting competitive requirements (sometimes known as the chip exercise) and preparing for steering team review number one.

Rules for the Chip Exercise

There are four attributes of supply chain performance (as defined in the second column of the metrics template, Tables 4-1a–c):

1. Delivery performance
2. Flexibility and responsiveness (combined)
3. Supply chain cost
4. Asset management efficiency

The objective of the chip exercise is to prioritize these attributes for each customer or market channel, determining whether the company needs to perform each attribute at a superior level, a level of advantage, or at parity with other providers.

There is a catch: For each customer or market channel, the team is only allowed to set one performance attribute at the superior level and one at the level of advantage. The other two attributes must be set at parity.

Finally, the requirements are established from the company's point of view as they relate to the competitive landscape of the future. This is not a goal-setting exercise; it's a strategic exercise, focused on how to differentiate against stiff competition in the future.

Many companies are using the strategic categories written about in *The Discipline of Market Leaders* (by Michael Treacy and Fred Wiersema) defining operational excellence, customer intimacy, or product innovation as the strategy driver. The results of the chip exercise should reflect and support the strategy driver. At the end of the exercise, the team must reach consensus on the requirements for each supply chain. On close calls, it might help to assign numeric values to each chip: three for superior, two for advantage, and one for parity.

This exercise needs to be performed three times. It's performed first by the design team. It will be performed almost immediately afterward by the full steering team. The third time it's performed by each relevant business team as the SCOR process is spun farther out through the enterprise. In each case, the coach should review the metric categories and definitions with the players, but actual data should not be revealed. That's because people tend to put the "superior" chip where they see the need for the most improvement, not necessarily where the strategic advantage lies.

At Fowlers, the coach facilitated as the design team went through the chip exercise (Figure 5-2). Using the five channels identified as being in scope (see Table 3-5) as a baseline, the team determined that there were really only three supply chains with unique requirements. All of Fowlers' U.S. retail markets had the same overall performance requirements regardless of the product group. Similarly, the U.S. distributor markets and U.S. government had similar requirements independent of product type. Lastly, the U.S. direct-to-consumer markets and U.S. OEM/key accounts were grouped together with similar delivery, cost, and inventory requirements—again, with little distinction required from one product to another.

The results of the chip exercise were clear. To differentiate in the U.S. retail channel, Fowlers needed to achieve superior delivery performance, advantage supply chain cost, and parity performance in flexibility and asset efficiency.

To differentiate in the U.S. distributor and government markets, Fowlers needed to achieve superior performance in supply

Figure 5-2. Fowlers' competitive requirements summary.

Performance Attribute or Category	Associated Level 1 Performance Metrics	Competitive Requirements S = Superior . . . 1 category per supply chain A = Advantage . . . 1 category per supply chain P = Parity . . . 2 categories per supply chain		
		U.S. Retail Markets	U.S. Distributor Markets U.S. Government	U.S. Direct to Consumer U.S. OEM Key Accounts
Supply Chain Delivery Reliability The performance of the supply chain in delivering the correct product, to the correct place, at the correct time, in the correct condition and packaging, in the correct quantity, with the correct documentation, to the correct customer.	Delivery Performance	S	P	P
	Fill Rates Substitute Line Item Fill Rate here			
	Perfect Order Fulfillment			
Supply Chain Responsiveness The velocity at which a supply chain provides products to the customer.	Order Fulfillment Lead Time	P	P	S
Supply Chain Flexibility The agility of a supply chain in responding to marketplace changes to gain or maintain competitive advantage.	Supply Chain Response Time			
Supply Chain Flexibility The agility of a supply chain in responding to marketplace changes to gain or maintain competitive advantage.	Production Flexibility			
Supply Chain Cost The costs associated with operating the supply chain.	Total Supply Chain Cost	A	S	A
	Warranty / Returns Processing Costs			
Supply Chain Asset Management Efficiency The effectiveness of an organization in managing assets to support demand satisfaction. This includes the management of all assets: fixed and working capital.	Cash-to-Cash Cycle Time	P	A	P
	Inventory Days of Supply			
	Asset Turns			

chain cost, advantage performance in asset efficiency, and parity on delivery performance and flexibility and responsiveness.

To differentiate in the demanding direct-to-consumer and OEM/key accounts, Fowlers needed to achieve superior performance in flexibility and responsiveness, advantage performance in supply chain cost, and parity on delivery performance and asset efficiency.

Preparing For Steering Team Review Number One

In advance of the first steering team review, consider the following points:

1. The project manager should be the principle person consolidating and preparing the presentation.
2. The project manager should conduct one-on-one discussions with steering team members who are responsible for key data, as they may be called on to provide explanation or detail.
3. Any rumors, objections, and other cultural issues that need to be addressed during the steering team meeting should be discussed candidly.
4. Speaking roles should be determined for the steering team review. In addition to David, design team members who did a lot of homework may be given a chance for exposure.

Overall, the objectives of steering team review number one are to review supply chain metric definitions and preliminary query data, conduct the competitive requirements chip exercise with the entire steering team, review preliminary industry comparison sample and benchmark data, and establish expectations for steering team review number two.

The corporate controller, the vice president of sales and marketing—food products group, the director of logistics, and the director of customer service worked with David to prepare the first steering team review. They established the following agenda:

- ❑ Project roadmap status
- ❑ Reminder—communications plan
- ❑ Conduct chip exercise with the steering team—review design team results
- ❑ Review preliminary supply chain metric data—Fowlers enterprise SCORcard
- ❑ Review preliminary benchmark data—Fowlers industry comparison
- ❑ Make decisions required today
- ❑ Set expectations for steering team review number two

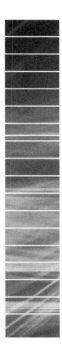

6

Week Four: SCORcards

Tackle the difference between competitive requirements
and actual performance.

After a proper debrief of highlights from the steering team meeting, the design team starts in on the objectives of Week Four:
Review all SCORcards, begin the process of calculating gaps,
and assign financial value to the gaps between competitive requirements and actual performance.

The SCORcard Review

For a SCORcard to be complete, it must include actual data for
each metric of each supply chain, as well as appropriate industry
benchmarks, competitive requirements, and gap calculations
completed for each metric for each SCORcard. In a perfect world
SCORcards would cascade neatly from the enterprise level to
each business, or from the enterprise level to each market segment. But that rarely happens, as the Fowlers design team
learned on Day One of the fourth week. As the review process

took shape for each of the three SCORcards (enterprise, food products, technology products) that the design team set out to create, reality checks were required to make sense of the data and focus the design effort. The first day focused on the actual and benchmark columns.

Discussion of the enterprise SCORcard (Table 6-1), lead by the corporate controller and director of logistics, considered three compromises. First, enterprise-wide customer facing data simply didn't exist in the Fowlers structure. But they did have data at the product group level, which they had combined (see Chapter 4) for surprising results on delivery performance, line item fill rate, etc.

A second compromise had to do with the fact that balance sheet data was only available at the corporate level; trying to allocate that information back to the product groups would have taken a major restructuring. As a result, the team simply left the "supply chain asset management efficiency" metrics blank on the product group SCORcards.

Third, and most important, the SCORcards weren't organized in the same way as the supply chain competitive performance requirements that had been generated during Week Three. The SCORcards were organized by business—because that's how the data existed. And the supply chain requirements were determined by market/customer channel—because that represented the ideal situation the team wanted to create. So translating from the competitive requirements to the SCORcard would be a challenge.

For example, the food products group supplied products to food service, retail, and government channels—each requiring its own priorities (summarized in Figure 5-2). How could these different requirement profiles be aligned on a single SCORcard for the food products group? Especially when the cash-to-cash, inventory, and asset turn data only showed up on the enterprise SCORcard.

"You'll come up against more than one roadblock like this," the coach said. "We're not always going to have complete data or perfect alignment. What do you want to do? Go back and do some more homework, or pick a direction to go forward?" The team was impatient, and a few minutes of conversation made it

Table 6-1. Fowlers' enterprise SCORcard.

	Performance Attribute or Category	Level 1 Performance Metrics	Actual	Parity Median of statistical sample	Advantage Midpoint of parity and superior	Superior 90th percentile of population	Parity Gap Parity—actual	Opportunity
External	Supply Chain Delivery Reliability	Delivery Performance		74.7%	85.0%	95.0%		$1,227,500
		Line Item Fill Rate		92.0%	95.5%	99.0%		
		Perfect Order Fulfillment		74.0%	81.0%	88.0%		
	Supply Chain Responsiveness	Order Fulfillment Lead Time		10 days	6.5 days	3 days		Enables Inventory and Delivery Reliability
	Supply Chain Flexibility	Supply Chain Response Time		60 days	45 days	29 days		
		Production Flexibility		42 days	26 days	10.8 days		
Internal	Supply Chain Cost	Cost of Goods	86%	69%	61%	53%	−17%	$58,600,000
		Total Supply Chain Cost	15.5%	9.5%	6.7%	3.9%	−6%	
		SGA Cost	7%	17%	12%	7%	10%	
		Warranty / Returns Processing Costs	0.7%	1.5%	1.0%	0.5%	0.8%	$1,250,000
	Supply Chain Asset Management Efficiency	Cash-to-Cash Cycle Time	197	97.9	63.8	29.7	−99	
		Inventory Days of Supply	91	74	48	23	−18	$18,099,583
		Asset Turns	1.5	2.5	4.7	7.0	−1.0	
Shareholder	Profitability	Gross Margin	14%	31%	39%	47%	−17%	$79,177,083
		Operating Income	7%	14%	19%	23%	−7%	
		Net Income	4%	5%	8%	11%	−2%	
	Effectiveness of Return	Return on Assets	10.7%	11%	15%	20%	−0.4%	

Source: © Copyright 2001 Supply-Chain Council, Inc. Used with permission.

clear that there probably was no perfect solution. So they agreed to apply the priorities of the retail channel because it represented the operating unit's largest share of revenue.

The food products SCORcard discussion (Table 6-2), lead by the vice president of sales and marketing—food products group, summarized four learning points and considered two compromises. Here was the first learning point: While it was perceived as superior in delivery performance, the food products group had an opportunity to improve and widen its competitive gap by focusing on delivery performance and perfect order metrics.

Here was the second learning point: Most of the supply chain cost factors were accounted for in the cost-of-goods-sold cost centers. Comparing individual components of these costs to industry benchmarks highlighted new opportunities for cost reduction that would help put the division at a more acceptable level of operating income.

The third learning point was that the food products business team, in order to focus on cash-to-cash efficiency, would first need to create new information tools for analysis and better leverage its new ERP system.

Fourth, for Fowlers Inc. to perform at the level expected by shareholders, the food products group needed to do better than achieve industry parity in operating income. It needed to achieve superior results.

In this way, the SCORcard exercise helped members of the food products business team to formalize a strategy of supply chain excellence as a means to compete not on list price of its products, but on total landed price to customers.

The first necessary compromise focused on how to distribute the market/customer channel performance requirements—the chip exercise priorities—onto the food products SCORcard. While their supply chain definition matrix identified four potential supply chains (Table 3-5) that were then consolidated to three distinct channels (Figure 5-2), the food products business team agreed to adopt the retail markets SPAP (superior/parity/advantage/parity) priorities for their SCORcard gap baseline because it was the largest and most profitable segment. Supply chain cost was a high priority in all segments; and lead time requirements for the direct-to-consumer markets and OEM/key accounts could initially be set up on a fee-for-service basis for requirements above parity.

The second compromise was recognized at the enterprise level. The competitive opportunity for asset management efficiency would be defined through the enterprise SCORcard until information systems and financial reporting could support truer activity-based definitions. In the meantime, to calculate opportunity the team used 25 percent of enterprise cash-to-cash and inventory numbers.

Discussion about the technology products group (Table 6-3), lead by David Able in his capacity as the group's operations vice president, summarized three unique learning points and considered necessary two compromises.

The first learning point was this: While the decision to outsource manufacture of several products succeeded at achieving lowest unit cost, it drastically reduced the responsiveness and flexibility metrics, which in turn impacted inventory levels. The second learning point was that the new metrics on service reliability provided empirical evidence to complaints by customers that the company was "hard to do business with." In the third learning point, by assembling supply chain costs it became clear that material acquisition expenses outpaced all other increases. And inbound transportation, normally calculated as a cost of material, was isolated for all to see. The last learning point was similar to one of the lessons for the food products group: There was considerable opportunity to improve operating income by attacking supply chain costs, improving utilization of working capital, and better leveraging the new ERP system.

Like the food products group, the technology products group's first necessary compromise focused on how to distribute the market/customer channel performance requirements onto the technology products SCORcard. The technology products business team agreed to adopt the direct-to-consumer and OEM/key accounts superior/parity/advantage/parity priorities for their SCORcard gap baseline. The second compromise was that competitive opportunity for asset management efficiency would be defined at the enterprise level based on information systems and financial reporting. In the meantime, to calculate the opportunity gap, David used 45 percent of the enterprise cash-to-cash and inventory dollars. That effort completed a full day of work.

The Gap Analysis

The agenda for Day Two is focused on completing the SCORcard gap analysis. The first step is to calculate the mathematical opportunity for each metric. This is done by calculating both the parity gap and the competitive requirement gap, and then subtracting actual performance for each metric from the benchmark number determined by the competitive requirement for the category.

If the gap analysis results in a negative number, it means actual performance is less than the benchmark (for example, the gap between an actual delivery performance of 78 percent and competitive requirements of 92 percent is 14 percent). The next step is to translate each gap number into a profit potential; the most frequently used measure is operating income.

The calculations are straightforward for the internal metrics but can be subjective for customer-facing metrics. The basic calculation that the design team, and ultimately the business team, must agree upon is the anticipated effect on operating income of improvements in delivery performance, responsiveness, and flexibility. This is often more art than science, but there are some accepted approaches:

❑ *The Lost Opportunity Measure.* This calculates the revenue lost before order-entry due to lack of availability of a product.
❑ *The Canceled Order Measure.* This measure calculates revenue lost after order-entry, due to canceled orders that result from poor delivery performance.
❑ *The Market Share Measure.* This attempts to project a revenue increase based on achieving competitive advantage in the customer-facing metric categories.

Because any approach will have its tradeoffs, just make sure to document your assumptions and details for the financial analysis, and identify some of the steering team or business team members to help validate preliminary numbers.

In Fowlers' case, the design team agreed on the organization of the gap analysis itself, deciding that all the opportunity dollars should be calculated using an operating income profit perspective that allowed them to add up the numbers in the "opportunity" column of the SCORcard. Here are some other decisions made by the team:

❑ Group all delivery reliability metrics, and use "lost opportunity" and "canceled order" calculation methods. The detailed calculation required an estimated revenue increase multiplied by the gross margin, resulting in an operating income opportunity.

❑ Use opportunities in the supply chain responsiveness and flexibility category to improve results in reliability and cash-to-cash. This minimized the risk of double counting.

❑ Group the supply chain cost category, and base the opportunity calculation on the total supply chain cost and warranty/returns processing cost metrics.

❑ Base the supply chain asset management efficiency category on the cash-to-cash metric. Because this data was only available at the enterprise level, the calculation first multiplied the enterprise working capital times the cost of capital, and then multiplied it by the percent of total revenue for each product group.

❑ Use the number in the profitability section as the sum total of the operating income improvements on the SCORcard.

Here are the assumptions made for the food and technology product group gap analysis (Tables 6-2 and 6-3):

❑ Food products delivery reliability assumed a one percent increase in revenue due to availability of product at the point of order using a 14 percent gross margin. The 1 percent was based on analysis of lost and cancelled orders, conducted by the customer service department over the course of one week.

(text continues on page 82)

Table 6-2. Fowlers' food products SCORcard with competitive requirements.

	Performance Attribute or Category	Level 1 Performance Metrics	Actual	Parity Median of statistical sample	Advantage Midpoint of parity and superior	Superior 90th percentile of population	Parity Gap Parity—actual	Requirements Gap	Opportunity
External	Supply Chain Delivery Reliability	Delivery Performance	68.4%	74.7%	85.0%	95.0%	-6.3%	-26.6%	$350,000
		Line Item Fill Rate	91.0%	92.0%	95.5%	99.0%	-1.0%	-8.0%	
		Perfect Order Fulfillment	35.0%	74.0%	81.0%	88.0%	-39.0%	-53.0%	
	Supply Chain Responsiveness	Order Fulfillment Lead Time	5 days	10 days	6.5 days	3 days	5 days	5 days	Enables Inventory and Delivery Reliability
	Supply Chain Flexibility	Supply Chain Response Time	90 days	60 days	45 days	29 days	-30 days	-30 days	
		Production Flexibility	61 days	42 days	26 days	10.8 days	-19 days	-19 days	
Internal	Supply Chain Cost	Cost of Goods	86%	69%	61%	53%	-17%	-25%	$25,750,000
		Total Supply Chain Cost	17.0%	9.5%	6.7%	3.9%	-7.5%	-10.3%	
		SG&A Cost	7%	17%	12%	7%	10%	5%	
		Warranty / Returns Processing Costs	1.5%	1.5%	1.0%	0.5%	0.0%	-0.5%	$1,250,000
	Supply Chain Asset Management Efficiency	Cash-to-Cash Cycle Time*	197	97.9	63.8	29.7	-99.1	-99.1	$6,464,137
		Inventory Days of Supply*	91	74	48	23	-17.4	-17.4	
		Asset Turns* Enterprise Data * .25	1.5	2.5	4.7	7.0	-1.0	1.0	
Shareholder	Profitability	Gross Margin	14%	31%	39%	47%	-17%	-8%	$33,814,137
		Operating Income	7%	14%	19%	23%	-7%	-5%	
		Net Income							
	Effectiveness of Return	Return on Assets							

*Allocation percentage of enterprise total for receivables and inventory dollars.

Table 6-3. Fowlers' technology products SCORcard.

	Performance Attribute or Category	Level 1 Performance Metrics	Actual	Parity Median of statistical sample	Advantage Midpoint of parity and superior	Superior 90th percentile of population	Parity Gap Parity—actual	Requirements Gap	Opportunity
External	Supply Chain Delivery Reliability	Delivery Performance	10.0%	74.7%	85.0%	95.0%	−64.7%	−64.7%	$877,500
		Line Item Fill Rate	85.0%	92.0%	95.5%	99.0%	−7.0%	−7.0%	
		Perfect Order Fulfillment	1.0%	74.0%	81.0%	88.0%	−73.0%	−73.0%	
	Supply Chain Responsiveness	Order Fulfillment Lead Time	8 days	10 days	6.5 days	3 days	2 days	−5 days	Enables Inventory and Delivery Reliability
	Supply Chain Flexibility	Supply Chain Response Time	110 days	60 days	45 days	29 days	−50 days	−81 days	$32,850,000
		Production Flexibility	58 days	42 days	26 days	10.8 days	−16 days	−47.2 days	
Internal	Supply Chain Cost	Cost of Goods	87%	69%	61%	53%	−18%	−26%	$0
		Total Supply Chain Cost	14.0%	9.5%	6.7%	3.9%	−4.5%	−7.3%	
		SG&A Cost	7%	17%	12%	7%	10.1%	5.1%	
		Warranty / Returns Processing Costs	0.7%	1.5%	1.0%	0.5%	0.8%	0.3%	
	Supply Chain Asset Management Efficiency	Cash-to-Cash Cycle Time*	197	97.9	63.8	29.7	−99.1	−99.1	$11,635,446
		Inventory Days of Supply*	91	74	48	23	−17.4	−17.4	
		Asset Turns* Enterprise Data * .45	1.5	2.5	4.7	7.0	1.0	1.0	
Shareholder	Profitability	Gross Margin	13%	31%	39%	47%	−18%		$45,362,946
		Operating Income	6%	14%	19%	23%	−8%		
		Net Income							
	Effectiveness of Return	Return on Assets							

*Allocation percentage of enterprise total for receivables and inventory dollars.

❑ Using the same study, the technology products group assumed a 1.5 percent increase in revenue using a 13 percent gross margin.

❑ Total supply chain cost was based on the cost centers allocated to material acquisition, order management, MIS
cost, planning, finance and administration, and inventory
carrying cost. Inventory carrying cost and warranty/re-
turns processing cost were eliminated from the opportunity column to avoid double counting.

❑ Warranty/returns processing cost was based on the cost
centers to support return transactions, warehouse storage, and transportation.

With a total enterprise working capital of $514 million and a
cost of capital at Fowlers of 10 percent, the economic profit potential for Fowlers is $51.4 million. This number was allocated
to food products at 25 percent and technology products at 45
percent representing their share of total Fowlers revenue.

The team's homework for the next week was to identify
steering team and extended team members to validate the calculations and, more important, the detailed assumptions behind
the numbers. The second part of the homework required some
thoughtful analysis of putting together the rational business
case for supply chain improvement for steering team review
number two.

Phase III

Design Material Flow

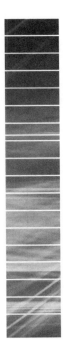

7

Week Five: Initiating AS IS Material Flow and Steering Team Review Number Two

Transition from analysis to action.

Week Five marks the close of the information gathering and analysis phase of the SCOR project life cycle and bridges to the third phase supply chain design. Specifically, the design team will launch the AS IS material flow analysis for logistical types. It's usually the most interesting part of the project with the biggest potential for improvement. The objectives for the week are to complete the supply chain opportunity summary including the SCORcard gap analysis, and initiate the AS IS material flow, including learning about SCOR Level Two classifications—raw material, work in progress, finished goods, or return; and make to stock, engineer to order, and make to order. Another objective is the assembly of a more detailed view of material flow. Lastly, the team needs to prepare and conduct the second steering team review.

▪ Validating Gap Analysis and Preparing Steering Team Review Number Two

The first agenda item for Day One is for each assigned subteam to review its SCORcard gap analysis and validation effort, including revised assumptions, calculations, and validation resources. The entire design team must ask enough questions to achieve consensus on the value of each metric and on the total opportunity calculated on the SCORcard.

The second agenda item is to identify the design team members who will make presentations in the second steering team review. The third and final agenda item is to prepare and conduct a dry run prior to the steering team review.

The SCORcard gap analysis, combined with the business context summary and project charter (Appendixes B and C), establishes the overall business case for a strategic effort of continuous supply chain improvement.

The agenda for the steering team review included:

❏ Project roadmap status
❏ Review consolidated competitive requirements by supply chain
❏ Review enterprise and product group SCORcards (Tables 6-1–6-3)
❏ Gap analysis and opportunity summary results
❏ Set expectations for steering team review number three

In preparation for the steering team review at Fowlers, the validation effort ultimately did not change the numbers or assumptions. But the process did reveal some change-management stages that would have to occur. The careful resource planning of the subteams for each SCORcard and the key validation resources helped to manage the length of these stages in advance.

Change Management: Dealing with Denial

In the first stage, reactions are predictable as the design team's work spreads through the organization: The numbers are wrong; we aren't that bad.

The technology and food products business teams, when presented with the SCORcard gap analysis, reacted predictably; they challenged the numbers. This happens in almost all projects. That's why it's important to have business leaders from each of the product groups present to explain the data and review the validation resources. This builds confidence that the numbers are, in fact, reliable and quickly puts the focus on the issues.

Change Management: Placing Blame

The second-stage reaction is to allocate blame, which is easier than taking responsibility for the results. Positioning design team members to share their personal perspectives on the gap analysis, and to review competitive performance facts, helps accelerate business unit leaders through this stage and moves them beyond the convenient catch-all phrase: "But we're unique."

Change Management: Book the Numbers

The third reaction is to confuse acceptance of the analysis with actually having solved the problem. Agreeing on the opportunity does not improve anything. At this point, the business team is excited at the value of improving supply chain performance; based on benchmarks and competitive requirements, the numbers can add up fast. But it's too soon to start booking the savings in corporate forecasts and memos to the board. The real value of change will show up as part of the next phase.

In closing out Phase II, the Fowlers project team accomplished a couple important points. First, they really learned that the main goal of the SCORcard analysis and validation effort is to manage change, not just to complete a deliverable. Second, they successfully transferred knowledge; the validation sources needed to learn and the design team needed to teach.

Launching Phase III: Design Material Flow

The third phase of the project life cycle focuses on supply chain design—the effort to identify organizational, process, personnel, and technology changes to close the metric gaps calculated in the SCORcards. The design is completed in two steps.

First, the design team focuses on physical material flow. Primary deliverables are AS IS material flow, disconnect and gross opportunity analysis, material flow strategy and appropriate leading practices, and TO BE material flow.

Second, the team aligns practices and looks at processes and systems involving work and information flow. Primary deliverables are AS IS work and information flow, transactional analysis, TO BE work and information flow, and productivity impact summary.

At the conclusion of the design phase, the project team combines, values, and prioritizes changes in material, work, and information flow. This portion of the schedule, as shown in the project charter (Appendix C) includes twenty-four design sessions conducted over twelve weeks. The primary cast of characters includes the executive sponsor, project manager, design team, and extended team members for transportation, data, and process step inquiries.

As noted in the project charter, there are seven steering team milestones: reviewing and approving 1) AS IS material flow and disconnect process; 2) material flow disconnects; 3) preliminary opportunity summary; 4) TO BE material flow recommendations; 5) work and information flow transactional analysis; 6) work and information flow baseline TO BE business blueprint; and 7) work and information flow productivity opportunity summary.

The design effort provides the basis for a project portfolio of supply chain improvements offering a six-month cost-neutral return on investment with two- to six-times return after a year. The portfolio (discussed in detail in Chapter 19) outlines work that will span twenty-four to thirty-six months.

■ Initiating AS IS Material Flow

Day Two of this week is occupied with learning about SCOR Level Two processes and mapping the current state of material flow. The design team must address three things: 1) appropriate

level of detail; 2) assembling the geographic maps and character-
izing each physical location using the SCOR Level Two process
types; and 3) assembling a material flow performance spreadsheet.

About The SCOR Level Two Process Types

The SCOR model version 5.0 decomposes from five Level One
process categories—PLAN, SOURCE, MAKE, DELIVER, and
RETURN—to twelve supply chain execution process types and
five planning process types. (See Figure 7-1.)

Level Two elements identify the types of items and consequent processes that are used to move material from location to
location.

Source

The SOURCE Level Two process types—source stocked product
(S1), source make-to-order product (S2), and source engineer-
to-order product (S3)—attempt to characterize how a company
purchases raw materials and finished goods. The key factors in
determining the source process types are the trigger event from
PLAN, MAKE, and DELIVER processes, and the state of the material at the supplier when the purchase order is placed.

S1—a make-to-stock environment—is generally triggered by
a forecast requirement from PLAN, MAKE, or DELIVER and the
supplier has the item available in a finished-goods inventory before the purchase order. S2—a make-to-order environment—is
usually triggered by a specific customer-order requirement from
MAKE or DELIVER, and the supplier must convert raw materials or semi-finished goods in response to a purchase order.
S3—an engineer-to-order environment—is most often triggered
by a specific customer order and design specifications from
MAKE or DELIVER. A qualified supplier must be identified before a purchase order is issued; the purchase order quantity is

Figure 7-1. SCOR level two process types.

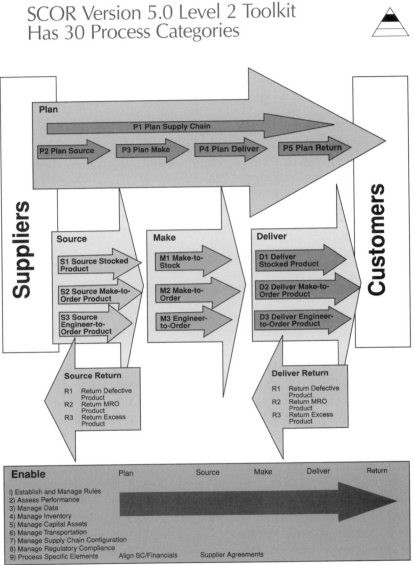

SCOR Version 5.0 Level 2 Toolkit Has 30 Process Categories

Source: © Copyright 2001 Supply-Chain Council, Inc. Used with permission.

dependent on specific customer order quantities and is often executed only once.

Frequently, the supply of a given raw material or finished good evolves through each of these process types over the course of its product life cycle. Just as frequently, a location may use one, two, or all three SOURCE process types.

Make

The MAKE Level Two process types—make-to-stock (M1), make-to-order (M2), and engineer-to-order (M3)—attempt to characterize how your company converts raw materials (RM) to work-in-process (WIP) to finished goods (FG) status. The conversion process generally is located in a manufacturing site or sites but can be applied to a warehouse as well. The key factors in determining the make process types are the trigger event from PLAN or DELIVER, and also the state of the material when the customer order is placed.

M1 is generally triggered by a forecast or replenishment requirement from PLAN; the conversion process is executed prior to the customer order. The work-order quantity is independent of specific customer order quantities, and is often related to a replenishment economic order quantity. M2 is generally triggered by a specific customer order requirement from DELIVER; the conversion of raw materials or semi-finished goods is executed in response to a customer order. The work order quantity is equal to customer order quantities. M3 is generally triggered by a specific customer order requirement and design specifications from DELIVER. Manufacturing engineering specifications must be completed prior to the issue of a work order. The work order quantity is dependent on specific customer order quantities, and is usually executed once.

As with raw materials, WIP items can evolve through each process type over the course of the product life cycle, and a location may use one, two, or all three MAKE process types.

Deliver

The DELIVER Level Two process types—deliver stocked product (D1), deliver make-to-order product (D2), and deliver engineer-to-order product (D3)—attempt to characterize how a company processes its finished goods in response to customer orders. The delivery process frequently is located in a warehouse site, but can be applied to manufacturing or supplier direct ships as well. The key factors in determining the deliver process types are the trigger event from PLAN or the customer, and the state of the material when the customer order is placed.

D1 is generally triggered by a forecast from PLAN that places finished goods in inventory on an available-to-promise basis prior to the customer order. Inventory levels are independent of specific customer order quantities. D2 is usually triggered by a specific customer order requirement of finished goods that are planned to be converted, assembled, or configured after the receipt of the customer order. The sales order quantity is equal to customer order quantities. D3 is triggered by a specific customer order requirement and design or manufacturing specifications to be completed prior to the issue of a sales order. The sales order quantity is equal to customer order quantities and is usually executed once. FG items can evolve through each process type over the course of the product life cycle, and a location may use one, two, or all three DELIVER process types.

Return

The RETURN Level Two process types—return defective product (R1), return maintenance, repair, and overhaul (MRO) product (R2), and return excess product (R3)—attempt to characterize how a company returns its finished goods in response to customer return authorizations. The return process frequently is located in a warehouse site but can be applied to a manufacturing or supplier direct ships as well.

There are two perspectives built into the return process types: returns from customers (DRx) and returns to suppliers (SRx). Key factors in determining the return process types are the trigger event from the customer of PLAN and the state of the material when the customer order is placed.

R1 is triggered on a small scale by a warranty claim initiated by a customer and on a large scale by a product recall triggered by internal resources executing the process steps in PLAN Return. R2 is triggered by planned maintenance event initiated by PLAN return, or an unplanned maintenance event initiated by engineering, maintenance, or other technical resources. R3 is triggered by planned inventory returns based on contractual agreements with specific customers, or unplanned inventory returns based on category management data for retail or distributor shelf space.

Plan

PLAN supply chain (P1) is the process of taking actual demand data and generating a supply plan for a given supply chain, as defined by the supply chain project scope matrix (see Table 3-5). The basic steps require:

❏ A unit forecast that is adjusted for marketing and sales events
❏ A supply plan that constrains the forecast based on availability or resources, such as inventory, manufacturing capacity, and transportation
❏ A balance step where demand/supply exceptions are resolved and updated on the system

This planning process type is most closely associated with the leading practice of sales and operations planning.

PLAN source (P2) is the process of comparing total material requirements with the P1 constrained forecast generated above and generating a material requirements resource plan based on P3 to satisfy landed cost and inventory goals by commodity type. This translates to a material release schedule that lets the buyer know how much product must be purchased based on current orders, inventory, and future requirements. It is carried out for items on the bill of materials and may be aggregated by supplier or commodity type. This planning process type is most closely associated with the leading practices in material requirements planning.

PLAN make (P3) is the process of comparing actual production orders plus replenishment orders coming from P4 against the P1 constrained forecast generated above and then generating a master production schedule resource plan to satisfy service, cost, and inventory goals. This translates to material requirements, P2, that tell the purchasing (or commodity) manager how much product is required by item and a master production schedule that lets the plant scheduler know how much total product must be made by ship date. It is carried out for each plant location and may be aggregated to region or another geography type. This planning process type is most closely associated with the leading practices of master production scheduling.

PLAN deliver (P4) is the process of comparing actual committed orders with the P1 constrained forecast generated above and developing a distribution resource plan to satisfy service, cost, and inventory goals. The plan generally translates to replenishment requirements that tell the plant manager how much product to plan for, P3; and visibility into available-to-promise inventory. P4 is carried out for each warehouse stocking location and may be aggregated to regional levels or another geography type. This planning process type is most closely associated with the leading practices of distribution requirements planning.

PLAN return (P5) is the process of aggregating planned returns and generating a return resource plan to satisfy service, cost, and inventory goals. The plan generally translates to return requirements that tell the manufacturing, maintenance, and logistics teams the type, volume, and schedule of planned and known unplanned returns. P5 is carried out for each warehouse and maintenance return and may be aggregated to regions or other geography type.

Level of Detail

The first job in material flow analysis is to determine the right level of mapping detail to identify inefficiencies. Here are some factors that help to determine the right level.

For the AS IS portion, it's often easier to map material flows from the row or product point of view of the supply chain definition matrix (Table 3-4), as opposed to the column, or customer point of view. The reason is that physical locations, raw material commodities, and key suppliers are grouped by row more frequently than the column.

Second, the SCORcard data must be able to cascade to the maps; there will be more on this subject in the material flow performance summary (Chapters 7 and 8).

Third, and most important to efficiency in the mapping process, is the level of the products to be mapped. Mapping material flow at the SKU level is more work than mapping at the product family level, which is more effort than mapping at the product line or group level. Which level is right? Use the highest level that can point to both tactical and strategic inefficiencies in service levels, transportation cost, lead-time (cycle time), and days of inventory.

AS IS Mapping at Fowlers

The Fowlers design team determined that two maps were necessary to illustrate inefficiencies in the food products material flow. The first map comprised key food product suppliers by commodity type (live produce, packaging, contract manufacturer of precooked food), manufacturing locations (Des Moines, Iowa; Madison, Wisconsin; and Minneapolis, Minnesota), and corporate distribution locations (Portland, Oregon; Atlanta, Georgia; Harrisburg, Pennsylvania; and Santa Fe, New Mexico) mapped by product family (fresh, frozen, and precooked).

The second map included Fowlers' corporate distribution locations on one layer, and on a second layer, a region-by-region breakdown of food products customer channel sales data (retail, distributor, direct-to-consumer, and government).

The design team also generated two maps for the technology products group. The first included key suppliers by commodity type (resins, packaging, a contract manufacturer that supplied optical media and computer hardware); manufacturing locations (San Jose, California; Chicago, Illinois; St. Paul, Minnesota; and Memphis, Tennessee) mapped by product family (CD-ROM replication, fulfillment, and life cycle management); and corporate distribution locations mapped by product family (optical drives and optical media). See Figure 7-2 for a summary of technological product locations.

The second map included Fowlers' corporate distribution locations on one layer and on a second layer a region-by-region breakdown of customer channel sales data (retail and OEM/key accounts).

Geographic Maps

With the level of detail defined, construction of the maps can begin. As with the SCORcard building process (Chapter 5), the design team is divided into appropriate subteams based on experience, change-management value in appropriate product groups, and division of work to complete the maps. Physical locations are usually placed on the map first, followed by the product-family routes between the locations.

There are two basic strategies to assemble the maps—by the type of material movement (inbound, intercompany, outbound, and returns) or by supply chain.

In the case of suppliers, many teams map the physical locations of a few top suppliers for each main commodity type. One strategy to gather accurate data on transportation routes is to focus a subteam on collecting and summarizing freight bills. Freight bills contain the important details of the item, quantity, sales value, freight expense, and delivery cycle time, point of origin, and destination. Depending on the transportation carriers used, much of this data may be available electronically.

In Fowlers' case, the technology products geographic map summarizes the material flow of four product families from supplier location to manufacturing site to warehouse location (Figure 7-3). It also highlights all warehouse-to-warehouse and warehouse-to-manufacturing moves. Return flow is not mapped on this figure; the team assembled it on a customer-facing map. Lastly, the import locations for optical media and drives—Seattle and Los Angeles—are included.

Figure 7-2. Technology products geographic map—locations.

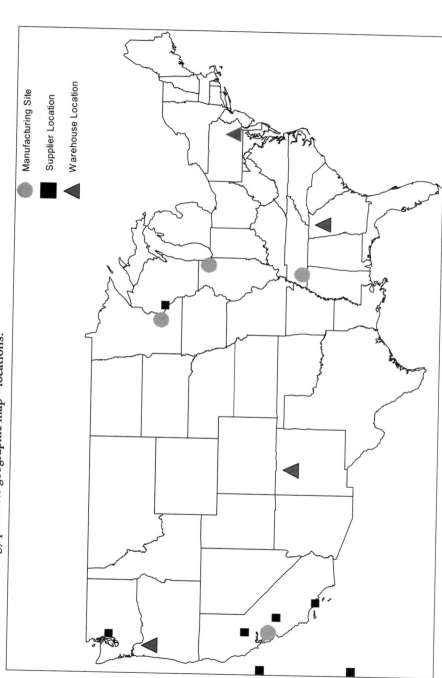

Manufacturing Site

Supplier Location

Warehouse Location

Figure 7-3. Technology products geographic map—flow.

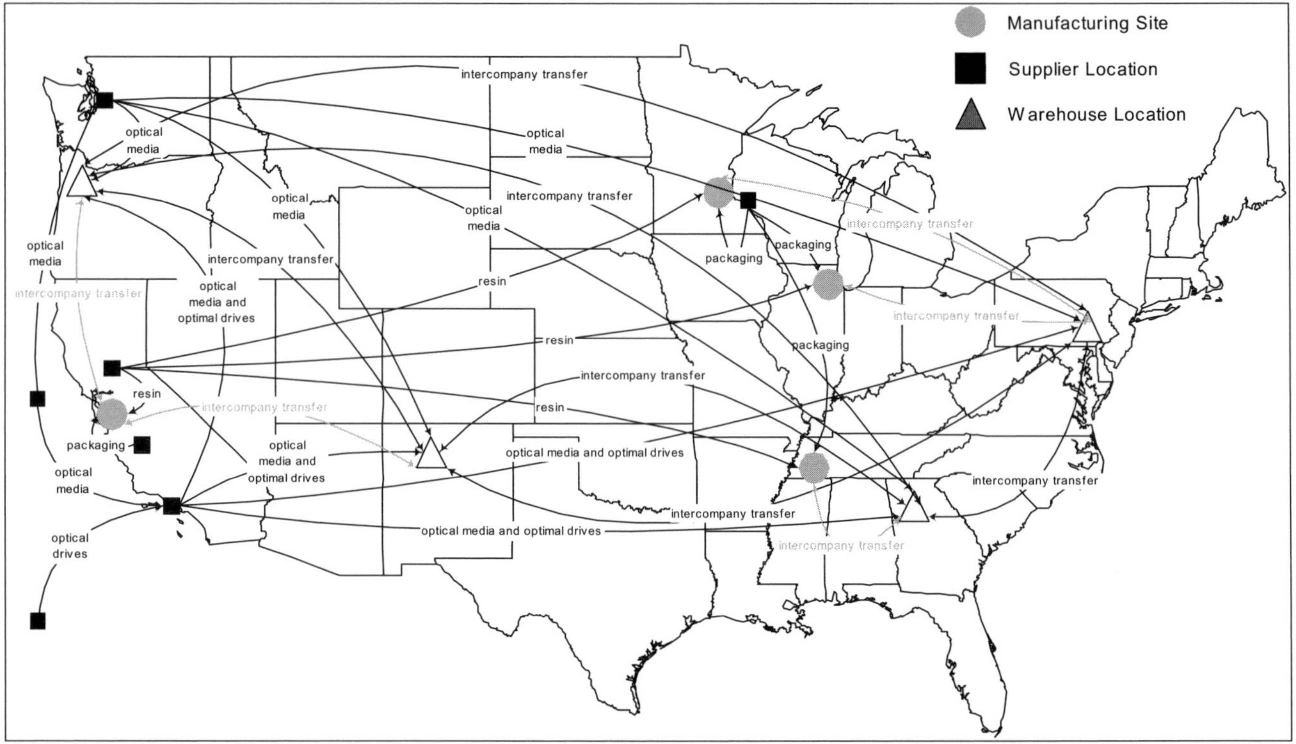

■ Location Level Two Processes

The next step is to determine SCOR Level Two process types used by each location on the geographic maps. Start by identifying appropriate process categories specific to the location—that is SOURCE, MAKE, DELIVER, and/or RETURN. The second step is to determine the process type—stock-to-order, engineer-to-order, defective, excess inventory, and MRO. A typical manufacturing location might have a profile defined by S1, S2, M1, and D2.

In this case D2 refers to direct shipments configured in the manufacturing warehouse to customer specs based on the exact customer order. Not all locations have to have all process categories. A warehouse, for example, may have only D1 and D2 profiles because the plan and deliver replenishment orders are driving the supply from manufacturing. The same warehouse that also issues purchase orders to a contract manufacturer for purchased finished goods may have a profile that includes S1, D1, and D2.

In Fowlers' case, the manufacturing locations utilized all process types for SOURCE, MAKE, and DELIVER and just R1 returns. The primary configuration was characterized as S2 for key suppliers of resins and packaging; S1 for contract manufacturers that supplied optical media and optical drives; M2 for CD-ROM replication, fulfillment, and life cycle management; and D2 customer direct parcel ship for CD-ROM replication, fulfillment, and life cycle management. The primary technology products configuration of the Fowlers corporate distribution locations was characterized as S2 and D1 for optical drives and optical media. Another common tool that SCOR users employ is the thread diagram (see Appendix A). The method allows for a more process-oriented picture of material flow. It is ultimately up to the teams to which methods are employed in this part of the analysis.

■ Material Flow Performance

Usually initiated after the first two steps, the third part of the AS IS analysis is to assemble a material flow performance spreadsheet. The objective is to collect and analyze key SCOR Level Two metrics for *each location*.

Supply chain metrics for Level Two (noted on metrics template, Tables 4-1a–c) include:

❑ Supplier on-time and in-full
❑ RM inventory days of supply at locations and in transit
❑ Transportation cost, calculated by inbound
❑ Backorder duration
❑ Source lead-time, defined by actual and contractual agreements

Manufacturing Level Two metrics include:

❑ Production schedule attainment or on-time shipment
❑ RM, WIP, FG, and returns inventory days of supply, at locations, and in transit
❑ Transportation cost, calculated by shipments between company locations
❑ Manufacturing lead-time, defined by actual and system setups

Distribution center Level Two metrics include:

❑ Order on-time shipment
❑ RM, Returns, WIP, and FG inventory days of supply at locations and in transit
❑ Transportation cost, calculated by outbound and returns
❑ Backorder duration
❑ Order drop-to-ship lead-time.

In Fowlers' case, the assembly of the freight payment detail and assembly of the material flow performance spreadsheet was homework for the rest of the week. The project team agreed that the workload for everyone would be greater in this phase than the SCORcard.

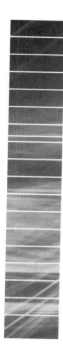

8

Week Six: The AS IS Material Flow Performance Summary

Get a full understanding of material flow.

This week, the design team will look at supply chain material flow from two perspectives: common sense and fact. Supply chains that have evolved one supplier at a time and customer by customer tend to be less strategic and more events driven than those that have been engineered. Common sense and fact are necessary to help align supply chain strategy with material flow efficiency. Common sense looks at the macro issues of how supply chain material flows relate to strategy and practices. This is the fun part. Fact looks at the micro issues of how the company utilizes its transportation and inventory dollars to meet service levels. This part is data intensive.

The amount of progress to be made this week depends on how easily transportation data can be assembled, the degree of financial sophistication of the inventory organizations, and the approach to inbound freight. For many design teams, assembling a geographic map or thread diagram (Chapter 7) is the company's first comprehensive look at the efficiency of how materials are moved from place to place. The material flow performance summary may be the first time value is assigned to the efficiency. Now is the time to cash in any outstanding favors with the transportation department and logistics service providers.

Reviewing the Material Flow Performance Summary and Refining Geographic Maps

Many design teams would prefer to evaluate their material flow work from the geographic map. This is the forest perspective, and it limits the ability to assign relative values needed to compare one issue or problem against another.

The other instinct is to try to resolve each material flow issue on its own. This is the trees perspective, and it fails to consider the most important outcome: efficiency of the total system. What's needed is balance between the two. For example, a point-to-point geographic map of distribution center shipments to customer locations graphically represents the inefficiencies that exist (Figure 8-1).

A map like this is a powerful graphic for executives. Similar maps can be developed for intercompany and inbound shipments. But this type of map doesn't provide a deeper understanding of the details needed to answer the ultimate question: What if I fix it? With that in mind, the only agenda item for Day One is to review the material flow performance spreadsheet.

The Material Flow Performance Spreadsheet

The main components of the spreadsheet (Table 8-1) are the location name, revenue, warehouse expense, transportation expense, inventory value, on-time performance, lead-time, and returns profile. The spreadsheet summary is just that—a summary. However, each component is fully supported with detail. Revenue data is the actual sales value of the shipments originating from the location. Other details that may be included in the

Figure 8-1. Outbound shipment summary.

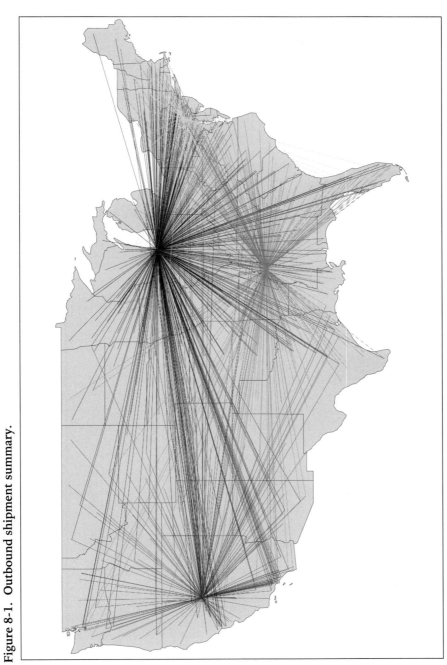

Table 8-1. Material flow performance spreadsheet.

Location	Revenues	Warehouse Expense		Transportation Expense				Inventory				On Time		Lead-time			Returns		
		RM & WIP	FG		Inbound	Inter-company	Outbound		RM	WIP	FG	Inbound Receipts	Outbound Shipments	Inbound Orders	Inter-company Orders	Outbound Orders	$	Inventory	Inbound Freight $
				$				INV $											
				lbs.				COGS $											
				$/lb.				Days											

analysis include number of shipments and number of customers counted by ship-to locations. The type of materials stored and handled summarizes warehouse expense data; RM/WIP and FG are the two inventory categories noted on the spreadsheet. Transportation expense data is aggregated to three categories: inbound freight expenses from suppliers, intercompany freight expenses (moving goods between locations), and outbound freight expenses to customers. For each category the dollars, weight, and number of shipments are other details needed to assess the efficiency of goods movement. Cost per shipment and number of shipments to complete a customer order are critical to quality measures here. Inventory data is categorized by type: RM, WIP, and FG. Calculating the days of stock requires knowing the annualized cost of goods sold (COGS) for each type. On-time performance is calculated for inbound receipts and outbound shipments. Many companies track both complete and line fill rate. Lead-time is calculated for all inbound (purchase) orders, intercompany (transfer) orders, and outbound (sales) orders. Data collected for this part of the spreadsheet includes both complete order duration and backorder duration. The returns data includes total dollar value of revenue returned, the inventory value and days of stock based on the annualized COGS, and the return freight weight and associated costs.

By the time they are done with this week, many design teams recognize for the first time how SCOR metrics cascade and how typical logistics measures relate back to the profit-and-loss statement. For example, total supply chain cost cascades to the sum of order management cost, material acquisition costs, planning costs, information systems costs, and inventory carrying costs. Order management costs cascade to customer service costs, outbound transportation cost, and finished goods warehouse costs. (For a refresher on the cascades, refer to the Level Two and Level Three components of Table 4-1a–c, SCOR metrics template.)

■ Fowlers' Material Flow Spreadsheet Review

In Fowlers' case, this spreadsheet review was coming on the heels of the most homework-intensive week of the project to date. The coach suggested organizing the review in two parts.

The first part was aimed at simply reviewing what was actually on the spreadsheet. The second, more important part was to start listing the important learning points of old-but-forgotten knowledge and new discoveries. This second part starts the kind of thinking that's needed in the disconnect analysis that begins in Week Seven (Table 8-2, technology products material flow performance spreadsheet).

The technology products group locations match up with the geographic map from the previous week. The first four locations represent corporate regional distribution centers, and the last four represent manufacturing locations. Revenues were collected by location. Manufacturing locations support direct sale of CD-ROM replication, fulfillment, and life cycle management services to the OEM channel. Corporate distribution centers support direct sale of optical drives and media to the retail channel. Adding up the numbers shows that of $450 million revenue in 2001, $150 million came from OEM sales and $300 million through retail. (Figure 8-2, technology products sales regions, shows how sales regions match up to specific distribution centers.)

Warehouse expense in the distribution centers was isolated to finished goods handling only, whereas the manufacturing sites accumulated expense for both finished goods and raw materials/work-in-process categories. Overall warehouse expense totaled $8.1 million—equivalent to 1.8 percent of sales, with most of the expense—13 percent—in the finished goods category.

Transportation expense in the distribution centers included all modes of transportation. Inbound was predominately from Japan and the Pacific Rim; intercompany involved material moves between distribution centers and manufacturing locations; outbound included all shipments to customers in and outside the region. Inbound and intercompany expenses for the manufacturing locations were similar; the OEM customer paid outbound freight. Overall transportation expense totaled $24.6 million (excluding customer-paid freight), or 5.4 percent of sales.

Inventory value for the distribution centers was isolated to FG only. Conversely, the manufacturing locations stored only RM and WIP. The distribution centers were a source of sup-

Table 8-2. Technology products material flow performance spreadsheet ($ and lbs. in million; $/lb. are actual).

Location	Revenues	Warehouse Expense RM & WIP	Warehouse Expense FG		Transportation Expense Inbound	Transportation Expense Inter-company	Transportation Expense Outbound		Inventory RM	Inventory WIP	Inventory FG	On Time Inbound Receipts	On Time Outbound Shipments	Lead-time Inbound Orders	Lead-time Inter-company Orders	Lead-time Outbound Orders	Returns $	Returns Inventory	Returns Inbound Freight $
Sante Fe	$82.0	$0.00	$0.87	$	$2.28	$0.85	$2.10	INV $	$0.0	$0.0	$22.0	67%	69%	62	3	5	$19	$20.0	$0.25
				lbs.	5.4	4.3	5.5	COGS $	$0.0	$0.0	$86.1							$86.1	1.2
				$/lb.	$0.42	$0.20	$0.38	Days	—	—	93							85	$0.21
Harrisburg	$70	$0.00	$1.04	$	$1.92	$0.72	$1.76	INV $	$0.0	$0.0	$20.0	59%	75%	59	4	4	$16	$16.8	$0.24
				lbs.	4.5	3.6	4.6	COGS $	$0.0	$0.0	$73.5							$73.5	1.0
				$/lb.	$0.43	$0.20	$0.38	Days	—	—	99							83	$0.24
Atlanta	$75	$0.00	$0.97	$	$2.07	$0.77	$1.90	INV $	$0.0	$0.0	$18.5	61%	77%	72	3	5	$17	$17.9	$0.23
				lbs.	4.9	4.0	5.0	COGS $	$0.0	$0.0	$78.8							$78.8	1.1
				$/lb.	$0.42	$0.19	$0.38	Days	—	—	86							83	$0.21
Portland	$73	$0.00	$1.03	$	$2.00	$0.77	$1.80	INV $	$0.0	$0.0	$18.6	66%	71%	69	3	4	$17	$17.9	$0.20
				lbs.	4.7	3.9	4.9	COGS $	$0.0	$0.0	$76.7							$76.7	0.9
				$/lb.	$0.43	$0.20	$0.37	Days	—	—	89							85	$0.22
San Jose	$56	$0.84	$0.73	$	$1.50	$0.58	$0.00	INV $	$6.0	$0.02	$0.0	50%	95%	62	3	4	NA	—	—
				lbs.	3.6	2.9	0.0	COGS $	$27.7	$2.0	$0.0							—	—
				$/lb.	$0.42	$0.20	—	Days	79	4	—							—	—
Chicago	$23	$0.35	$0.30	$	$0.60	$0.23	$0.00	INV $	$3.1	$0.02	$0.0	67%	96%	63	3	4	NA	—	—
				lbs.	1.4	1.2	0.0	COGS $	$9.2	$1.1	$0.0							—	—
				$/lb.	$0.43	$0.19	—	Days	123	5	—							—	—
St. Paul	$22	$0.33	$0.29	$	$0.60	$0.24	$0.00	INV $	$2.8	$0.02	$0.0	70%	97%	61	3	4	NA	—	—
				lbs.	1.3	1.1	0.0	COGS $	$9.0	$1.0	$0.0							—	—
				$/lb.	$0.46	$0.22	—	Days	114	7	—							—	—
Memphis	$49	$0.74	$0.64	$	$1.30	$0.51	$0.00	INV $	$6.2	$0.02	$0.0	59%	98%	64	3	4	NA	—	—
				lbs.	3.1	2.6	0.0	COGS $	$23.0	$2.0	$0.0							—	—
				$/lb.	$0.42	$0.20	—	Days	98	4	—							—	—
$Total	$450.00	$2.25	$5.85	$	$12.3	$4.7	$7.6	INV $	$18.1	$0.1	$79.1						$69.0	$72.5	$0.9
%Total		0.5%	1.3%	lbs.	28.9	23.6	20.0	COGS $	$68.9	$6.1	$315.0							$315.1	$4.2

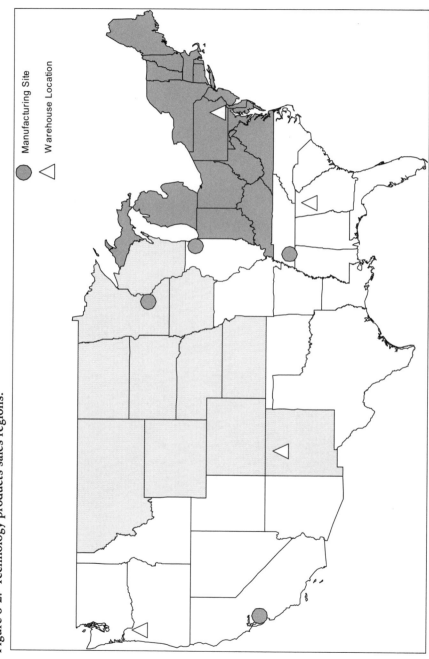

Figure 8-2. Technology products sales regions.

Manufacturing Site

Warehouse Location

ply for optical media for the manufacturing locations. FG media was reclassified upon receipt in the factory as RM. Overall inventory value totaled $97.3 million. Against an annual $390 million COGS, this represented ninety-one days of supply.

On-time performance is measured in two categories: inbound receipts from purchase orders or transfer orders, and outbound shipments of transfer orders or sales orders. In either case, the raw data is based on the actual orders themselves. As with the overall SCORcard metric of delivery performance, the formula here requires data for on-time and complete shipments. On-time performance for inbound receipts is consistently poor, while results for outbound deliveries to the OEM group are among the industry's best. The performance of the distribution centers in servicing products is a contributing factor to the critical issues of delivery reliability and the perception that the technology products group was hard to do business with. On the spreadsheet, lead-time data is consolidated into three categories: inbound (purchase orders), intercompany (transfer orders), and outbound (sales orders). The data represents the total number of days to finish an order for both complete order duration and backorder duration.

Finally, the return data categories include total revenue returned, the inventory value and days of stock based on annualized COGS, and the return freight detail including expense, pounds, and per-pound expense. The total value of goods returned is $69 million, or 23 percent of the sales value through the distribution centers. The inventory value of $72.5 million is calculated by taking the sales value and multiplying by the gross margin percent. Transportation cost of $4.2 million represents 0.9 percent of sales.

While compiling this information, the design team encountered typical issues: maps with too much or too little detail; unavailable customer data; general confusion using SCOR language S1, M1, and D1. But they continued on, refining metric data for each lane and location. They had trouble pulling intercompany and inbound freight costs out of cost of goods sold, which is a common problem. Further, they found that supplier metrics in general were not calculated consistently. It was the same with backorder duration. Nevertheless, they were able to finish this part of the process by validating their calculations while noting disconnects and absent measures.

Here's what they learned about material flow through Fowlers:

❑ Transportation cost accounted for more than 6.3 percent of total supply chain costs, which in turn represents 14 percent of total company costs. The cost per pound demonstrated the impact of allowing expedited shipping and airfreight to creep in as standard practice. The picture would have been worse if true customer-paid costs for shipments from manufacturing sites were added in.

❑ Return performance was somewhat hidden because the inventory was accounted for through accruals and write-offs on the balance sheet. More direct data simply wasn't being collected on returns. This was also the first time the freight expense was aggregated—regardless of return type—for all to see. Another discovery was that return transportation combined two sets of cost: moving goods to the initial return center and then making an intercompany move to wherever the goods would end up.

❑ Each location had latitude to designate the mode of transportation for inbound materials, based on its own production schedule and delivery requirements. Suppliers moved the same material to multiple Fowlers locations using multiple modes, frequently including costly airfreight.

❑ "Free freight" was provided to the retail segment as an informal practice that had evolved over time. It started as a way to close sales or to appease retailers over any number of problems, but it became an expectation, regardless of mode or required delivery time. This was a vicious circle that contributed to Fowler's high transportation cost. Efforts to contain that cost led to poor delivery performance, which contributed to the large account receivables and a slow cash-to-cash cycle.

❑ Poor assimilation of the new Tier One ERP system left the team without basic analytical reports for inventory, cost, and order status, which made problem-solving activities event based rather than a more proactive hunt for root causes.

❑ On products with six-month lifecycles—as is common in electronics—lead-times of sixty days or more made inventory planning impossible. The team realized the implication: The business unit consistently had to guess the total product volume required across its entire lifetime, with only one or two chances to make adjustments.

Planning For Disconnect Analysis

The search for understanding of disconnects in material flow offers content value as well as an opportunity for important leaps in change management. The content value is the process of identifying and valuing supply chain improvement opportunities, using established problem-solving techniques. The change-management value is taking advantage of the opportunity to include more people in the design process. The brainstorming activities of this work can engage as many as fifty people. The agenda for Day Two focuses on finishing the material flow summary, updating the geographic maps, and planning for the disconnect analysis.

In planning for the disconnect analysis, first identify the brainstorming team—a group that includes design team members plus other experts in the various material flow locations and lanes who know where problems exist. Second, assemble the brainstorm meeting agenda and invitation letter.

Finally, assign owners to complete any remaining homework on the material flow performance summary.

The brainstorm meeting agenda should include:

❑ A one-hour premeeting for those who have not participated in SCOR education, to familiarize them with SCORcard gap analysis, review of AS IS material flow maps, and review of the AS IS material flow performance summary
❑ Brainstorming individual disconnects noting location and lane of impact
❑ Arranging the disconnects into groups with similar causes and clearly defining problem statements for each group
❑ Reviewing problem statements with entire team
❑ Documenting

9

Week Seven: Material Flow Disconnect Analysis and Steering Team Review Number Three

Add up the value while getting the whole company involved.

What do the numbers fifty, twenty, 1,000, and fifteen have in common? They're the typical results of a successful material flow disconnect brainstorming event, focused on identifying all the issues, inefficiencies, and assorted problems of moving goods from suppliers through the company and on to customers.

Fifty is the typical number of people who participate in the daylong event. Twenty is how many problems or issues a person can brainstorm in an hour. A thousand is the number of issues or problems the whole team can generate in the same amount of time. And fifteen is approximately the number of unique issues common among the 1,000. In other words, if you get to the root cause for the fifteen major issues, you're most of the way to solving 1,000 perceived problems.

As a rule of thumb, these fifteen unique issues will represent profit improvement potential of at least 3 percent of the supply chain's sales value. A team brainstorming issues for a supply chain supporting $100 million in revenue typically will identify $3 million in gross opportunity savings.

The objectives of the seventh week are to conduct the disconnect analysis; initiate the fishbone analysis to find root causes for the common issues; and prepare for the third steering team review—providing the first look at the relationship between numerical SCORcard gaps (last three columns of enterprise, technology group, and food group SCORcards, Tables 6-1 through 6-3) and the causes of the inefficiencies that have evolved in the supply chain over time.

Planning the Brainstorm Session

A well-planned brainstorm event results in fast and efficient collection of data and creation of a positive feeling of teamwork through a common understanding of the project expectations. It offers a shared vision of the path forward and gives those who aren't on the design team a sense of the project's organization and pace. It empowers agents of change to carry the project values to their respective departments.

There are five ingredients to a good brainstorming session:

1. An appropriate invitee list
2. Effective communication including an invitation, project overview, and instructions for event preparation
3. Predefined brainstorm categories
4. An appropriate venue
5. Predefined leadership roles for the design team that carries through to the TO BE material flow phase

Invitees

Select people who are close to the day-to-day and week-to-week details of all facets of the movement of materials. Using the process categories of the SCOR model, identify people who can point to problems at the purchase order, work order, and sales order level. At this phase, quantity of issues, with examples, is the most important factor. Don't reach too high in the organization; participants at higher levels of management have more trouble generating a comprehensive list and often cannot point to specific examples. The examples are what help drive the root cause analysis.

Effective Communication

The invitation letter needs to clearly convey the purpose of the event, preparation instructions, and the basics of where, when, and so on. The invitation needs to be in participants' hands one to two weeks in advance; anything less gives the impression that the project is poorly planned and limits the quality of individual preparation.

A SCOR overview session conducted before the event provides participants with a wide-angle view of the project and gives them a status report on the key deliverables of the SCORcard gap analysis, AS IS geographic map, and the material flow performance summary spreadsheet.

Predefined Brainstorm Categories

Setting up discussion categories in advance helps the participants generate more detail faster. There is no single method of selecting categories. You can use SCOR process categories— PLAN, SOURCE, MAKE, DELIVER, RETURN, and Enable. Or you can use physical locations and metrics based on those in the material flow spreadsheet (Table 8-1)—such as revenue, warehouse expense, transportation expense, inventory, on-time, lead-time, and return.

The Appropriate Venue

The ideal venue is a large rectangular room with enough theater seating for all attendees. The category labels are taped high on the wall and spaced equally around all four walls of the room. The activity does not work as well as in a small conference room.

Predefined Leadership Roles

At this session, design team members formalize their role in the knowledge-transfer process from student to teacher. The project manager serves as the master of ceremonies, reviewing the agenda and instructions for each step. He or she also serves as pace keeper, moderator of conflict, and general role model for everyone.

A different design team member is assigned to facilitate the brainstorming steps for each category. Once the individual issues are placed under the appropriate category, each facilitator works with a subteam of attendees to group similar issues, define problem statements for the group, and own the assembly of the opportunity assessment.

◼ Conducting the Brainstorm Session

The Fowlers brainstorm team named itself "team disconnect." Its members included the entire design team; COO Brian Dowell; product development managers; buyer/planners; customer service representatives; cost accountants; marketing analysts; material planners; focus factory managers; sales managers; product line managers from both the technology and food products groups; functional experts for purchasing, order management, planning, distribution, and manufacturing from the corporate applications group; a transportation manager; an import/export manager; a warehouse manager from corporate logistics; a market research analyst; forecast analysts for each of the product families; and a business development manager from the corporate marketing group. In all, there were forty people on the list.

For discussion categories, the design team agreed on SCOR Level One processes: PLAN, SOURCE, MAKE, DELIVER, RETURN, and Enable. The rationale was to get people thinking about categories of how things should be. The first rule for the session was that each person who identified a disconnect must also identify the metric impact, using the material flow performance spreadsheet, noting location, and metric columns.

The PLAN category includes issues in sales and operations planning, unit forecasting, materials requirements planning, master production scheduling, distribution requirements planning, planned maintenance of capital parts, long-term capacity, and supply planning.

The SOURCE category includes issues in requisitioning and purchase orders, scheduling individual releases, paying suppliers, receiving, short-term material availability, inbound transportation, and raw material inventory.

MAKE includes issues in scheduling production lines, manufacturing and testing, packaging, releasing products to warehouses, intercompany transportation, work-in-process inventory, utilization, product yield, and short-term capacity.

DELIVER includes issues in order fulfillment such as quotes and inquiries, entering and confirming orders, and allocating inventory; also, such warehouse issues as consolidating orders, building loads, customer routes, receiving, picking, loading, receiving at the customer location, installation, and invoicing.

RETURN includes warranty returns, product recall, excess inventory returns in the pipeline, and return of maintenance, repair, and overhaul items.

The Enable category includes issues relating to information, relationships, and other factors that allow the supply chain to plan and execute effectively. Business rules, performance management, data collection, capital assets, transportation, network configuration, regulatory requirements, and compliance are all issues that fall under the Enable process.

The planning director was assigned team leader for the PLAN category. SOURCE was led by the purchasing director; the director of manufacturing oversaw discussion of MAKE; DELIVER was handled by the director of logistics/customer services; the corporate controller led the return discussion; the vice president of sales and marketing for the food products group led Enable with help from the director of applications. David Able served as the master of ceremonies, while the coach was available to provide role modeling as needed during the day.

Fowlers' Disconnect Analysis Brainstorming

The agenda for the disconnect analysis session at Fowlers had five line items and looked like this:

1. *Introduction.* David reviews the agenda, room layout, brainstorm categories, and introduces the category facilitators.

2. *Initial Brainstorm.* David facilitates the brainstorming activity to identify individual disconnects and issues known by participants. Everyone should be equipped with a pad of sticky-back notes. Participants get an hour to write as many disconnects as possible—one per note. Each person should be able to contribute at least twenty disconnects. A good disconnect contains an accurate description of the issue, using a full sentence, a reference to real examples (list an item, supplier, customer, etc.), a frequency estimate (daily, weekly, monthly, etc.), and the initials of the person who wrote it.

3. *Category Organization.* The master of ceremonies assigns people to categories where they have knowledge and experience. Then, each category team spends two hours reading through the disconnects and grouping them appropriately. Then the subteam members are tasked with writing a problem statement that accurately represents each grouping. A good statement is usually a combination of three sentences—one that describes the problem, one that describes an example, and one that lists metrics affected on the material flow performance summary.

4. *Question and Answer Review.* The master of ceremonies facilitates a question-and-answer review of each category team's problem statements with the entire group. Plan for an hour to ninety minutes for this exercise.

5. *Documentation.* The category team leaders document the category, disconnect groups, and individual disconnects. David makes sure the Post-Its are properly labeled and transcribed into an electronic version. A simple, effective system is to label each main category with a number, each

subcategory with a decimal number, and each individual disconnect with a third digit (PLAN disconnects would be 1.1.1, 1.1.2, etc.).

Fowlers' disconnect analysis session yielded 838 individual disconnects in six brainstorm categories and thirty-two disconnect groups with their own problem statements. For a detailed example, consider the PLAN category, which yielded eight disconnect groups with problem statements representing 258 individual disconnects.

❏ 1.1 included problem statements on inaccurate product forecasts resulting from a lack of reliable market information, poor demand signals, proliferation of items, and poor data integrity results in excess inventory or lost revenue opportunity. For example, CDR item 7890987 under-forecasted while PC card item 3443939 over-forecasted. Metrics impacted included forecast accuracy, revenue, on-time performance, transportation expense, and inventory.

❏ 1.2 included problem statements on ineffective interdepartmental communication and coordination results and diluted corporate goals and objectives. For example, there was no alignment between unit cost goals driven through purchase price variance (PPV) and manufacturing variance with logistics goals of service and inventory levels and warehouse and transportation expenses. Metrics impacted included revenue, on-time performance, and inventory.

❏ 1.3 included statements on a lack of clearly defined and communicated new product introduction priorities resulting in lost revenue or inappropriately allocated product development resources. For example, 1325644 item memory cards took too long to develop while item 1299987 manuals were considered obsolete due to revision changes. Metrics impacted included net new revenue, inventory, and potential accruals.

❏ 1.4 showed that there are multiple technology platforms that exist between manufacturing, purchasing, order fulfillment, and planning that lead to MRP errors and inconsistent priorities between suppliers and plants, impeding delivery effectiveness when multiple plants were required to produce products. For example, a purchase order for CDR was placed while a work order was cut in spite of a declining forecast trend. Metrics impacted included COGS and inventory.

❑ 1.5 revealed there was no current sales and operations plan to align the financial and unit plans of the business. For example, the operating unit plans differed between the manufacturing production plan driven for unit cost, the marketing sales plan, and the sales forecast and compensation plan. Metrics impacted included revenue, transportation expense, warehouse expense, on-time performance, and lead time.

❑ 1.6 showed no definition of lead times for proper promotion planning and communication to all affected parties when plans were changed. Take, for example, the identified items that represented lead violations where promotions were increased, decreased, cancelled, or delayed. Metrics impacted included revenue, inventory, warehouse cost, and transportation cost.

❑ 1.7 showed there were ineffective warehouse-to-warehouse transfers and/or inventory balancing resulting in longer lead times and ineffective use of inventories. Shipping finished goods item 7687878 from Santa Fe to Portland to support inventory replenishment of a back order situation was given as an example. Metrics impacted included revenue, inventory, transportation expense, and warehouse expense.

❑ 1.8 showed that supply planning was difficult due to mismatches between purchase price variance goals, demand requirements, supplier minimum order quantities, and manufacturing economic order quantities. For example, the minimum order quantity to achieve PPV goals for buyer 123 resulted in stocking 365 days' worth of goods for an item forecasted to decline 20 percent. Metrics impacted included inventory and COGS.

Here are a few examples of the individual disconnects for 1.1—inaccurate unit forecasts:

1.1.1   New product forecasts are inaccurate and result in lost opportunities.

1.1.2   Inaccurate forecasting on new products

1.1.3   Better market information for new product forecast

1.1.4   Forecast at product family level does not help with individual SKU variance

1.1.5   Integrate new product growth rates into sales budgets and forecasts.

1.1.6   Too heavy a reliance on sales forecasts for new products

1.1.7   Repair parts are not forecasted as separate demand points.

1.1.8   Item master data setup errors that cause lack of planning passing to plants or vendors

1.1.9   Lack of accountability between field forecasting, marketing forecasting, and supply chain forecasting

1.1.10 No visibility of sales to end customers and sales to dealers clouded by return

For ideas on documenting the mass of data to be assembled during this day, see Table 9-1.

The Fishbone Analysis

After an exhausting exercise, the first agenda item for the design team on Day Two of this week is to consolidate similar problem statements within and between brainstorm categories. It's reasonable to assume, for instance, that a problem describing poor inventory planning might show up in PLAN, SOURCE, DELIVER, and perhaps other categories. The design team needs to determine if consolidation is appropriate, then rewrite the combined problem statement to reflect the changes. This is where specific examples of the problem or issue are important.

Table 9-1. Disconnect summary template.

1.1 Enter disconnect group statement here for Category 1	
Description for Disconnect or Cause	**ID**
Enter individual disconnect for Group 1 here	1.1.1
Enter individual disconnect for Group 1 here	1.1.2

1.2 Enter 2nd disconnect group statement here for Category 1	
Description for Disconnect or Cause	**ID**
Enter individual disconnect for Group 2 here	1.2.1
Enter individual disconnect for Group 2 here	1.2.2

1.3 Enter 3rd disconnect group statement here for Category 1	
Description for Disconnect or Cause	**ID**
Enter individual disconnect for Group 3 here	1.3.1
Enter individual disconnect for Group 3 here	1.3.2

Source: © Copyright 2000 Pragmatek Consulting Group, Ltd. Used with permission.

When in doubt, leave problems separate; there will be other opportunities to consolidate. To keep track of the changes, include the original documentation numbers with the consolidated problem statements. These will be needed later as the team begins to fill in the fishbone diagram. In Fowlers' case, the thirty-two disconnect groups were consolidated to twelve unique problems:

1. *Inaccurate Forecasts.* These were due to poorly defined practices, underutilized modeling techniques, and untrained personnel.
2. *Inconsistent Supply Management Practices.* These focused mainly on tactical aspects of some suppliers.
3. *Disparate Systems.* These were defined as poor integration, and as low utilization of planning and forecasting with enterprise resource planning.
4. *Poor Data Integrity.* This was defined as the ineffective management of supplier, item, and customer master data.

5. *Supplier Inflexibility.* This was defined as the vendors' inability to respond to near-term demand fluctuations for source-to-stock and source-to-order items.

6. *Hit and Miss Product Life Cycle Management.* This problem was defined as ineffective processes to manage all phases of the business life cycle, from introduction through commercialization to retirement.

7. *Poor Inventory Planning.* This was defined as the reactive tactical management of stocking levels, and replenishment orders to factories and suppliers.

8. *No Sales and Operations Planning.* This was defined as lack of a process to integrate new demand and supply planning with business plan reconciliation to financial objectives.

9. *Reactive Logistics Planning and Execution.* This problem concerned physical goods movement.

10. *Undisciplined Order Management.* This problem covered inquiry and quote through order entry and inventory allocation.

11. *No Formal Return Management.* This problem included reverse logistics processes to goods movement to policy to the authorization process.

12. *Poor Inventory Control Practices.*

After consolidation, David Able assigned the problem statements to the appropriate Fowlers design team members to lead both the root cause and opportunity analysis; depending on the number of teams and problems, it may sometimes be necessary to assign multiple problems to a leader. The leader is responsible for getting the work completed and validated.

Distribute a blank fishbone analysis sheet (Figure 9-1). Each problem statement becomes the head of the fish. With a group, role-model a detailed root cause analysis, going to the second level of bones for each cause. Use a problem statement from the day before and facilitate the exercise with the group. Use appropriate detail from the brainstorm categories, original problem statements, and individual disconnects to help fill in the cause-and-effect bones. Finally, have the design team category leaders put together a plan to complete their fishbone analysis

Figure 9-1. Blank fishbone template.

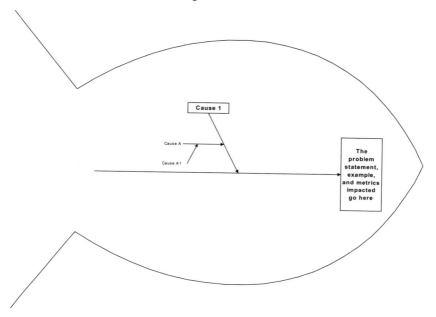

by the next session, using any necessary resources to accurately portray the fish.

▪ Conducting Steering Team Review Number Three

Prepare and conduct steering team review number three with the following agenda:

- ❑ Project roadmap status
- ❑ Education on disconnect process
- ❑ Introduce team disconnect
- ❑ Share disconnect statistics
- ❑ Review group problem statements
- ❑ Decisions required today
- ❑ Expectations for steering team review number four

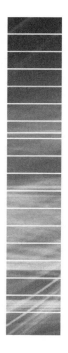

10

Week Eight: The Disconnect and Opportunity Analysis

Identify and solve the big-fish problems.

There's no end to the comic relief that the fish analogy offers when a hard-working design team feels like it's swimming upstream. Here are some actual statements that have been tossed out by team members who were starting to flounder:

- ❑ A big-fish story is a supply chain problem that's rumored to be bigger than it really is—and that gets even bigger with each retelling.
- ❑ Big fish are big savings opportunities while little fish are small opportunities; sometimes it's easier to catch little fish.
- ❑ Filleting the problems means eliminating all the bones.
- ❑ You need the right tackle to catch the right fish.
- ❑ Conducting the opportunity analysis is just a matter of putting meat on the bones. Remember timing is everything.

The homework for this week focuses on the brainstorm subteams and other resource experts on completing the fishbone analysis for their respective problems. By using effective problem-solving techniques, the subteams prepare to review their findings with the rest of the team and get started on calculating the savings opportunity.

Specifically, the objectives of Week Eight are to review and refine the fishbone analysis and initiate the gross opportunity analysis and prioritization.

Reviewing and Refining the Fishbone Analysis

On Day One, the review and refinement process provides another chance to consolidate problems (some call them schools of fish) before starting the opportunity analysis. The process follows three basic steps, and the goal is to end up with uniquely defined problems to minimize the risk of overestimating potential savings.

The first step is for each subteam to review its fishbone chart, starting with the problem statement at the head, then branching out to the bones and the sub-bones. The group should discuss any changes—and the rationale behind those changes—and identify the resources used in the analysis process.

The second step is to consolidate or expand fish based on the details of the cause-and-effect analysis. When in doubt, let an example of the problem be the tiebreaker. The objective is to get to a point where each fish represents a unique problem that can be analyzed financially, and at this point, the process is as much art as science.

The third step is to validate that each fishbone problem statement can be traced backward to the original brainstorm category from which it derived and then a step further to the individual disconnects and examples. When this is done, and the number of fish has been locked down, the design team moves to the next step: opportunity analysis.

In Fowlers' case, the twelve fish distributed for homework the previous week consolidated to eight after the fishbone review and refinement process. "Inaccurate forecasts" and "poor inventory planning" consolidated with "no sales and operations planning," to form a new fish with the simplified title "poor planning."

"Inconsistent supply management practices" consolidated with "rigid supplier flexibility and responsiveness," and became, simply, "supply management."

"Poor inventory control practices" was rolled into "reactive logistics planning and execution."

The remaining fishbone diagrams—disparate systems, poor data integrity, hit-and-miss product life cycle management, undisciplined order management, and no formal return management—all remained unchanged.

The final list at Fowlers looked like this:

- ❑ Poor planning
- ❑ Supply management
- ❑ Disparate systems
- ❑ Poor data integrity
- ❑ Hit-and-miss product life cycle management
- ❑ Reactive logistics planning and execution
- ❑ Undisciplined order management
- ❑ No formal return management

The trick is to understand the causal relationships of each bone in relation to the main problem. (Figure 10-1 is an example of the Poor Planning Fishbone.)

In the original three fish that were combined into the poor planning fish, there had been many overlapping bones, both at the primary-cause level and the secondary-cause level. By consolidating, the opportunity analysis would be simplified, and the potential savings estimate would be more accurate.

■ Initiating the Opportunity Analysis

The objective for the design session on Day Two is to educate the team about the process of quantifying opportunity, to identify the appropriate documentation tool, to demonstrate how to

Figure 10-1. Poor planning fishbone chart.

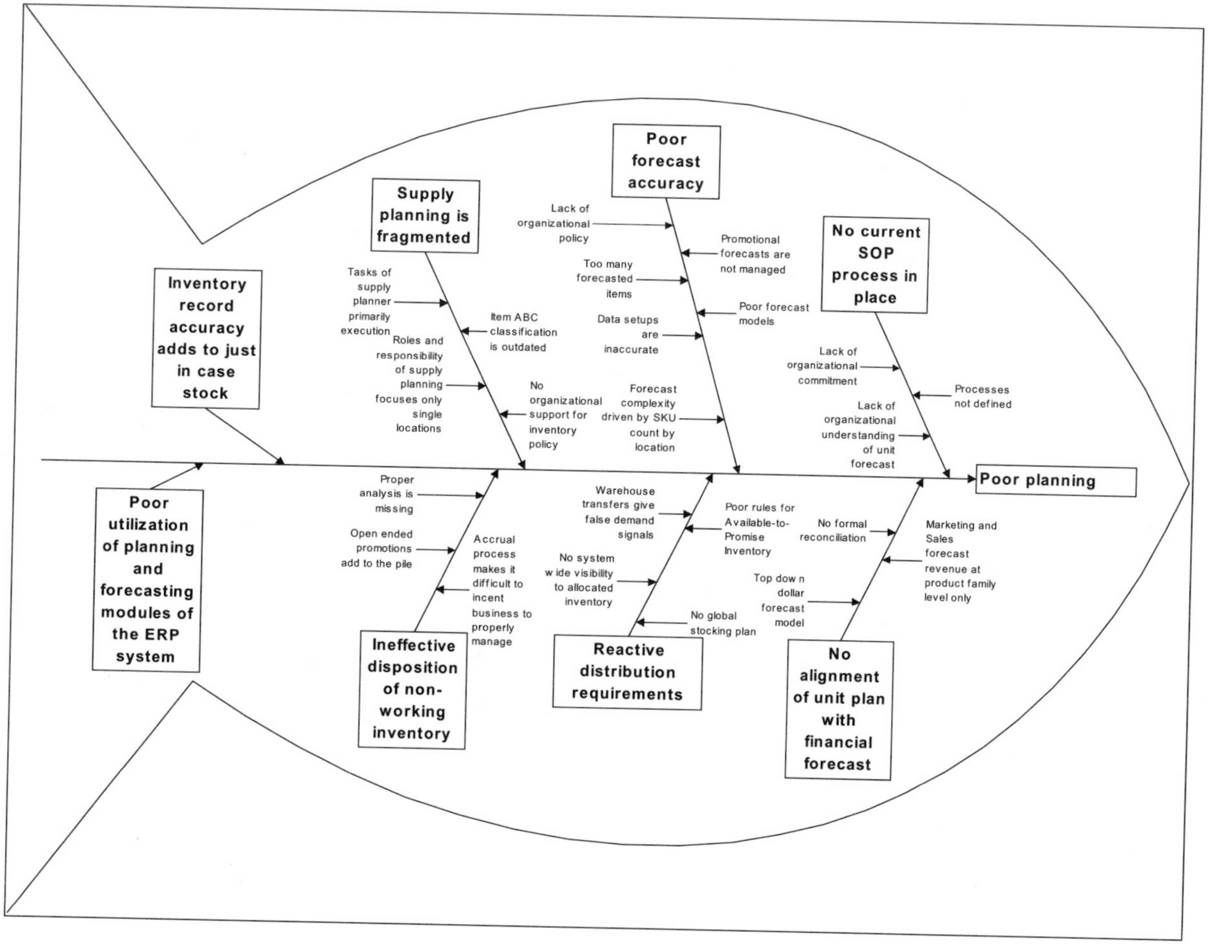

create a test scenario, and to clarify the homework for next week—that is, completing the opportunity analysis.

The quantification process follows five principles.

❏ *Principle One.* At a minimum, the subteams must determine the value of killing the fish using locations and measures from the material flow performance spreadsheet (Table 8-2).

❏ *Principle Two.* Factor out the effect of forecasted growth by assuming constant revenue for the financial period; usually savings are annualized. It's acceptable to include the profit improvement of revenue growth as a result of solving the problem.

❏ *Principle Three.* Be realistic in the savings estimates; the steering team and ultimately the executive team should add the appropriate safety buffer to the numbers, observing the doctrine of "underpromise and overdeliver." Conservative realism is normal; gross sandbagging is not helpful at this point.

❏ *Principle Four.* Document all assumptions behind the savings estimates. This is the most important principle; any pushback by the steering team typically has more to do with the assumptions than the numbers.

❏ *Principle Five.* Identify validation resources that can objectively test or spar with the numbers and assumptions—before the estimates are shared with the steering team. There are two kinds of value that result from this effort: change management and content. The validation team accomplishes both, giving others the opportunity to participate and feel ownership while making the content more accurate.

Documenting the opportunity analysis varies from sophisticated supply chain modeling and simulation software tools to simple spreadsheets. In all cases, the true challenge is to represent the value of eliminating each fishbone problem in the context of the profit and loss statement and balance sheet.

This part of the process makes many people uncomfortable. Engineers and other detail-minded folks on the project team have a difficult time getting comfortable with estimating opportunity. Even with sophisticated modeling tools, acronyms like WAG (wild ass guess) and SWAG (super wild ass guess) frequently show up at this phase of the analysis. But there should be some comfort in the fact that you'll round to the nearest $100,000 or $50,000. Some teams choose to value every major bone and then total them. Other teams focus on valuing the whole fish. Either way works as long as assumptions are documented.

Table 10-1 is a reasonably complicated sample opportunity spreadsheet. It is comprised of three main columns:

❏ Baseline represents actual data on the SCORcard and the material flow spreadsheet (Table 8-1)
❏ Test scenario represents the impact of eliminating the fish problem
❏ Change is where the change estimates are entered

The rows are organized by SCOR Level Two categories using order service level, lead-time, cost, working capital, and profit.

This spreadsheet will change a little for each project depending on how the cost centers and inventory organizations are allocated. In other projects, the material flow performance spreadsheet (Table 8-2) is used to show changes in appropriate locations and performance categories.

Try not to spend time estimating bones or fish related to work flow and information flow issues—things like customer service cost, purchasing cost, and planning cost. The next design phase will focus on indirect labor productivity to handle transactions such as purchase orders, work orders, sales orders, return authorizations, forecasts, and replenishments. Things get a little fuzzy in warehouse cost, because moving or eliminating such a facility involves both labor and physical cost. If the focus of the opportunity is the warehouse, then keep it as part of the material flow opportunity assessment. If the focus of the opportunity is on the productivity improvement of the process, then save the analysis for work and information flow.

Table 10-1. Sample opportunity spreadsheet.

	Baseline		Per Piece/Order		Test Scenario		Per Piece/Order	%Change	$ Change
Transaction Summary									
Revenue	$450,000,000				$450,250,000			0.00%	$ 250,000
Orders	1,326,632		$339.20		1,326,632		$339.39	0.00%	0
Total Items on Orders	1,340,900,800		$0.34		1,340,900,800		$0.34	0.00%	0
Purchase Orders	35,678		$9,809.97		35,678		$9,803.82	0.00%	0
Total Items Purchased	10,457,862		$33.47		10,457,862		$33.45	0.00%	0
Service Level								%Change	
Supplier Fillrate	62.4%				62.4%			0.00%	
Order Fillrate	84.7%				84.7%			0.00%	
Order Fulfillment Lead Time								Days	
Re-Plan Time	0.0				0.0			0	
Order Processing Time	6.8				6.8			0	
Outbound Transit Time	3.0				3.0			0	
Item Total Source Lead Time	63.8	100.0%			63.8	100.0%		Days	Mix Change
S1 Days, % of Total	30.0	46.0%			30.0	46.0%		0	0%
S2 Days, % of Total	90.0	52.0%			90.0	52.0%		0	0%
S3 Days, % of Total	160.0	2.0%			100.0	2.0%		0	0%
Production & Merchandise Cost			Per Piece:				Per Piece:	%Change	$ Change
COGS Material Cost	$350,000,000	77.8%	$33.47		$349,780,760	77.7%	$33.45	0.00%	$ (219,240)
COGS Labor Cost and Intercompany Freight	$44,700,000	9.9%	$0.03		$40,625,000	9.0%	$0.03	0.00%	$ (4,075,000)

#	Supply Chain Cost	%	$	Per Piece	%	$	Per Piece	%Change	$ Change
26									
27	**Supply Chain Cost**								
28	**Order Management Cost**	**3.2%**	**$14,350,000**	**$0.01**	**3.3%**	**$14,878,000**	**$0.01**	%Change	$ Change
29	*Customer Service*	0.0%		$0.00	0.0%	$0	$0.00	0.00%	$ —
30	*FG Warehouse*	1.3%	$5,850,000	$0.00	1.3%	$5,850,000	$0.00	0.00%	$ —
31	*Outbound and Return Transportation*	1.9%	$8,500,000	$0.01	2.0%	$9,028,000	$0.01	0.00%	$ 528,000
32									
33	**Material Acquisition**	**3.2%**	**$14,550,000**	**$1.39**	**2.8%**	**$12,720,000**	**$1.22**	%Change	$ Change
34	*Purchasing*	0.0%		$0.00	0.0%	–$210,000	–$0.02	0.00%	4 $ (210,000)
35	*RM Warehouse*	0.5%	$2,250,000	$0.22	0.5%	$2,250,000	$0.22	0.00%	$ —
36	*Inbound Transportation*	2.7%	$12,300,000	$1.18	2.4%	$10,680,000	$1.02	0.00%	$ (1,620,000)
37									
38									
39	**Operating Margin Impact %**	94.1%			1.3%			0.00%	
40	**Operating Margin Impact $**					$ 5,831,573			
41									
42	Write-offs %	–16.00%			%Change	–16.00%			
43	Write-offs $	$ —				$ (72,040,000)			
44									
45	Total Income Impact					$ (66,208,427)			
46									
47	**Assets**								
48	Working Capital							%Change	Days Change
49	*Inventory, Days—$*	91.0	$97,300,000		91	$97,300,000		0.00%	0
50	*Payables, Days—$*	34.4	$33,000,000		34.4	$33,000,000		0.00%	0
51	*Receivables, Days—$*	140.0	$172,600,000		140	$172,600,000		0.00%	0
52	*Working Capital Total, Days—$*	196.6	$236,900,000		196.6	$236,900,000			
53									
54	**Working Capital Impact %**				0.0%			Cost of Capital	
55	**Working Capital Impact $**	$0			$0			10%	

11

Week Nine: Opportunity Summaries, Initiating TO BE Material Flow, and Steering Team Review Number Four

Add up the opportunities.

As described earlier, 3 percent profit improvement to the sales value of the supply chain: That's the rule-of-thumb opportunity before the data is prepared (read: sanitized) for presentation to executives and the board. For every $100 million in revenue, that means an opportunity for an extra $3 million dollars in earnings. This gem is worth repeating.

Where any given team comes in against this rule, however, depends on the supply chain competency of the organization. The more competent a company is at managing its supply chain, the more likely it is that the discovery and analysis process will yield opportunity of less than 3 percent. Companies with less maturity will yield opportunities in excess of that amount. It's possible to gauge this maturity level in advance by checking your company against a set of basic questions (Figure 11-1). The more yes answers, the more competent.

Why is this the first time you'll address the question of the company's fundamental culture for managing its supply chain? Because there are two reasons to do so. First, it should be an

Figure 11.1. Supply chain competency matrix.

	Goals—Supply Chain Strategy	Design	Management and Measurement
Organization	Has the organization's supply chain strategy/direction been articulated and communicated? Does the supply chain strategy make sense in terms of external threats and opportunities and the internal strengths and weaknesses? Given this supply chain strategy, have the required outputs of the organization and the level of performance expected from each output been determined and communicated?	Does the formal organization structure support the supply chain strategy and enhance the efficiency of the system? Are all relevant functions in place? Are all the functions necessary? Is the current flow of inputs and outputs between functions appropriate?	Is customer-facing, internal-facing, and shareholder-facing performance measured? Have the appropriate supply chain performance requirements, priorities, and goals been set? Are resources appropriately allocated?
Process	Are goals for plan, source, make, deliver, and return processes linked to customer/organization requirements? Are the appropriate enable processes in place to support supply chain planning and execution?	Are these the most efficient/effective plan, source, make, deliver, and return processes for accomplishing the plan, source, make, deliver, and return processes goals?	Have the appropriate plan, source, make, deliver, and return process subgoals been set? Are the plan, source, make, deliver, and return processes performance managed? Are sufficient resources allocated to each plan, source, make, deliver, and return process? Are the interfaces between plan, source, make, deliver, and return process steps being managed?

(continues)

Figure 11.1. (Continued).

People/Jobs	Are job outputs and standards linked to plan, source, make, deliver, and return process requirements? (and cascaded from the organization level?)	Are plan, source, make, deliver, and return process requirements reflected in the appropriate jobs? Are job steps in a logical sequence? Have supportive policies and procedures been developed? Is the job environment sound?	Do the performers understand the job goals (outputs they are expected to produce and standards they are expected to meet?) Do the performers have sufficient resources, clear signals and priorities, and logical job design? Are the performers rewarded for achieving job goals? Do the performers know if they are meeting job goals? Do the performers have the necessary knowledge/skill to achieve the job goals? If the performers were in an environment in which the five questions above were answered, "yes," would they have the physical, mental, and emotional capacity to achieve the job goals?
Technology	Are goals for technology linked to customer/organization requirements? Do the technology goals support plan, source, make, deliver, and return processes and people/jobs?	Is the most efficient/effective technology being put in place to accomplish the plan, source, make, deliver, and return processes	Have the appropriate technology subgoals been set? Is the technology performance managed? Are sufficient resources allocated to support effective use of technology? Are the interfaces between technologies being managed?

easy assessment by this point in the process. Second, it's an interesting exercise to help launch the start of a potentially frustrating week.

Depending on how experienced design team members are at the budgeting process, the opportunity assessment homework may have ranged from simple to mind-bending. At best, the result of the opportunity assessment will be a rough estimate. The objectives of Week Nine are to review, refine, and prioritize opportunity analyses; initiate the TO BE material flow, and prepare for the fourth steering team review.

◼ Completing the Opportunity Analysis

There are three steps to complete the opportunity analysis: review and refine the assumptions and associated financial and service numbers; identify further validation resources for content as well as change-management value; and prioritize them. These activities take up Day One and part of Day Two.

Review and Refine Assumptions

Each opportunity analysis spreadsheet (Table 10-1) needs to be refined. The process focuses on testing the soundness, precision, and relevance of the assumptions and the consequent calculations. This is the point when you'll be glad to have documented all the assumptions made since the brainstorm session (Chapter 9).

There's no magic to assembling a good written assumption; it's a matter of format. Each spreadsheet—or opportunity fish—gets its own statement of assumption. It should include an item number or numbers by type (that is, RM, WIP, FG, or Return); estimated volume, calculated using such data as market share, geographic segment, unit volume, or unit forecast; cost or revenue impact, calculated by cost per unit or margin per unit; delivery reliability, lead time, and necessary business conditions. It takes a paragraph to write such an assumption.

The number—the size of the opportunity—that results from the paragraph is simply a calculation. If the number doesn't feel right—and there is a certain amount of feel to this part of the job—don't change the numbers. Change the assumptions.

There are different kinds of assumptions. One kind describes the impact of cost reduction or productivity improvement in direct or indirect categories. Another kind describes the revenue impact of delivery reliability through fewer lost opportunities or pure growth. Another type of assumption describes the working-capital impact of lead time and delivery performance, as measured in inventory, payables, and/or receivables. It's common that a fish assumption paragraph will contain multiple types of assumptions.

At Fowlers, the team started with the "poor planning" fish (Table 11-1). Members identified six major profit opportunities that would result from "killing" this fish. They aligned these opportunity assumptions with the numbers in the last column as summarized below:

1. Reduce lost opportunity orders, calculated as one percent of total orders, or 26,532 orders missed on account of no immediate material availability. At $339.20 average value per order with a 50 percent gross margin, the profit opportunity calculates to $4,500,000.
2. Improve order fulfillment lead time by 5.8 days excluding transit time for all stocked parts to support lost opportunity revenue increase.
3. Achieve a one percent decrease in price per part for the ability to provide accurate forecast data to all suppliers. At $349,780,000 COGS, that equates to a $3,497,800 annualized cost decrease.
4. Have inventory immediately available. This will reduce 10 percent of the amount of time spent per order picking multiple times, expediting inventory transfer orders, and providing phone status to customer service representatives. At $4.40 warehouse cost per order with 1,326,632 orders per year, this equates to $583,718.
5. Reduce unplanned changes to purchase orders, decreasing the number of instances of expedited transportation

Table 11-1. Fowlers' opportunity analysis for the poor planning fishbone chart.

	B	C Baseline	D Per Piece/Order	F	G Test Scenario	H Per Piece/Order	I	J
Transaction Summary								
			Per Piece/Order			Per Piece/Order	%Change	$ Change
Revenue	$450,000,000			$454,500,000			0.00%	$ 4,500,000
Orders	1,326,632		$339.20	1,326,632		$342.60	0.00%	0
Total Items on Orders	654,000,000		$0.69	654,000,000		$0.69	0.00%	0
Purchase Orders	35,678		$9,809.97	35,678		$9,711.93	0.00%	0
Total Items Purchased	10,457,862		$33.47	10,457,862		$33.13	0.00%	0
Service Level							%Change	
Supplier Fillrate	62.4%			62.4%			0.00%	
Order Fillrate	84.7%			84.7%			0.00%	
Order Fulfillment Lead Time							Days	
Re-Plan Time	0.0			0.0			0	
Order Processing Time	6.8			1.0			−5.8	
Outbound Transit Time	3.0			3.0			0	
Item Total Source Lead Time	63.8	100.0%		63.8	100.0%		Days	Mix Change
S1 Days, % of Total	30.0	46.0%		30.0	46.0%		0	0%
S2 Days, % of Total	90.0	52.0%		90.0	52.0%		0	0%
S3 Days, % of Total	160.0	2.0%		160.0	2.0%		0	0%
Production & Merchandise Cost			Per Piece:			Per Piece:	%Change	$ Change
COGS Material Cost	77.8%	$350,000,000	$33.47	76.2%	$346,502,200	$33.13	0.00%	$ (3,497,800)
COGS Labor Cost and Intercompany Freight	9.9%	$44,700,000	$0.07	9.8%	$44,700,000	$0.07	0.00%	

Assumptions

1 Reduce lost opportunity orders calculated at 1% of total orders or 26,532 orders missed on account of no immediate material availability. At $339.20 average value per order, there is a $4,500,000 opportunity.

2 Improve order fulfillment lead time by 5.8 days excluding transit time for all stocked parts to support lost opportunity revenue increase.

3 Achieve a 1.0% decrease in price per part for the ability to provide accurate forecast data to all suppliers. At $349,780,000 COGS, that equates to a $3,497,800 annualized cost decrease.

(continues)

Table 11-1 (Continued).

#	Supply Chain Cost	%	$	Per Piece:	%	$	Per Piece:	%Change	$ Change	Notes
27										
28	**Supply Chain Cost**									
29	Order Management Cost	3.2%	$14,350,000	$0.02	3.0%	$13,766,282	$0.02	0.00%		
30	*Customer Service*	0.0%	$0	$0.00	0.0%	$0	$0.00	0.00%		
31	*FG Warehouse*	1.3%	$5,850,000	$0.01	1.2%	$5,266,282	$0.01	0.00%	$ (583,718)	4 Having inventory immediately available will reduce 10% of the amount of time spent per order picking multiple times, expediting inventory transfer orders, and providing phone status to customer service representatives. At $4.40 warehouse cost per order with 1,326,632 orders per year, this equates to $583,718.
32	*Outbound and Return Transportation*	1.9%	$8,500,000	$0.01	1.9%	$8,500,000	$0.01	0.00%		
33				Per Piece:			Per Piece:			
34	Material Acquisition	3.2%	$14,550,000	$1.39	2.3%	$10,250,000	$0.98	0.00%		
35	*Purchasing*	0.0%	$0	$0.00	0.0%	$0	$0.00	0.00%		
36	*RM Warehouse*	0.5%	$2,250,000	$0.22	0.5%	$2,250,000	$0.22	0.00%		
37	*Inbound Transportation*	2.7%	$12,300,000	$1.18	1.8%	$8,000,000	$0.76	0.00%	$ (4,300,000)	5 Reduce unplanned changes to purchase orders reducing the number of instances of expedite transportation within lead time. 65% of the purchase orders are currently expedited incurring 35% higher inbound transportation costs than necessary. Inbound transportation totals $12.3 million; improvement would reduce cost by $4.5 million.
38										
39										
40	**Operating Margin Impact %**	94.1%			2.8%					
41	**Operating Margin Impact $**					$ 12,617,518		%Change		
42										
43	**Write-offs %**	−16.00%			−16.00%					
44	**Write-offs $**	$ 69,000,000				$ (72,720,000)				
45										
46	Total Income Impact					$ (60,102,482)				
47										
48	**Assets**									
49	Working Capital							%Change	Days Change	
50	*Inventory, Days—$*	91.0	$97,300,000		91	$65,223,077		0.00%	−30	6 Cut non-working inventory in half, from 25% of overall inventory value to 12.5% of overall inventory value equivalent to $8,152,884 or 7.6 days. Accrual is already in place for the 25% level. First year is working capital only. 2nd year benefit would directly impact profit by eliminating the accrual. Leverage sales and operations planning process to align inventory position in each warehouse to support parity days of supply additional $23,924,039 or 22.4 days.
51	*Payables, Days—$*	34.4	$33,000,000		34.4	$33,000,000		0.00%		
52	*Receivables, Days—$*	140.0	$172,600,000		140	$172,600,000		0.00%		
53	*Working Capital Total, Days—$*	196.6	$236,900,000		166.6	$204,823,077				
54									Cost of Capital	
55	**Working Capital Impact %**	15.3%				$32,076,923			10%	
56	**Working Capital Impact $**	$32,076,923				$3,207,692				

within lead time. Sixty-five percent of purchase orders are currently expedited, incurring 35 percent higher inbound transportation costs than necessary. Inbound transportation totals $12.3 million; improvement would reduce cost by $4.3 million.

6. Reduce nonworking inventory by 50 percent—from 25 percent of overall inventory value to 12.5 percent of overall inventory value, equivalent to $8,152,884 or 7.6 days. Accrual is already in place for the 25 percent level, so first-year benefit is working capital only. Second-year benefit would directly impact profit by eliminating the accrual. Leverage the sales and operations planning process to align inventory position in each warehouse to achieve inventory-competitive requirements, as specified on the SCORcard (Figure 5-1), of 22.4 days—or $23,924,039 in profit opportunity.

The Fowlers team wrestled with where to put other obvious benefits—things like reducing accruals for returns, reducing days sales outstanding, and optimizing outbound transportation. All of these are benefits of improved sales and operations planning, which could be included in a number of fish. To avoid the risk of double-counting the savings, the team was careful to discuss each opportunity and assign by consensus to a single fish.

Identify Further Validation Resources

The second step naturally follows the first. As the team tweaks the assumptions, it also reviews the list of names of people involved in building them and considers additional validation resources.

There are two reasons to add more names. First, it may be necessary to add more content expertise about details to further refine assumptions. For example, one might include a marketing research analyst to help refine market share and volume numbers, or a cost accountant to calculate the impact of accruals or balance sheet changes. Second, adding these topical experts gives them extra time to digest the information before deciding to stand behind the numbers and therefore widen support for the project.

Prioritizing the Opportunities

The last part of the day is devoted to assembling the disconnect opportunity grid (see Figure 11-2). The grid is a simple quadrant chart, identifying projects by how tough or easy they are to implement and by how big or small the impact. The size of impact is taken directly from the opportunity spreadsheet for each fish. Assigning a degree of difficulty is subjective, based on such factors as required technology, reliance on a supply chain partner to change behavior, and multiple functions involving corporate and business unit resources.

Figure 11-2. Disconnect opportunity grid template.

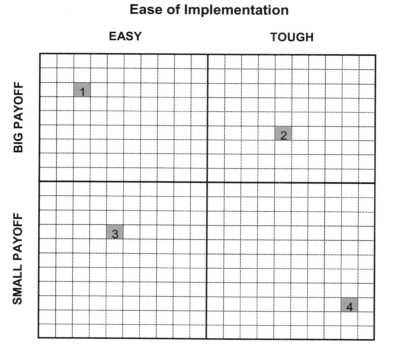

The most desirable projects are those in the easy/big quadrant. At the opposite end are tough/small. Each quadrant is set up as a ten-by-ten grid, allowing fine-tuning of projects with similar degrees of difficulty and opportunity. The objective is to define the scale factors for every fish, and then place them all on the grid.

The Fowlers team had eight fish (see Chapter 10) and supporting opportunity analyses:

1. Poor planning
2. Supply management
3. Reactive logistics planning and execution
4. Disparate systems
5. Poor data integrity
6. Hit-and-miss product life cycle management
7. Undisciplined order management
8. No formal return management

The team agreed that any fish with an impact of $250,000 or more would be considered a big payoff. Any fish requiring changes in technology, or in behavior of customers or suppliers, would be considered tough.

The rest of the scales were subjectively defined by consensus using the number of functions required to support a project to kill the fish (Figure 11-3). The returns accrual was the biggest surprise to everyone except the corporate controller. Its classification as "tough" was based on the need for an enforced returns policy. Fish marked WI indicated that the financial analysis would be determined in the "work and information flow" transaction analysis still to be completed. Besides the accrual, the total of about $24 million in opportunity—about 5 percent of supply chain sales—put Fowlers right about where it belonged, based on the team's assessment that the company was on the immature side of the supply chain competency scale.

▆ Initiating TO BE Material Flow

By the afternoon of Day Two, brains are frying in the pan. The only activities being started are to find leading practices in the

Figure 11-3. Fowlers' disconnect opportunity grid.

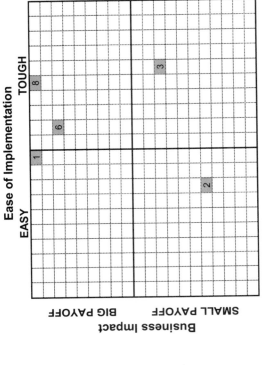

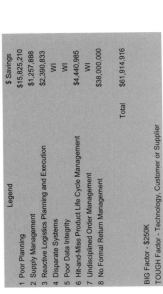

Legend		$ Savings
1	Poor Planning	$15,825,210
2	Supply Management	$1,257,888
3	Reactive Logistics Planning and Execution	$2,390,833
4	Disparate Systems	WI
5	Poor Data Integrity	WI
6	Hit-and-Miss Product Life Cycle Management	$4,440,985
7	Undisciplined Order Management	WI
8	No Formal Return Management	$38,000,000
	Total	$61,914,916

BIG Factor - $250K
TOUGH Factor - Technology, Customer or Supplier

SCOR dictionary (available to members of the Supply-Chain Council as a downloadable file from the council's website, supply-chain.org), validate customer delivery requirements by segment, and locate potential internal sources of leading practices.

Conducting Steering Team Review Number Four

Prepare and conduct steering team review number four with the following agenda items:

- ❑ Project roadmap status
- ❑ Review disconnect grid
- ❑ Review opportunity analysis
- ❑ Decisions required today
- ❑ Expectations for steering team review number five

12

Week Ten: TO BE Material Flow

Design a better business.

The first two days that the team spends identifying TO BE material flow changes often seem anticlimactic. From the first day of the first week, people had ideas on how to fix things. By this point in the analysis, it's usually already clear what changes are needed to improve profits and customer satisfaction. Sometimes, identifying the TO BE change is as simple as adding the phrase "thou shalt not" to the problem statement on the head of the fish. However, you can't count on it being that easy. So the objectives of Week Ten are to identify appropriate leading practices and other necessary changes in material flow to kill all the fish.

The TO BE phase of the project is where sophisticated modeling tools come in handy. There are modeling tools for processes, logistics networks, and data flow. Some of these tools combine SCOR elements with process and material flow. Others act as a workflow interface to ERP systems. The Supply Chain Council has examples on their Web site of tools that incorporate SCOR elements.

◼ Identifying Changes and Initiating TO BE Models

Analysis of AS IS material flow has been conducted by subteams. For some reason, TO BE solutions are best developed by the entire group. It may be more time consuming, but in a discipline that is as much art as science, it just seems to work better. Based on experience, the same rule is true for work and information flows: AS IS by subteams; TO BE by the whole group.

On Day One, the first step is to develop a short list of leading practices (from the homework) appropriate for your company and industry. Sources for this list include the SCOR dictionary; experience and education of design team members; professional and industry associations; and disciplines learned from such initiatives as business process reengineering, quality function deployment, Six Sigma continuous improvement, efficient consumer response, total quality management, theory of constraints, lean manufacturing, and so on (Appendixes D and F).

The second step—and it takes some research—is to find a good case study for each of the leading practices on the short list; "good" in this case is measured by at least three criteria:

1. The case study should describe detailed characteristics of the desired state. These include strategy, design, and management factors for the organization, processes, job tasks, and technology.
2. The case study should describe the transition from current practices to the end state, including lessons learned.
3. The case study should have relevance by industry, by the role in a supply chain, or, preferably, both.

With background for each leading practice on the short list, the design team can begin identifying and documenting necessary changes and assumptions. Each fish gets its own discussion. To outline these discussions, use the supply chain competency matrix (Figure 11-1) as a checklist.

For each fish, ask, "Is a leading practice necessary to eliminate this problem?" If yes, then use the case study information to identify necessary changes, answering the questions in each cell on the supply chain competency matrix. Some cells are noted as not applicable. It usually takes changes in several cells on the matrix to implement a leading practice. If your answer is no, then use the "thou shalt not" approach.

The number of cells that will require change depends on the complexity of the fish. Changing policy on late payments is relatively simple and might affect only a few cells. Changing the way an enterprise executes sales and operations planning will likely affect every cell. The design team that can eliminate the most fish with the fewest changes tends to build the best supply chain.

Finally, assemble a business use case or scenario that illustrates the before-and-after geographic material flow and material flow spreadsheet along with the assumptions for change captured in the competency matrix.

■ Leading Practices at Fowlers

In Fowlers' case, the technology products short list included two leading practices for planning: sales and operations planning (SOP) and collaborative planning, forecasting, and replenishment (CPFR). In truth, SOP straddled the definition of a leading practice and the common sense statement, "Thou shalt not have an ineffective SOP process." CPFR, on the other hand, was well beyond Fowlers' current practices; forecast and replenishment variability from large retail customers was wreaking financial havoc in returns, inbound and outbound transportation cost, poor inventory positions, and inconsistent delivery reliability. CPFR was clearly needed, and it would depend on a good SOP process.

Leading retailers have been practicing CPFR for years with their largest suppliers. As technology solutions helped bring down the cost of communication infrastructure and forecast analytics, the number of suppliers investing in CPFR competency was growing. So the team had little trouble finding good information.

The Voluntary Interindustry Commerce Standards (VICS) organization proved a rich source of research data through its

> *Collaborative Planning, Forecasting and Replenishment Voluntary Guidelines* published in 1998. Its 1999 *Roadmap to CPFR* provided case studies. The Fowlers team utilized the VICS website—vics.org—and also the CPFR website—cpfr.org—to locate a case history that addressed these critical issues: Why CPFR? What are the steps to CPFR? How is CPFR aligned with SCOR? What are some step-by step guidelines? And where can further references be found?
>
> As the team identified CPFR changes as described in the supply chain competency matrix, they found changes would be needed in all twelve cells.

■ Refining TO BE Models and Initiating Quick-Hit Plans

There is no firm rule on how many days should be allocated to developing TO BE solutions. It depends on the scope and complexity of the problems. But Day Two, defined as the day after a first-draft solution has been developed for each fish, begins with another round of review and editing.

The appropriate question at this point isn't whether the solutions and associated assumptions need revision; it's how many and how much?

Also, before-and-after illustrations will demand more detail and clarity—all with the goal of delivering a clear financial picture. In next week's steering team review, the executives are anticipating seeing the first clear map of the company's future, and the solutions need to be delivered simply enough for fast and easy understanding—yet with enough detail for full appreciation of their impact.

For Fowlers, the TO BE material flow for CPFR involved four key changes. First would be more direct ships from suppliers to targeted retail warehouses; this changed connector lines on the geographic map. Before, material flowed from supplier to Fowlers warehouse to Fowlers warehouse to customer retail location. In the TO BE map, material would flow from supplier to customer regional warehouse.

In the second key change, consigned inventory would be consolidated to fewer locations closer to the customer point of sale. Before, a specific inventory item was stored in all Fowlers warehouses. In the TO BE, the item would be stored in a single Fowlers warehouse and in designated customer regional warehouses.

In the third key change, lead-time expectations were eased due to improved inventory position and aggregation; the result would be improved delivery reliability and reduced transportation costs.

The fourth change optimized the flow of returned goods. Before, returns moved from customer locations to the closest Fowlers warehouse. In the TO BE, returned goods were consolidated at the customer regional warehouse and then shipped to a single Fowlers warehouse designated to accept all returns.

The second agenda item on Day Two is to initiate quick-hit plans—one or two projects that will deliver fast ROI with a minimum of cultural change. There are two guidelines for this activity. First, the design team needs to prioritize the TO BE material flow solutions in a way that allows a certain number of changes to surface that can be acted on immediately without disruption to the greater effort. This quick-hit pile forms the basis for the goal of six-month cost neutral, and it builds momentum and credibility to reach two- to six-times return on investment over twelve months.

You'll start with the disconnect opportunity grid (Figure 11-2), but will then take some of that information to create a new matrix. A balanced project mix grid (Figure 12-1), the new matrix considers a project's scope—tactical versus strategic—and the pace of change—fast versus measured. To find the quick hits, examine only the opportunities in the "easy" portion of the disconnect opportunity grid and place them on the new balanced project mix grid. Then, for quick hits, consider only those projects in the tactical/fast quadrant.

The second guideline for initiating quick-hit plans is to effectively move ownership of quick-hit implementations to extended team members and others in the organization by developing a mini-charter. It's like the original project charter, but specific to the quick hits. Elements of the mini-charter include a summary of the issue and root cause analyses; recom-

Figure 12-1. Balanced project mix grid.

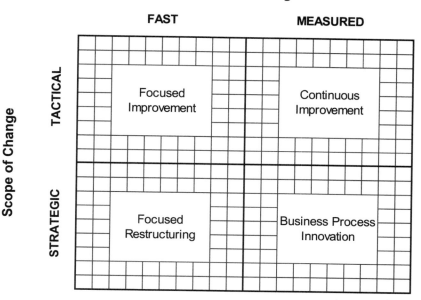

mended changes; action plans, responsibility, and timing; benefits as calculated in the opportunity spreadsheets; an implementation leader (extended team or other resources); implementation resources (including capital, expense, and people); and an implementation sponsor (steering team).

In Fowlers' case, the quick-hit plan involved supplier shipments from the Pacific Rim (Figure 12-2).

Figure 12.2 Fowlers' Asia-Pacific transportation consolidation quick-hit mini-charter.

ISSUE & ROOT CAUSE ANALYSIS
Inbound shipments from Asia are consolidated by each supplier in quantities large enough to support full container shipments. While each shipment has low transportation cost, inventory value is high while flexibility and responsiveness are low.

RECOMMENDATION
Set up a regional consolidation for all suppliers in the region.

ACTION PLAN	**RESPONSIBILITIES/TIMING**
1. Identify suppliers 2. Identify service provider 3. Define and pilot process 4. Roll out changes	1. Sort supplier list and validate with business team—two weeks—Buyer/Planner Analyst 2. Define third-party logistics requirements and issue request for proposal—four weeks—Transportation Analyst 3. Develop and pilot changes—two weeks—Joint 4. Plan and roll out consolidation—four weeks—Joint

PAY-OFFS	**IMPLEMENTATION RESOURCES**
Quantify in terms of cost, cycle time, quality, and/or customer service 1. $1,750,000 annualized transportation cost reduction 2. 6 weeks lead time improvement 3. 35% improvement in delivery reliability by purchase order	Full Time Equivalent (FTE) Personnel, Capital, and Expensed Items 1. Two FTEs as identified for the duration defined in the responsibilities/timing section including a Buyer/Planner and Transportation Analyst

IMPLEMENTATION LEADER	**IMPLEMENTATION SPONSOR(S)**
1. Buyer/Planner	1. Directors of Purchasing and Logistics

CHARTER STATUS
1. Approved as of Steering Team Review Five

13

Week Eleven: Quick-Hit Plans, Steering Team Review Number Five, and Initiating the Work and Information Flow Analysis

Dig into work and information flow.

There are several points during a SCOR project that seem to draw people into reflection on the significance of their work relative to the potential opportunity for their company—as opposed to thinking about next week's homework. The SCORcard gap analysis during Week Five (Chapter 7) is often such an occasion. This is another.

At this point, members of the design team have reason to feel like they've produced something of great value to their company—measured in millions of dollars of potential profit improvement. Better still is the feeling that they've created a detailed understanding of what improvement will be achieved. If this swagger shows up in the confidence level of presenters at the steering team review, the steering team gets excited too.

By this time, project momentum has reached something close to full speed, and other people throughout the organization are looking for ways to participate and saying things like, "This is the best thing our company has ever done."

A careful mix of common sense, analysis, and measurable results has moved the project to the executive team's center of attention. And the organization stands poised for a transition to something big and new. So does the design team. After six weeks of work on metrics and material flow, everyone will be eager to put the geographic maps behind and move on to work and information flow.

With these thoughts as background, the objectives for Week Eleven are to review and refine quick-hit mini-charters, prepare for and conduct steering team review number five, to approve material flow changes, and, finally, to initiate analysis of work and information flow.

■ Reviewing and Refining Quick-Hit Mini-Charters

Day One begins by focusing on the people who will take on the quick-hit projects, including the implementation leaders and sponsors. To identify these people, the project manager and sponsor must complete four tasks:

1. Identify and rank a short list of potential implementation leaders—ideally from the group of people who have already participated as members of the extended project team. The short-list candidates also should report up through one of the departments represented on the steering team.
2. Discuss the list with the steering team and gain consensus on the leading candidate for the quick-hit project or projects (no more than one or two). This is followed by a phone call from a steering team member to each candidate's boss to endorse the recommendation and discuss time commitments.
3. Meet individually with each leading candidate's boss to describe the contents of the mini-charter and seek commitment to support the time allocation.
4. Meet individually with the candidates to discuss the mini-charter and any changes or suggestions brought out through this process.

This common sense but time-consuming activity is an important piece of the change-management work that must accompany a supply chain improvement. Ultimately, the implementation leader—after dealing with the stress of suddenly having so much more to worry about—will start to show ownership by tweaking the mini-charter action steps, timing, and responsibilities given his or her own personal expertise and style. This leader's role in establishing early success is critical; the candidates should understand that fact and be recognized for taking on the responsibility.

As part of the knowledge-transfer process, the project manager acts as the personal coach for the quick-hit implementation leader, providing background on the issue and benefit analysis and the incorporation of the changes into the greater SCOR design process.

In Fowlers' case, David Able and Brian Dowell identified two short-list candidates: a buyer/planner for largest commodity purchases in Asia and a logistics engineer specializing in import/export. Both candidates, they reasoned, had knowledge of logistics solutions and relationships with suppliers in a region at the center of the quick-hit project. Further, they both had participated in the material flow disconnect brainstorm session and reported through the directors of purchasing or logistics.

With both candidates being highly considered, specific supplier relationships became the tiebreaker, and the buyer/planner got the nod. After meeting with the commodity manager in charge, David and Brian shared the good news.

■ Initiating AS IS Work and Information Flow

The primary agenda for Day Two is to plan and initiate the transactional analysis; the activity itself is similar to the brainstorming event that launched the material flow-disconnect analysis. There are three initiating tasks to complete: Brush up on the SCOR Level Three process elements; identify the transaction analysis teams; and plan the "staple yourself to an order" kickoff event.

Using SCOR Level Three elements is like speaking a foreign language; if you don't use it, you lose it. At the end of this phase of the project, the whole design team will be fluent in SCOR. To accelerate fluency, it's helpful to have a quick-reference resource and dictionary. *The SCOR Quick Reference Guide* provides a summary of just the elements. *The SCOR Dictionary* provides individual definitions for each element, along with suggested metrics, leading practices, inputs and outputs, and supporting technical features (see Appendix E and Figure 13-1).

(For members of the Supply-Chain Council, the dictionary can be downloaded from the council website, supply-chain.org.)

The brush-up involves brief discussion on each element in the quick reference guide, with reference to the dictionary for official definitions and an example of the process steps in action. As with any language, there is room for interpretation. This is the moment to achieve consensus on the elements that cause contention.

Identifying the transaction analysis team—"team staple" if you will—is not trivial. The objective, like the brainstorm activity, is to assign members of the design team to lead subteams focused on each of the six SCOR Level Three transaction types. These transactions are aligned with the SCOR processes. They are: purchase order—SOURCE; work order—MAKE; sales order—DELIVER; return authorization—RETURN; forecasts—PLAN; and replenishment orders—PLAN.

The transaction team leader uses the SCOR Level Three process steps to identify a group of individuals who know the details of each step. For example, in SOURCE, the purchase order transaction leader needs to assemble a team that can conduct a guided tour of how purchase orders move through:

- ❏ S1.1—schedule product deliveries
- ❏ S1.2—receive product
- ❏ S1.3—verify product
- ❏ S1.4—transfer product
- ❏ S1.5—authorize supplier payment

This SOURCE team might be one person or five, depending on the expertise. The notion of a guided tour is discussed in the classic *Harvard Business Review* article, "Staple Yourself to An

Figure 13-1. Level three dictionary sample.

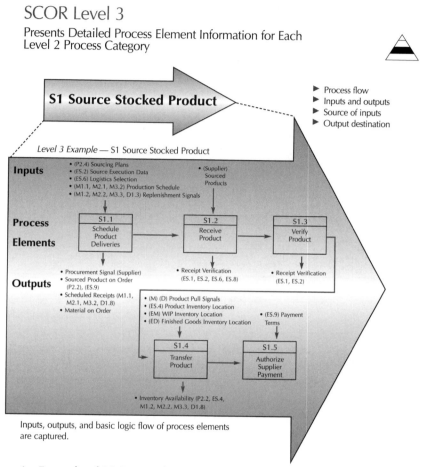

An Example of SCOR Level 3 Process Element Logic Flow

Order" (July 1, 1992; Benson P. Shapiro, V. Kasteri Rangan, John J. Sviokla).

Planning the Staple Yourself Analysis

The objective of the staple yourself transaction analysis is to collect AS IS data for each relevant SCOR Level Three element by

Examples:

SCOR Level 3 Standard Process
Element Definition, Performance Attributes, and Accompanying Metrics

Process Element: **Schedule Product Deliveries**	Process Number: S1.1

Process Element Definition

Scheduling and managing the execution of the individual deliveries of product against an existing contract or purchase order. The requirements for product releases are determined based on the detailed sourcing plan or other types of product pull signals.

Performance Attributes	Metric
Reliability	% Schedules Generated within Supplier's Lead Time
	% Schedules Changed within Supplier's Lead Time
Responsiveness	Average Release Cycle of Changes
Flexibilty	Average Days per Schedule Change
	Average Days per Engineering Change
Cost	Product Management and Planning Costs as a % of Product Acquisitions Costs
Assets	None Identified

SCOR Level 3 Best Practices and Features

Process Element: **Schedule Product Deliveries**	Process Number: S1.1

Best Practices	Features
Utilize EDI transactions to reduce cycle time and costs	EDI interface for 830, 850, 856, and 862 transactions
VMI agreements allow suppliers to manage (replenish) inventory	Supplier managed inventories with scheduling interfaces to external supplier systems
Mechanical (Kanban) pull signals are used to notify suppliers of the need to deliver product	Electronic Kanban support
Consignment agreements are used to reduce assets and cycle time while increasing the availability of critical items	Consignment inventory management
Advanced ship notices allow for tight synchronization between SOURCE and MAKE processes	Blanket order support with scheduling interfaces to external supplier systems

Source: © Copyright 2001 Supply-Chain Council, Inc. Used with permission.

physically following it from the moment it's opened until the moment it's closed. The AS IS data categories include steps to complete the process; input trigger events and key process outputs; enabling technology (including system modules); manual steps right down to the level of Post-it notes; business rules— both formal and informal; and disconnects or issues that cause cycle-time delays and rework of the transaction.

An effective data collection plan has three components. First, there is a staple yourself to an order kickoff event that officially launches the data collection. A proper invitation should be sent out for the event, an appropriate venue chosen, and preread material included with the invitation. The agenda includes:

❑ A one-hour premeeting for those who have not participated in SCOR education, including review of the SCOR-card gap analysis and TO BE material flow maps
❑ A review of the transactional analysis process
❑ An overview of the staple analysis activity and documentation of results

The second component of a good plan is a map that details the interview path within and between locations to follow the life of a transaction. The map identifies interviewees by name and title. It's not possible to cover all locations and all transactions; the map should represent the best opportunity to collect the most representative data.

The third component is an effective communication plan to notify locations of what is going to happen and how much time interviewees can expect to spend on the project.

■ Fowlers' Staple Yourself Structure

At Fowlers, the staple teams were organized in the following manner:

❑ *PLAN.* The director of planning (team leader) focused on the aggregate unit forecast and replenishment plans with extended team members from corporate supply planning; forecast analysts from each of the business groups; and the president, controller, and vice president of operations for the technology products group.

❑ *SOURCE.* The director of purchasing (team leader) focused on the entire acquisition process with extended team members from corporate accounts payable; requisition agents from both Food and Technology Products; a warehouse supervisor to support receipts; and a buyer/planner from the technology products group (not the same individual who was chosen to lead the quick-hit projects).

❏ *MAKE.* The director of manufacturing (team leader) focused on scheduling, staging, and releasing work orders with team members from plant scheduling; materials control; and manufacturing.

❏ *DELIVER.* The director of customer service (team leader) focused on quotation to order promise, credit check, inventory allocation, and the warehouse processes from order consolidation through shipment and receipt at the customer's site. Enlisted to help were customer service managers from both food and technology products; a manager from corporate credit and accounts receivable; and warehouse managers from two of the Fowlers warehouses.

❏ *ENABLE.* The directors of applications and logistics (co-team leaders) focused on master data integrity including supplier, item, and customer with team members from engineering at both food and technology products; corporate customer service; and corporate purchasing.

❏ *RETURN.* The vice president of sales and marketing/food products group (team leader) focused on return authorization and goods movement with team members from corporate customer service; a warehouse supervisor from the largest returns site; corporate credit; and corporate quality assurance.

◼ Conducting Steering Team Review Number Five

Prepare and conduct the next steering team review meeting with the following agenda items:

❏ Project roadmap status
❏ Review TO BE geographic maps
❏ Review quick-hit plans
❏ Work and information flow overview with introduction of the staple teams and tour maps
❏ Decisions required today
❏ Expectations for steering team review number six

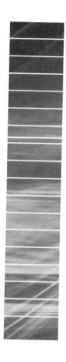

Phase IV

Work and Information Flow
Analysis and Design

14

Week Twelve: The Staple Yourself Analysis

Follow the information step by step.

This week marks the second time during the project when a large group of people from across the organization is pulled in for both change and content value. The first time—the material flow-disconnect analysis—the extended resources came to the design team. This time, the design team will travel to them.

The staple yourself analysis is fieldwork. Guided by each transaction's tour map, the appropriate subteam travels to where the transaction is created and follows it to closure, as framed by the SCOR Level Three element, conducting interviews along the way. In many cases, the field trip starts at a salesperson's home office, where the quote is generated, then moves back to headquarters to see that the order is received, validated, and entered. The whole week is dedicated to gathering and summarizing this critical information. The objective for Week Twelve is to kick off the staple analysis, collect, and summarize the AS IS data.

The Staple Yourself Kickoff and Analysis

After the premeeting to the kickoff, which reviews progress (Chapter 13), the main content of the meeting is to teach the team about the transaction analysis process, how to model a good example, and to launch the activity. The most effective structure is the proven teaching method of "tell 'em, show 'em, have 'em try it together, and have 'em try it alone."

The transaction analysis process is comprised of three steps. First, collect AS IS work and information flow data using the transaction analysis worksheet (Figure 14-1) as a guide for the interview.

Second, collaborate with subteam members to ensure nothing has been overlooked. Third, document the consolidated results for each SCOR Level Three element. The critical component is to understand the transaction analysis worksheet and the information to be gathered for each SCOR Level Three element.

Understanding the Transaction Analysis Worksheet

On the transaction analysis worksheet, *process* refers to the SCOR Level Three process summarizing the element under analysis, including both abbreviation and words. In the sample case in Figure 14-1, the process—M1.2 issue material—refers to the pull and staging of component material in advance of a manufacturing run of make-to-stock product.

Input/output refers to the primary trigger to start the process and primary output of the process. In the sample case, production schedule and pull instructions were triggers to the material handler issuing material to the production line; staged material was the primary output as a result of four processing steps.

Process steps refers to a maximum of ten tasks to complete the SCOR Level Three process element. In the sample case, the material handler completed four tasks: locating, transferring, physically moving, and sequencing the components to be staged.

Figure 14-1. Sample transaction analysis worksheet.

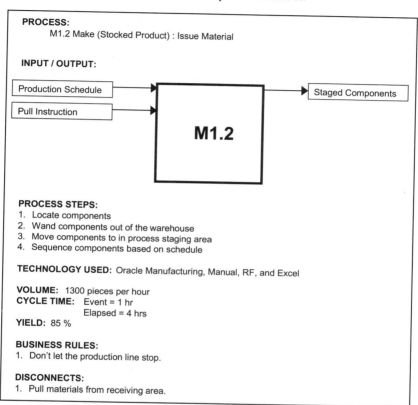

PROCESS:
M1.2 Make (Stocked Product) : Issue Material

INPUT / OUTPUT:

Production Schedule → M1.2 → Staged Components

Pull Instruction →

PROCESS STEPS:
1. Locate components
2. Wand components out of the warehouse
3. Move components to in process staging area
4. Sequence components based on schedule

TECHNOLOGY USED: Oracle Manufacturing, Manual, RF, and Excel

VOLUME: 1300 pieces per hour
CYCLE TIME: Event = 1 hr
Elapsed = 4 hrs
YIELD: 85 %

BUSINESS RULES:
1. Don't let the production line stop.

DISCONNECTS:
1. Pull materials from receiving area.

Source: © Copyright 2000 Pragmatek Consulting Group, Ltd. Used with permission.

Technology used refers to the information tools utilized to complete the tasks identified in the previous step. The tools can range from an ERP module or Internet signal to a fax, phone call, or simple Post-It note. In the sample case, the material handler used the Oracle manufacturing module, a manual entry on a Microsoft Word form, a radio frequency (RF) device, and a reference document on an Excel spreadsheet.

The next three items on the worksheet are factors in calculating transaction productivity. Productivity refers to three simple metrics: volume, cycle time, and yield.

Volume is the number of transactions of the primary output over a specified period of time (ultimately expressed on an annual basis). In the sample case, the material handler staged 1,300 pieces per hour, representing 2,704,000 pieces a year.

Cycle time is defined two ways: *event time*—the time spent from start to finish on the tasks assuming no lag time; and *elapsed time*—the actual time that passes from start to finish, including wait time for steps like "get approval." In the sample case, it took the material handler an hour to complete all four tasks without wait time and four hours in elapsed time. The difference between event time and elapsed time can be dramatic, such as three minutes to enter a purchase order and two days for approval to complete the work. Lean manufacturing principles would associate this measure with process-cycle efficiency.

The constraint is somewhere in the approval process. If the issue is policy, then no amount of technology will break the constraint. When a transaction is viewed this way, shortening event time will only make a nominal productivity improvement in most transactions. The real improvement is in elapsed time and yield.

Yield is the number of transactions requiring no rework. It's measured as a percentage of the total. This concept places a value on purchase, work, and sales orders that need to be reopened to change or complete data, such as bad addresses, incorrect unit prices or terms, quantities, and so on. A customer service representative who enters 1,000 orders today and has to reenter 250 tomorrow because of such errors has a yield of 75 percent. In the sample case, the material handler had to restage fifteen component pulls out of one hundred due to materials that were poorly labeled, incorrectly placed in inventory, inaccurately counted, and so on.

Business rules are policies and informal guidelines that govern decisions and behavior. Processing all orders by 3:00 P.M. may be a policy, but onsite supervisors might enforce an unwritten practice of accepting an order an hour later—with the same delivery expectations—as part of a customer-focused culture. Both are business rules. In the sample case, the most significant business rule supporting the material handler's decision and behavior is informal; don't let the production line stop.

Disconnects are issues that result in gaps in elapsed time or event time, and bring yield below 100 percent. In the sample case, the material handler would often respond to the informal business rule to keep the production line moving by pulling material from receiving. This reduced transaction yield, because it created discrepancies in documentation of where materials were located.

■ ## Fowlers' Staple Yourself Analysis

In Fowlers' case, the first draft of the consolidated transaction analysis for D1.2 receive, enter, and validate order transaction analysis is summarized in Figure 14-2.

The tour stop for this process element included customer service representatives in each of the business groups, corporate credit, and corporate customer service. It's noted in the interviewee summary at the end of the document that six people were interviewed in this staple yourself exercise. The team agreed that the analysis should focus on sales orders of stock items (D1) as well as configure-to-order items (D2). Types of inputs are summarized including customer call, fax, or email; web order; field sales call-in; and customer master setup. The output was appropriately called an entered order.

The subteam finished their staple yourself tours for the duration of Week Twelve, documenting all thirteen DELIVER elements (see Appendix E). The other subteams gathered the rest of the forty-seven other processes spanning PLAN, SOURCE, MAKE, and RETURN.

The goal for homework is to complete the transaction analysis worksheets for distribution on Day One of Week Thirteen. This data packet will be the source for building both the AS IS swim diagram and the productivity summary. Extra time may be needed, and more resources should be brought in to complete this step promptly to keep up the project momentum.

Figure 14-2. Fowlers' transaction analysis worksheet.

PROCESS:
D1.2 Receive, Enter & Validate Order (Deliver Stocked Product)
D2.2 Receive, Configure, Enter & Validate Order (Deliver Make to Order Product)

INPUT / OUTPUT:

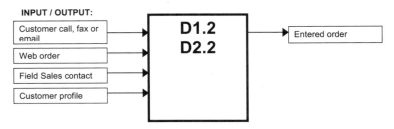

PROCESS STEPS:
1. Retrieve or enter new customer master record.
2. Verify ship to/bill to addresses.
3. Review customer special notes.
4. Enter customer contact, payment terms, ship method and P.O. number.
5. Enter requested ship date.
6. Enter part number and quantity.
7. Review part description and modify as necessary.
8. Input default price and unit of measure.
9. Update or save order record.
10. Call back customer when inventory allocation fails and re-date the order.

TECHNOLOGY USED:	MS Word, Access, and Excel; Legacy Mainframe; Fax; Email; Fowlers Website
VOLUME:	100,000 orders/year
CYCLE TIME (EVENT):	Average – 15 minutes
CYCLE TIME (ELAPSED):	Average – 6 hours
YIELD:	60% - meaning 40 orders out of 100 need to be reopened to rework data

BUSINESS RULES:
1. Formal - orders can be held waiting for payment for a maximum of 30 days after stock is committed.
2. Formal – Credit reviews holds once daily.
3. Informal – Once an order is entered, each order line is manually reviewed for correct quantity, part number and price.
4. Informal – If the ship-to address or bill-to address is modified or a new address is added, the order will go on a sales hold. Customer Service must review and approve the address change/addition before it becomes a permanent change/addition.

DISCONNECTS:
- Critical yield factors for valid orders include five factors: correct price, customer setup, item setup, terms, complete special customer instructions.
1. System pricing does not match spreadsheet version of the customer price – 40%
2. Manual entry to add new customer ship-to addresses for drop shipments from suppliers – 20%
3. Customer requests different terms than contract – 17%
4. Customer order incorrect increments, i.e., unit of measure and order minimums – 10%
5. Customer part number cross-reference is not correct – 7%
6. New items aren't setup – 2%
7. For EDI orders the item is not available at default source of supply – 2%
8. Missing instructions on customer special instruction orders – 2%

INTERVIEWEES: Susan, Terri, Julie, Jane, Dan, and Mike

15

Week Thirteen: The AS IS Swim Diagram and Steering Team Review Number Six

Learn exactly how much there is to fix.

Coming off an intense week of travel, the design team is armed with a packet of transaction analysis summaries covering all the SCOR Level Three process elements. Members have discovered unwritten rules, policy shortcuts and workarounds, and real-time validation of how silo mentality is destroying productivity. Now they're ready to start assembling the big picture of how their supply chain processes function (or not) in the current state. The main objective of Week Thirteen is to assemble the AS IS swim diagram using the data summarized in the transactional analysis worksheets. The data will be validated and refined during this process.

▩ Assembling the Preliminary AS IS Swim Diagram

A swim diagram is not a new technique for process mapping. Its effectiveness rests in the ability to illustrate organizational responsibility with process flow and performance measures—the who *and* the what *and* the how.

The SCOR approach to process mapping considers both work and information flow (Figure 15-1). The basic swim diagram (usually drawn in its first draft on a whiteboard or legal pad) contains the main functional departments that have some role in the process being mapped. In the sample purchase order, the functional departments include the warehouse, purchasing, accounts payable, and the supplier. A swim diagram then illustrates how tasks are carried out in the organization by placing the appropriate process step in the appropriate swim lane. In cases where there are multiple functions participating in tasks, the process step is drawn across all appropriate swim lanes.

In the sample case, the SOURCE Level Three processes were placed in the swim lanes performing the tasks. Schedule product deliveries and receive product both require purchasing; receive product, verify product, and transfer product all require warehouse personnel; and authorize supplier payment requires accounts payable analysts. In this oversimplified example, the warehouse performs the physical receipt of the raw materials

Figure 15-1. Sample purchase order swim diagram, whiteboard version.

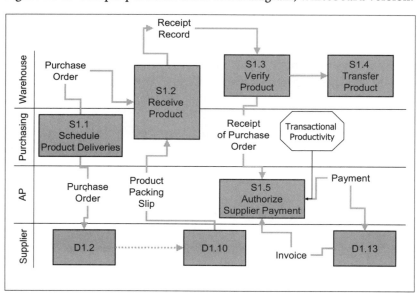

and purchasing personnel perform the electronic receipt. The SOURCE processes illustrate the work. A swim diagram then illustrates as inputs and outputs the important information flow necessary to enable the processes.

Continuing, the purchase order record on the system and the physical delivery of the material and packing slip triggers receive product. The output that triggers the next process step—verify product—is a receipt record. Inputs and outputs illustrate the information. The last major components of the swim diagram are process performance measures. They illustrate what is being measured at a particular point in the process flow. In the sample case, transactional productivity (defined by purchase order volume, elapsed cycle time, and yield) is measured at the completion of authorize supplier payment.

With the swim diagram discussion as background, building the AS IS diagram involves three steps: First, construct a dynamic white board preliminary diagram; second, refine an electronic document; and third, identify business case examples for each transaction type—not just sales forecasts, but also purchase, work, replenishment and sales orders, and return authorizations.

Dynamic white board refers to a design team group activity to construct the swim diagram live and on the fly without a starting template. When a generic AS IS diagram is used to start discussion, the results are usually not as good. Building a current-state diagram of any process as a group exercise helps disparate functions learn how all the pieces fit together; it facilitates team learning.

For building an electronic document, there are a number of modeling tools. Some of these tools are quite complex and expensive with automated SCOR process mapping and simulation functions to help speed up the work. Microsoft Visio is not designed specifically for SCOR; it basically automates the paper-and-pencil process. However, it's a strong tool because it is easily available and supportable in just about any corporate environment. The Supply-Chain Council maintains a list of other tools in the membership portion of its website. You can bring whatever level of technology you want to this process; pencil and paper will work. But long-term productivity can be greatly enhanced with some kind of process-mapping software.

As you begin to map, consider two other user tips. For the sake of productivity, an appointed scribe, or recorder, should build the Visio version on the spot, as the elements are confirmed on the white board. A good starting point for the white board activity is with the execution processes SOURCE, MAKE, and DELIVER, which is a perspective from the supplier and working forward. In other cultures, it might be just as comfortable to work from the customer back, which would be DELIVER, MAKE, and SOURCE. In any case, don't start with PLAN or RETURN—the processes at which most companies are least competent.

Second, start with three basic questions for each SCOR Level Three element as it's placed on the swim diagram. Who is involved in the process steps to complete the work? What is the primary information trigger to begin the work? What is the primary information output that describes the trigger of the next process?

■ Fowlers' First Swim Diagram

In Fowlers' case, here is the thought process that team members followed as they assembled the white board for P1—PLAN supply chain.

P1.1—Identify, Prioritize, and Aggregate Supply Chain Requirements

The Fowlers team asked: Who is involved in the process steps to complete the work? During the staple yourself activity it was discovered that five functions compiled a forecast—each somewhat independently of the others and with different objectives in mind. The marketing function developed a net revenue forecast in dollars, based on assumptions for product mix and average selling price. The sales function developed a gross revenue forecast as the largest factor in personal compensation plans, independent of product mix and discounts. Sales and marketing fought to gain consensus, with issues of

Figure 15-2. Fowlers' P1 swim diagram summary.

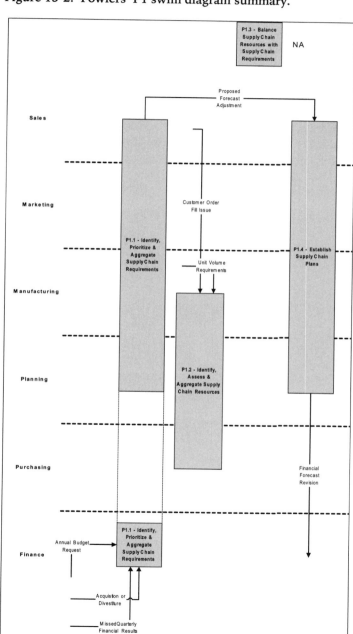

control involving pricing approval and promotional programs. The manufacturing function developed a history-
based unit forecast to support volume and unit-cost goals in
the budgeting process. Marketing relied on the manufacturing unit plan to guess at the right product mix. Meanwhile,
the planning department assembled a forecast to estimate inventory needed to support forecasted revenue; planning
didn't trust marketing's product mix forecast and it didn't
trust the manufacturing unit plan. Finally, the finance department assembled annual budget data for all of the above, ran
a pro forma profit and loss statement, then usually sent the
numbers back for each function to rework because the profit
picture wasn't ideal.

"So what is really the primary piece of information that triggers work to begin?" they asked. Three things trigger work
to produce a forecast. First is the annual budget cycle that
starts in July and is supposed to wrap up in November but
usually extends into January. Second is the event of a missed
quarterly profit plan, where some line on the income statement or balance sheet—whether it's revenue, cost, or inventory—is off. Third are acquisitions and divestitures.

And what is the primary information output from this work
that triggers the next process? The only consistent information output is a revised financial forecast in dollars, which is
notorious across Fowlers for having almost nothing to do
with actual production of units. The disconnects on this
transaction analysis summary were staggering.

P1.2—Identify, Assess, and Aggregate Supply Chain Resources

The team then asked: Who is involved in the process steps to
complete this work? The answer was: manufacturing, planning, and purchasing. Manufacturing responded to volume
fluctuations; demand was created and pushed to the warehouses based on unit-cost goals. Planning responded to
short-term order-fill issues by moving inventory from warehouse to warehouse and expediting factory replenishment
orders. And purchasing wagged the tail of the plan by expe-

diting and de-expediting supplier purchase orders in response to actions taken by manufacturing and planning.

The next question was: What is the primary information trigger to begin the work? Sadly, it was not the sales forecast generated in P1.1. It was order-fill problems that resulted from a chronically poor inventory position.

The team then wondered: What is the primary information output that describes the trigger of the next process? An expedited supply plan to support individual order-fill issues.

P1.3—Balance Supply Chain Resources with Supply Chain Requirements

Next came this question from the team: Who is involved in the process steps to complete the work? There were no functions formally involved in a balancing process; the means to address delivery issues was an 8:00 A.M. meeting that lasted three hours that was lead by manufacturing, with supporting from planning and purchasing. What is the primary information trigger to begin the work? The agenda for the 8:00 A.M. meeting was set by a daily backorder report showing the status and age of everything in the backorder pool.

The next question generated was: What is the primary information output that triggers the next process? The answer turned out to be a set of action items to expedite and de-expedite customer deliveries, inventory transfers, purchase orders, and replenishment orders.

P1.4—Establish and Communicate Supply Chain Plans

"Who is involved in the process steps to complete the work?," asked the team. The budget update was driven by the president of each business group. What is the primary information trigger to begin the work? It was the forecast adjustment generated in P1.1. What is the primary information output that triggers the next process? It turned out to be a revised budget and review for the executive team and board of directors.

As the Fowlers design team worked on the white board draft, the electronic version of the swim diagram was being built in real time. Refining a "Visio" not only involves representing the results of the white board discussion, it also attempts to insert the right amount of background data to portray the disconnects as clearly as possible. Information about productivity and technology tools—it's usually identification of module and submodule—are the most common data added to the electronic version. There is no standard format for the electronic modeling (see Figure 15-2).

The last steps in the AS IS process are to identify real examples for each transaction type and to continue to refine the productivity measures. The business cases help bring past experience forward—reinforcing the fluency of translating SCOR Level Three elements to current practices. It also sets the stage for logical testing of the TO BE solution, building confidence that desired state is more effective and efficient than the AS IS state.

The most important aspect of refinement at this stage is the data used to measure the transactional productivity. Industrial engineers using time and motion studies or human resource professionals conducting job task analysis are the closest in method to collecting legitimate data. As with the material flow spreadsheet and disconnect analysis, the accuracy of assumptions in relation to volume, event time, elapsed time, and yield are the basis for calculating savings opportunity. So any time dedicated to refining these assumptions is well spent.

▪ Conducting Steering Team Review Number Six

Prepare and conduct steering team review number six with the following agenda:

❏ Project roadmap status
❏ Anecdotal remarks from the "staple yourself" activity with

sample productivities including the tour maps, interviews, etc.
- ❏ Preview of transactional productivity data
- ❏ Quick lesson on swim diagrams and the business blueprint
- ❏ Expectations for steering team review number seven

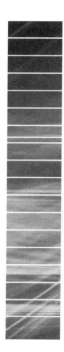

16

Week Fourteen:
The AS IS
Productivity Summary

Put dollar signs on work and information flow
opportunity.

The theme of this week is "Show me the money, Part II." The
primary objective is to summarize the productivity data—
volume, cycle time, and yield—from the sixty or so transactional
analysis worksheets (Figure 14-2) and associated swim diagrams (Figure 15-2) into six spreadsheets—one for each purchase order, work order, sales order, return authorization,
forecast, and replenishment order. The second objective is to
introduce the SCOR baseline business blueprint, which starts
the design team thinking about how transactions flow *should*
work.

Assembling the AS IS Productivity Summary

The activity for Day One, assembling a transaction productivity
summary, involves three steps: First, transfer the productivity

data to the spreadsheet template; second, group and transfer disconnects from the worksheets to the spreadsheet template and weight their impact on productivity; third, reconcile disconnect groups back to the fishbone diagrams created in material flow analysis (Chapter 10).

A generic transaction productivity summary looks complicated, but on further examination, it is like a fill-in-the-blanks worksheet. Let's focus on column one, "As Is," first (Table 16-1). In the sample, the headings are self explanatory: The first and second rows identify a SCOR Level Three element; the third row summarizes AS IS productivity including transaction volume, event time, elapsed cycle time, and yield; the fourth row summarizes the disconnect as drawn from the transactional analysis worksheet (Table 14-1) and the relative weight against all the others listed for this process. The weight category should add up to 100 percent. What's important is to get a sense of how each disconnect affects overall productivity. The last two columns are reserved for the TO BE solution summary, which helps calculate overall opportunity for the process.

In Fowlers' case, Table 16-2 is the transaction productivity summary/S1.1—schedule product deliveries—for products stocked at supplier storage facilities. The products include resin, packaging, and CD-ROM products from contract manufacturers. Fowlers employees spend about 80,000 hours a year performing this process step. The transaction volume (10,000/year) multiplied by event time (eight hours) and divided by 2,080 (a year of forty-hour work weeks) delivers an approximate number of people involved—in this case, about thirty-eight.

The director of purchasing at Fowlers was especially interested in another efficiency measure—the ratio of elapsed time to event time, which was 72:8, or 9:1. It meant nine hours of valueless waiting, reworking, expediting, and fighting other associated fires to schedule one purchase order. And then, based on the yield number, 3,900 out of those 10,000 purchase orders had to be rescheduled. As noted, the purchase order team identified and weighted five disconnects; the two biggest involved the purchase-order batch update cycle and the amount of time spent closing partial supplier orders. Lean research supports this anal-

Table 16-1. Transaction productivity summary sample.

AS IS Productivity	Volume	Disconnect Weight	Transaction Volume
	Event Time		Event Time (0 lag)
	Elapsed Time		Elapsed Time (with lag)
	Yield		% Without Rework
Disconnect	% out of 100 compared to other disconnects		Disconnect transferred from Transactional Analysis Worksheet

TO BE Productivity	Volume	Transaction Volume affected by change
	Event Time	TO BE Event Time
	Elapsed Time	TO BE Elapsed Time
	Yield	TO BE Yield
Recommendation	Description of changes to work and information flow	

Improvement Summary	Volume	Transaction Volume affected by change
	Event Time	AS IS—TO BE
	Elapsed Time	AS IS—TO BE
	Yield	AS IS—TO BE
Comments		

Source: © Copyright 2000 Pragmatek Consulting Group, Ltd. Used with permission.

Table 16-2. Fowlers' transaction productivity summary/S1.1—schedule product deliveries.

S1.1			
Schedule Product Deliveries			
AS IS Productivity	Volume	Disconnect Weight	10000
	Event Time		8
	Elapsed Time		72
	Yield		61%
Disconnect		30%	16- to 20-hour wait for overnight PO batch update and print
Disconnect		30%	Closing a partial shipment or back-orders takes 24 to 144 hours
Disconnect		25%	Large number of dis-crepancies including shipping product not ordered, shipping in different multiples, and price
Disconnect		15%	Checking on sup-plier status adds time because suppli-ers do not provide firm estimated time of arrival

ysis, stating that 95 percent or more of processing time is wait time.

Initiating TO BE Work and Information Flow

Like the TO BE material flow process, the TO BE work and infor-mation flow process seeks to improve transactional productivity by leveraging appropriate leading practices and eliminating disconnects. Unlike material flow, it starts with a template blueprint. The SCOR baseline business blueprint in swim diagram form shows the integrated processes for five leading practices: sales and operations planning, distribution requirements planning, master production scheduling, material requirements planning, and available to promise. The blueprint also incorporates closed-loop execution processes for all SCOR Level Three SOURCE, MAKE, DELIVER, and RETURN process elements (Table 16-3). This template is the starting point for the TO BE work and information flow. In this specific example, RETURN was not modeled.

The Baseline Business Blueprint Education

The blueprint is not a simple document, no matter how you try to describe or deconstruct it. Its purpose is to picture a more effective way to work than the tangle of evolutionary procedures that holds most businesses together (or tears them apart).

So the main objective for Day Two is to educate the design team on how integrated supply chain processes should work together. Some people find this to be an energizing part of the project. Executive reaction to the blueprint is—to use G-rated language—arm's length. And design teams, after coming this far, don't usually stop at G-rated language.

That was the case for the Fowlers design team. It was the coach who kept Day Two focused and effective. He did so by first explaining the strategic intent of the process and then tracing the flow on the blueprint diagram. It was conducted like a tour. The whole process took about three hours, and with team members contributing true examples of poor practices at Fowlers, the group's humor quickly improved.

The tour took the team from PLAN P1 to P4 to P3 to P2 to the SOURCE execution processes S1.1 through S1.5. Then it went on to the MAKE execution process M1.1 through M1.6 and finally to DELIVER execution processes D1.1 through D1.13.

Table 16-3. Sample SCOR baseline business blueprint.

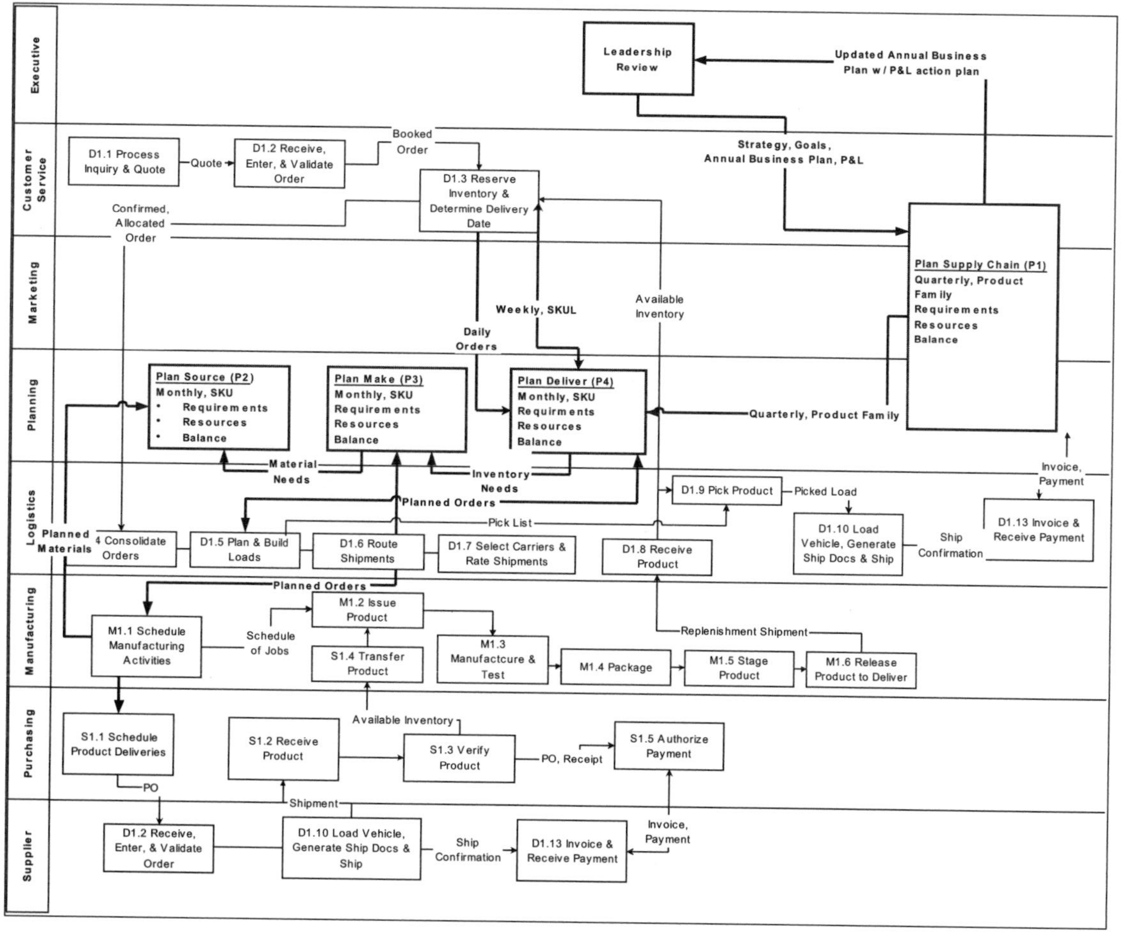

Finally, the tour ended with the RETURN execution processes DR1.1 through SR1.6 and DR3.1 through SR3.7. The epilogue covered one of the most frequently asked SCOR questions, "What do the enable processes do?"

■ The Fowlers SCOR Blueprint Tour

The following elements comprised the tour:

❑ *PLAN Supply Chain—P1.* This is the process of taking actual demand data and generating a supply plan for a given supply chain (defined in this case by customer, market channel, product, geography, or business entity). This process step is most closely associated with the discipline of sales and operations planning. The basic steps require a unit forecast that's adjusted for marketing and sales events; a supply plan that constrains the forecast based on resource availability (resources could be inventory, manufacturing capacity, or transportation); and a balance step where demand/supply exceptions are resolved and updated on the system. The output between this process step and the next—PLAN DELIVER (P4)—is a "constrained unit plan."

❑ *PLAN DELIVER—P4.* This is the process of comparing actual committed orders with the constrained forecast generated above and generating a distribution resource plan to satisfy service, cost, and inventory goals. It is carried out for each warehouse stocking location and may be aggregated to region or another geography type. This process step is most closely associated with the discipline of distribution requirements planning. The relationship between this process step and PLAN MAKE (P3) are "replenishment requirements," which tell the plant manager how much product to plan for. Reserve inventory and promise date (D1.3) is a "distribution requirements plan," which lets customer service know how much inventory will be available to promise.

❑ *PLAN MAKE—P3.* This is the process of comparing actual production orders plus replenishment orders with the constrained forecast generated above and then generating a master production schedule resource plan to satisfy service, cost, and inventory goals. It is carried out for each plant location and may be aggregated to region or another geography type. This process step is most closely associated with the discipline of master production scheduling. The relationship between this process step and PLAN SOURCE (P2) are "replenishment requirements," which tell the purchasing manager how much product to plan for. It's all rolled up into schedule manufacturing activities (M1.1), which is the master production schedule that lets the plant scheduler know how much total product must be made by the ship date.

❑ *PLAN SOURCE—P2.* This is the process of comparing total material requirements with the constrained forecast generated above and generating a material requirements resource plan to satisfy landed cost and inventory goals by commodity type. It is carried out for items on the bill of materials and may be aggregated by supplier or commodity type. This process step is most closely associated with the discipline of material requirements planning. The relationship between this process step and schedule product deliveries is the "material requirements plan," which lets the buyer know how much product must be purchased based on current orders, inventory, and future requirements.

❑ *SOURCE—S1.* This set of execution processes involves the material acquisition process—initiating and scheduling the purchase order, receiving and verifying product, transferring the product to available raw material, and authorizing supplier payment through. In the case of sourcing engineer-to-order products, there are accommodations to identify and select appropriate suppliers.

❑ *MAKE—M1.* This set of execution processes encompasses the conversion process of raw materials to finished goods—scheduling production activities, issuing and staging the product, producing and testing, packaging, and release of finished goods to customers or warehouses. In the case of making engineer-to-order products there are accommodations to finalize engineering specifications prior to initiating a manufacturing work order.

❑ *DELIVER—D1.* This set of execution processes involves the order fulfillment process—processing inquiries and quotes, entering orders, promising inventory, consolidating orders, planning and building loads, routing shipments, selecting carriers and rating shipments, receiving, picking, shipping, customer receipt, necessary installation, and final invoicing. In the case of delivering engineer-to-order products there are accommodations to include the request for proposal or quote and negotiating contracts prior to order entry.

❑ *RETURN—R1 and R3*. This set of execution processes involves the return authorization process, return shipment and receipt, verification and disposition of product, and replacement or credit process for defective and excess inventory. In the case of R2, a more detailed scheduling, determination of product condition, and transfer of maintenance, repair, and overhaul items is modeled.

❑ *ENABLE Processes*. Enable processes prepare, maintain, and manage information or relationships on which planning and execution processes rely. There is no decomposition of enable elements. Think of them as necessary processes. There are eight management categories of enable that are applied appropriately to PLAN, SOURCE, MAKE, DELIVER, and RETURN. They are business rules, performance improvement, data collection, inventory, capital assets, transportation, physical network configuration, and regulatory compliance. Another enable process, unique to PLAN, manages alignment of the financial and unit plans; another enable process—this one unique to SOURCE—manages supplier agreements. Supply chains can have well-integrated planning and execution processes and still underperform if enable processes are poorly managed. For example, a good sales and operations planning process cannot overcome a poor EP.9—align unit and financial plans.

With this education, the design team was ready to begin building their own blueprint for Fowlers' work and information flow.

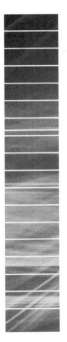

17

Week Fifteen: The TO BE Work and Information Flow Blueprint and Steering Team Review Number Seven

Document how the business should work.

The goal of brainstorming, any facilitator will tell you, is to "think outside the box." There was some kind of brain research from a college psychology class that indicated children who haven't yet started school will score an average of 95 percent on a creativity test, while third-graders score 30 percent on the same test, and adults in the workplace score 5 percent. So much for "outside the box."

Blend brain research with the fact that the relationships between supply chain processes are integrated and complex, and it's too much to ask for a design team to start building TO BE processes from scratch.

So the objective for this week is not fluid creativity. Rather, it's to figure out how the business should work by reviewing the SCOR Level 3 Baseline Blueprint (refer to Table 16-3), adjusting SCOR Level Three processes between swim lanes, incorporating transaction language for the specific technology application that will be used, conducting logical business transaction tests, and calculating productivity improvements based on the changes.

◼ Reviewing the SCOR Level Three Baseline Blueprint

The first agenda item on Day One is to convert the baseline blueprint. Chapter 16 provided generic commentary around the "work" part of work and information flow. Here is some necessary background on the "information" part.

In the language of SCOR, information flow is represented in inputs and outputs—definitions that are detailed in the SCOR dictionary (refer to Figure 13-1). There are two points to make regarding the inputs and outputs as summarized in the dictionary. First, what's represented on the picture and in the definitions section are a laundry list, there are no required links. And the format of the documentation is not in a true process flow. For example, the input to S1.2—receive product is the product and the output is receipt verification; the picture is not specific about the information link between each Level Three process. Users need to use the diagram as a guide, deciding which inputs and outputs are appropriate for their own blueprint.

Second, the inputs and outputs must be translated into the language of the application that will be used to create them. The application can be phone, fax, paper forms, voicemail, or digital through web-based data entry or modules of an ERP system. The tactics of the company's e-business strategy need to be reflected in the signals between elements. The inputs and outputs can be put in a variety of digital forms, such as electronic data interchange (EDI), extensible markup language (XML), etc. The information flow needs to reflect the TO BE solution environment.

With that as background, here is brief tour part two of the TO BE blueprint (Table 16-3).

The signals required to complete a sales order include a customer quote request, quote record, booked order, available inventory status, confirmed allocated order, pick list, customer master data containing routes, transportation master data containing rates and carriers, picked load, shipment record, advanced ship notice, customer receipt, and customer invoice.

The signals required to complete a work order or production job include planned orders, production schedule (by line or cell or process), material pull request, work order, replenishment order, and shipment.

The signals required to complete a purchase order include a requisition or other replenishment input, purchase order, receipt record, quality record, and supplier invoice. The signals required to complete a return authorization include customer request or planned return schedule, return authorization record, credit or replacement record, receipt record, disposition record, requisition for parts, material move request, return authorization to the supplier, and shipment record.

The signals required to support a forecast and supply replenishment plan include actual demand records, statistical forecast, forecast adjustments, supply plan exceptions, constrained unit plan, allocated orders by stock keeping unit by location, distribution resource exceptions, distribution requirements plan by location, replenishment order, master production schedule, planned orders, and material requirements plan.

This entire list—plus any others specific to the company—needs to be translated into appropriate labels in a packaged application.

The PLAN changes identified in the Fowlers case (Figure 17-1) include different signals that trigger a new unit forecast (P1.1), such as sales history; promotion; revised item master; other special causes; and annual unit and financial forecast. Sales history in this case refers to the month-end update of the planning software, based on actual demand. Promotion refers to the revised promotional calendar for specific customer or item events, as well as the general marketing campaigns. Revised item master refers to changes in item data that would change the method of forecast; for example, corporate marketing needs to release new products and a list of rationalized items to be retired. In either case, the history will need to be adjusted in some way during the work part of P1.1.

Examples of special causes that are inputs to the forecast

Figure 17-1. Fowlers' TO BE PLAN processes with inputs and outputs.

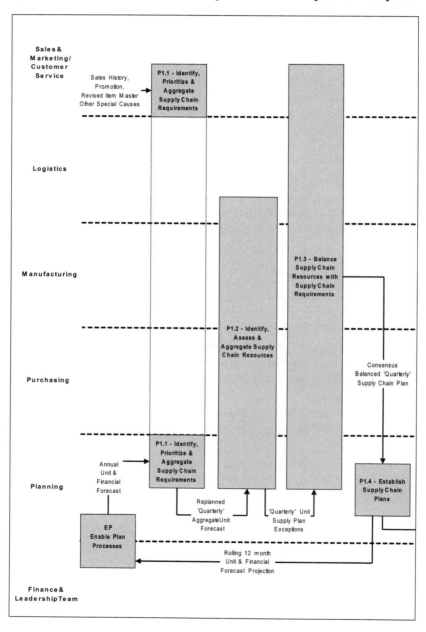

process include significant changes in the customer base, large trade shows where product is given away, and new market share acquisitions. The annual unit and financial forecast is the month's previous agreed-to plan—the most recent sales and operations plan.

Signals that trigger a new supply plan (P1.2) to support the forecast focus primarily on the replanned quarterly aggregate unit forecast. In this case, Fowlers is assuming that the capacity assumptions, inventory stocking strategies, and other essential supply planning setups are completed in the Enable PLAN elements prior to the actual P1.2 work. Replanned quarterly aggregate unit forecast refers to the unconstrained unit forecast generated by the demand planner in the previous step, when he or she hit the "done" button for the demand plan. Signals that trigger balance activity between requirements and resources are the quarterly unit supply plan exceptions. In supply planning terms, this is the exception list identified by item and location where there is real potential to miss designated customer service levels. Exceptions also point out where there is too much inventory.

Signals that trigger an update process include consensus balanced quarterly supply chain plans. Fowlers is seeking to formalize agreement to the exceptions and officially update a constrained unit plan that will feed the rest of the planning elements with an updated quarterly unit plan. It also would contribute to the revised financial projection needed in the leading practice of sales and operations planning with rolling twelve-month unit and financial forecast projections.

■ Adjusting Swim Lanes

The second agenda item is to adjust the configuration of swim lanes to streamline the work. Sometimes this will even involve adding lanes or taking some out altogether.

Some of these changes are little—such as rearranging how sales personnel help a forecast analyst adjust unit forecasts. Others are big. For example, transitioning an enterprise from corporate management of supply chain functions, which creates disconnects with and among business units, to a matrix that focuses corporate resources on Enable and work processes, while the business units focus on executing the signals (Table 17-1). That would be a big change.

In fact, that's the biggest change the design team made in Fowlers' supply chain: the way that functional responsibilities are allocated to minimize overlap and to integrate continuous improvement of the supply chain. In the before view, functional silos had evolved in such a way that personal agendas and internally focused metrics were allowed to get in the way of the overall goal of achieving efficiency across the whole system. In the after view, the design team assigned corporate responsibility for leading process improvement and developing Enable elements; the business units were charged with the single focus of executing the processes to perfection.

Because Fowlers' manufacturing facilities do most of their own purchasing of raw materials and contract manufactured

Table 17-1. Fowlers' supply chain matrix organization.

	Corporate Process Owners Process improvement, support, and resource development		
Supply Chain Organization Matrix	**Enable** System Engineers to support technical improvements to transaction productivity	**Plan** Corporate Manager of Planning owns the complete sales and operations planning process	**Source—Make** Corporate Manager of Materials Acquistion owns the process to acquire and transition material from raw materials to finished goods
Business Unit Execute processes on behalf of the business	System Engineers to extract information relevant to the business	General Manager, Demand Managers, and Supply Managers to execute effective SOP processes	Sourcing Managers, Materials Managers, Plant Managers execute the source and manufacturing processes

products, the design team combined SOURCE and MAKE. It also combined DELIVER and RETURN, both handled by the logistics and customer service functions. Each corporate manager had responsibility for measuring overall process performance and putting together plans for corrective action, including appropriate use of Enable elements.

Identifying Transaction Examples

The third agenda item for what turns out to be a long Day One is to identify real transaction examples and logically illustrate them with the TO BE blueprint to gain confidence that it works and to estimate productivity impact. The objective is to begin the bridge process for "how it works today" to "how it should work tomorrow." Document the business scenarios; they'll provide the framework for any functional and integrated system tests. Also take the temperature of the design team's confidence that the blueprint logically supports each scenario (Table 17-2).

In Fowlers case, Figure 17-2 illustrates the TO BE test of the SOURCE processes.

TO BE Productivity Improvement

As with the TO BE guidelines for material flow, we are leveraging the SCOR baseline blueprint for leading supply chain practice. However, just as important is the use of common sense to eliminate obvious inefficiencies. The process of arriving at what to change, the agenda for Day Two, is similar to material flow disconnects. For each disconnect documented in the transactional worksheets, describe the changes in process flow, swim lanes or organization, and technology. Next, for each change, have the subteam assess productivity impact as measured in the transaction productivity of the changes (documented on the transaction analysis worksheet, Figures 14-1 and 14-2). The more thorough the AS IS work, the better the estimated impact of the TO BE solution. Last, have the team accurately update the

Table 17-2. Business test scenario template.

Business Test Scenario 1—Sales Order
Test Description:
Insert a paragraph here describing the actual background of the sales order test and attached documents (invoice, sales order, inventory report, pick list, etc.).
Test Summary by Element:
D1.1   Insert a description here of the key aspects of how the TO BE solution would handle the business case. Use the recommended changes on your TO BE worksheet as a minimum building block.
Assumptions for Change:
Insert bullets here describing assumptions used in the element test summaries.

Source: © Copyright 2000 Pragmatek Consulting Group, Ltd. Used with permission.

changes on the TO BE blueprint. Each subteam should logically walk through the business scenarios with each iteration of the revised blueprint and assess the confidence level of team members. Extended team members who helped in the staple yourself activity (Chapter 14) may be appropriate resources to validate changes before next week's solution review.

Conducting Steering Team Review Number Seven

Prepare and conduct steering team review number seven with the following agenda items:

❑ Project roadmap status
❑ Productivity summary by transaction type
❑ Business test scenario to provide initial insight into the TO BE scenario
❑ Expectations for steering team review number eight

Figure 17-2. Fowlers' business test scenario—purchase order.

Business Test Scenario 1—Purchase Order.

Test Description:

The following test scenario describes the process followed in order to create a Purchase Order (non MRO) through the ERP System PO module. It describes the complete process from create to close.

Test Summary by Element:

S1.1, S2.1 SCHEDULE PRODUCT DELIVERIES (Create PO)

1. POs are created based on input from demand planner/forecasting (ERP system planning). Orders are placed as they are needed (or as reorder points designate), they are not placed according to the past order cycle period of one month (specific day of the month for a supplier).
2. Is the supplier new? If Yes, then contact purchasing to have the new supplier set up in ERP System.
3. If not, then using ERP system purchasing, the PO is created. The supplier is looked up and selected with the appropriate address for that site. Are the items set up in the system? If Yes, then the items are entered on the PO lines. For each item, quantity, requested delivery date, price, and ship to address are entered (accounts are auto-generated via account generator).
4. When all the data is entered on the ERP System PO, it is saved and a PO number is automatically generated. The PO is then routed for Approval. (This is done online.) The approval routing is based on hierarchical structure.
5. The PO arrives in the inbox/notifications of the appropriate person based on the dollar limits, and accounts on the PO. They then either approve or reject the PO.
6. If the PO is rejected, it would go back to the original creator, they would make the necessary changes, and it would be rerouted. If it was rejected because it was sent to the incorrect person, the original creator would then forward it to the correct approver. If it was rejected because it should not have been created, it would then be canceled.
7. If the PO was approved, it is either autofaxed to the supplier or web-enabled viewed.
8. A web-enabled acknowledgment is obtained from the supplier with the acceptance of the order and requested delivery date.

18

Week Sixteen:
The TO BE Summary
and Project Portfolio

The SCOR baseline blueprint makes the defining of new supply chain processes easier, but make no mistake, there's still heavy lifting to do, as the design team discovered with the homework from the previous week. The subteams were assigned with validating and finalizing recommended changes to supply chain work and information flow, including the swim diagrams, productivity summaries, and system changes using the business case scenarios to test each transaction.

Ultimately, though, all of this fun has to translate back to improved transaction productivity. So this week's primary objectives are a gut-check of the numbers, reviewing and refining the TO BE productivity spreadsheets, and initiating assembly of the overall project portfolio and associated return on investment summary.

Refining TO BE Productivity Spreadsheets

The Fowlers design team had five productivity spreadsheets to refine—one each for PLAN, SOURCE, MAKE, DELIVER, and

RETURN; that was the agenda for Day One. Figure 18-1, the TO BE Productivity Summary for S1.1—Schedule Product Deliveries, is just one example. It serves as a good example. First, not all purchase orders are affected by this particular solution; this targets the 5,000 purchase orders for stocked raw materials. (The business case scenario in Figure 17-2 addressed the other 5,000 purchase orders for to-order raw materials.)

Second, the summary recommendations description is just that—a summary. Addition of SCOR Level Four business requirements and a high-level set of systems requirements make the detailed documentation complete. The objective for this set of requirements is to help scope and sequence necessary system implementation, which provides a path for the corporate director of applications. For emphasis, the summary does *not* replace detailed system requirement definitions, solution design, functional and integrated testing, and go-live activities.

Third, the performance improvement is a simple calculation multiplying the number of purchase orders (5,000) by the estimated savings in event cycle time (eight hours)—an improvement of 40,000 hours. The team factored in yield by multiplying the number of purchase orders (5,000) by the amount needing rework under the improved process (5 percent)—250 orders. When multiplied by the new event cycle time (one hour), the total amount of rework needed under the improved process would be 250 hours. This was compared to the old process, in which 5,000 orders at 61 percent yield would result in 1,950 orders requiring rework at an event cycle time of nine hours per order—a total of 17,550 hours.

The before-and-after swim diagrams associated with the TO BE productivity summary for S1.1 are summarized in Figures 18-2 (before) and 18-3 (after). There are three significant changes to the schedule product deliveries process. First, the material flow previously scheduled to-order items, while it now stocks those items based on anticipated consumption; this is noted by the use of S1.1 rather than S2.1. The second change is in the placement of the process element on the swim diagram; the supplier (using self-service technology) is now responsible for carrying out the tasks as defined in the S1.1 Level 4 process steps.

(text continues on page 199)

Figure 18-1. Fowlers TO BE productivity summary/S1.1—schedule product deliveries.

S1.1 — Schedule Product Deliveries

	AS IS Productivity	TO BE	Improvement Summary
Volume	10000	5000	5000
Event Time	9	1	8
Elapsed Time	72	1.5	70.5
Yield	61%	95%	34%

Disconnect	Disconnect Weight	Disconnect	Recommendation
	30%	16- to 20-hour wait for overnight PO batch update and print	Leverage current functionality and processes for supplier self service including availability to create, process, and send purchase orders; automatic purchase order signoff hierarchy with Fowlers managing account security centrally; automated purchase order creation based on designated order points or other consumption trigger points, i.e., forecasts; align purchasing organization to effectively support more planning than execution steps
	30%	Closing a partial shipment or backorder takes 24 to 144 hours	Institute supplier performance scorecards to review delivery performance to at least party levels of competitive advantage for on-time and in-full delivery
	25%	Large number of discrepancies including shipping product not ordered, shipping in different multiples, and price	Item classification and unit of measure conversions should be automatically available; eliminate manual entry of default item attributes; establish Fowlers owner for item master accuracy and maintenance
	15%	Checking on supplier status adds time because suppliers do not provide firm estimated time of arrival	Web enable order status functionality as part of supplier self service including order event notification

Figure 18-2. Fowlers' before swim diagram S1.1.

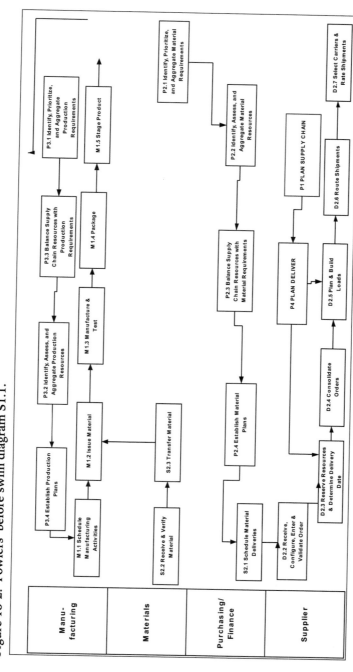

Figure 18-3. Fowlers' after swim diagram S1.1.

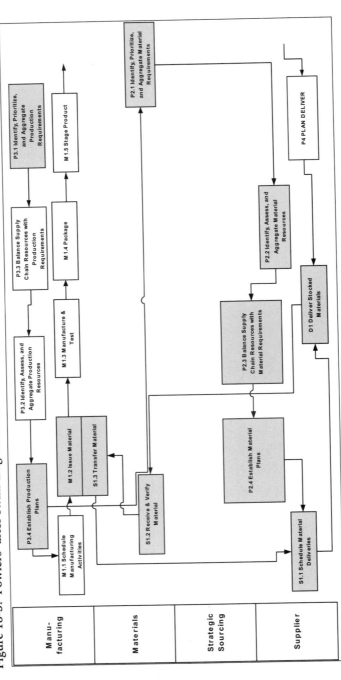

Third, the purchasing/finance swim lane is changed to strategic sourcing; the roles are reflected in the involvement in the P2—PLAN SOURCE elements. For example, while the supplier has responsibility (through real-time order status technology) to calculate material resources (P2.1), strategic sourcing has the shared responsibility of working with the supplier to communicate material requirements or forecast data (P2.1) and to balance demand and supply issues (P2.3).

Establishing the Overall Project Portfolio and Initiating the Return-on-Investment Analysis

There are some best practices to apply when building a credible overall project portfolio, which is the first agenda item for Day Two. The first best practice is no double-dipping. It gets harder at the end; here are some tips the Fowlers team used:

❑ Help the people in the finance function to understand where the savings are by speaking in their language, which tends to be oriented toward cost centers rather than supply chains. To this end, leverage the cost-center mapping to total supply chain cost, and warranty and return cost developed in the SCORcard phase of the project (Chapter 4).
❑ Use the Level Three metrics for the internal measure of total supply chain cost and warranty and return cost (Table 4-1), to sort between material flow measure versus work and information flow.
❑ Count customer service cost, returns authorization processing cost, purchasing cost, labor part of FG warehouse cost, labor part of RM warehouse, labor part of return maintenance cost demand planning, and supply planning costs as work and information flow as they generally are transaction related.
❑ Count inventory carrying cost, outbound transportation cost, inbound transportation cost, returns transportation cost, physical asset (lease or owned) part of FG warehouse cost, physical asset part (lease or owned) of RM warehouse, physi-

cal asset part (lease or owned) returns warehouse cost as material flow as they are material related.
❑ Use information technology costs, as a percent of sales, to combine labor expense to support IT operations with fixed assets and leases for software and hardware.

These are not strict rules to enforce, but rather guidelines to help keep the money straight and count it only once.

Using these guidelines, the Fowlers team made the following adjustments to the material flow disconnect opportunity grid (Figure 18-4):

❑ $1,500,000 was added to (2) supply management, based on purchase order productivity improvements.
❑ $2,349,080 was added to (7) undisciplined order management, based on sales order productivity improvements.
❑ $2,134,530 was added to (5) poor data integrity, based on data accuracy and maintenance productivity to customer, item, and supplier master data.
❑ $1,246,238 was added to (4) disparate systems, based on productivity improvements made through elimination of enable costs to support customized partially integrated systems.

Another best practice is to incorporate known processes for requesting and gaining approval of capital expenditures. Model the supply chain portfolio after successfully approved capital improvements, noting the format of the business case description, financial calculations and assumptions, situation analysis, and time-and-material descriptions for internal and external resources.

In Fowlers' case, the team established a return-on-investment summary modeled after one of their most successful capital projects (Figure 18-5).

The basic format translated each project (and associated profit improvement) on the list into a three-year benefit schedule, detailing a cost estimate for the first-year expenses to get the implementation pilot and roll-out plan completed. For each benefit year, the team estimated the percent of the benefit to be

Figure 18-4. Fowlers' updated disconnect opportunity grid.

Ease of Implementation (EASY — TOUGH)
Business Impact (BIG PAYOFF — SMALL PAYOFF)

Legend	$ Savings
1 Poor Planning	$15,825,210
2 Supply Management	$2,757,888
3 Reactive Logistics Planning and Execution	$2,390,833
4 Disparate Systems	$1,246,238
5 Poor Data Integrity	$2,134,530
6 Hit-and-Miss Product Life Cycle Management	$4,440,985
7 Undisciplined Order Management	$2,349,080
8 No Formal Return Management	$38,000,000
Total	$69,144,764

Adjustments to

Added $1,500,000 to 2-Supply Management.
Added $2,349,080 to 7-Undisciplined Order Management.
Consolidated customer, item, supplier master data savings to 5-Poor Data Integrity, totaling $2,134,530.
Added IT $1,246,238 to 4-Disparate Systems estimated as the cost to support customized partially integrated systems totaled.

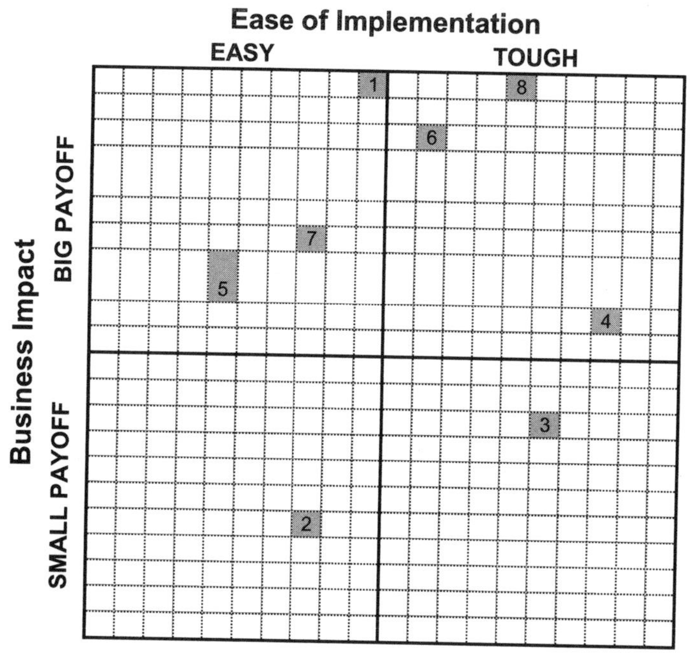

Figure 18-5. Fowlers' project portfolio.

Gross P&L Impacts ($ in 000's)	1st Year Cost Investment	3-Year Benefit		
		FY 1	FY 2	FY 3
Scalable Improvements	100%	25%	40%	100%
Project 1: Poor Planning				
Project 2: Supply Management				
Project 3: Reactive Logistics Planning and Execution				
Project 4: Disparate Systems				
Project 5: Poor Data Integrity				
Project 6: Hit-and-Miss Product Life Cycle Management				
Project 7: Undisciplined Order Management				
Project 8: No Formal Return Management				
Grand Total	$ —	$ —	$ —	$ —

Source: © Copyright 2000 Pragmatek Consulting Group, Ltd. Used with permission.

realized based on the pilot results and an estimate of the percent of the rollout completed. The cost breakdown was a gross estimate of the expense to institute all recommended changes, including material, work, and information flow. The benefit analysis for each project netted out any increase in ongoing operating costs that would result from the changes.

The Fowlers design team invited controllers from each business group to help educate everyone on the finer points of the necessary detail required as backup to the summary. This added content and change-management value in preparation for the final steering team review during the last week.

An updated disconnect opportunity grid, advice and counsel from the controllers, and a blank project portfolio and return-on-investment profile provided the obvious homework assignment heading into the last week of the analyze and design phase of the supply chain project.

19

Week Seventeen: Implementation Planning and Steering Team Review Number Eight

You can move beyond supply chain design.

The finish line! Or is it? In one of the hardest graduate classes at the University of Minnesota, as Professor Richard Swanson handed out the final exam after a grueling semester, he said, "True learning is a painful experience. I can see that all of you have learned a great deal in this course." As the last of the students left the room at the end of the class, he offered one more piece of advice: "Remember," he said, "that the road never ends. It's the journey that must be your home."

Design teams end this sixteen-week process weary, but also transformed, enlightened, broadened, deepened . . . changed; and they are excited to go get the dough. Closing out the final week of the project and moving on to implementation requires attention to detail: polishing up the project portfolio and projected return-on-investment spreadsheet and guiding the design team through reflection and transition. Achieving the improvements—the develop and implementation phases of the SCOR project roadmap—are the subject of another book.

◼ Fowlers' Project Portfolio and Projected Return on Investment

On Day One, the Fowlers design team met to review the project portfolio and projected return-on-investment (Figure 19-1). The numbers provided some surprises. The first was in Project Number Four: Disparate Systems. Nearly everyone had fit into one of two camps at the start of the project. The "rose-colored glasses" group saw the new Tier One ERP system as having achieved all that it was engineered to achieve; it was in and that was the goal, right? Those in the "system is the problem" group viewed the ERP system's implementation over the last couple of years as the main reason the company wasn't as successful as it had once been. But now, looking at the project portfolio, both groups agreed that in order to improve performance, more investment was needed to use the system to its fullest. The ROI value of Project Number Four was low—particularly in relation to the high level of first-year investment. This helped bring the camps together on prioritizing supply chain improvement elsewhere before putting more money into the system. It was clear that Project Number Four would start well after the rest of the projects on the chart.

Another surprise was in Project One: Poor Planning. Nobody had realized the tremendous cost of poor planning; it was the second biggest opportunity for profit improvement. The entire company had practiced execution and fire fighting until it was an art form. In fact, service awards were given to Fowlers employees who effectively responded to the most fires in a quarter. All of that could now change. The processes to be implemented that would improve the company's planning efforts were leading practices, but not rocket science. Of more concern was the human discipline needed to make, follow, and appropriately adjust plans. There were a thousand-and-one behaviors to change—from the executive team all the way to the manufacturing scheduler. Only a third of the cost for this project actually went to improving forecast analysis functionality; the rest was process and change management.

The third surprise was in Project Number Eight: No Formal Return Management. The financial impact of poor product re-

Figure 19-1. Fowlers' project portfolio and projected return on investment.

Gross P&L Impacts ($ in 000's)	1st Year Cost Investment	3-Year Benefit		
		FY 1	FY 2	FY 3
Scalable Improvements	100%	25%	40%	100%
Project 1: Poor Planning	(2,200.0)	3,956	6,330	15,825
Project 2: Supply Management	(150.0)	690	1,102	2,757
Project 3: Reactive Logistics Planning and Execution	(250.0)	598	956	2,390
Project 4: Disparate Systems	(6,500.0)	311	498	1,246
Project 5: Poor Data Integrity	—	533	853	2,134
Project 6: Hit-and-Miss Product Life Cycle Management	(500.0)	1,110	1,776	4,440
Project 7: Undisciplined Order Management	(250.0)	587	939	2,349
Project 8: No Formal Return Management	(1,200.0)	9,500	15,200	13,300
Grand Total	$ (11,050)	$17,285	$27,654	$44,441

turn is the first low-hanging fruit of the twenty-first century. Accruals, obsolescence, return policy, reverse logistics, customer service, technical support, inventory disposition, product recall, and consigned excess inventory have all evolved to a point where a well-designed RETURN element can deliver significant financial impact on every income statement and balance sheet.

The fourth surprise was in Project Number Five: Poor Data

Integrity. This project had the best ROI profile and the fewest required changes of all projects in the portfolio. The work is not glamorous, but improvements are exponential. If just one data field of the item master is off by just one digit, it cascades throughout the enterprise until, over time, inventory, cost, and service go out of control.

For each project in the portfolio, risk was assessed and strategies were put in place. Risk assessment included both gross dollar impact and probability of occurrence. Strategies were as simple as to avoid the risk or to accept it. When applicable, means to mitigate the risk were included.

The Final Steering Team Review

The day is finished with the eighth steering team review, with the following agenda:

- ❑ Project roadmap status
- ❑ Review the project portfolio and return-on-investment profile
- ❑ Discuss risk for each project
- ❑ Expectations for transition to implementation

Reflection and Transition at Fowlers

The agenda for Day Two was simple: a celebratory lunch. It was a large table, with most of the design team present. The conversation started the period of reflection and transition that comes on the heels of any successful supply chain design effort.

"What I want to know," one of the members asked, "is how we can be sure to keep up the momentum when we start to implement? I mean, look at the trouble they had with the ERP system. So how do we take all of this good energy and make sure that it brings fast enough results that supply chain improvement takes on a life of its own?"

It started a passionate discussion about change in an organization. It happens 1) when the balance between people's abilities and business challenges tips toward the challenges; 2) when, as a result, it becomes difficult to anticipate the future; and 3) when past expectations aren't relevant anymore.

"It seems to me," said another usually quiet member of the team, "that people can get behind change when they feel like they're able to respond to whatever new expectations are set for them."

"And if the expectations aren't reasonable, or if they're not based on some logical approach, then people run the other way," countered someone from the other end of the table.

"But not everyone has the same capacity for change, no matter how well the new expectations are documented," added yet another voice.

The coach couldn't help comparing this observation to the best-selling business book *Who Moved My Cheese* (Penguin Putnam Inc.). In it, author Spencer Johnson writes about four characters (Sniff, Scurry, Haw, and Hem), each with a different change capacity.

Sniff sniffed out change early and Scurry scurried into action to make change happen. Hem denied and resisted change and Haw, after initial resistance, learned to see that change was better and adapted accordingly. Sniff and Scurry had high-change capacities, easily learning to find new cheese. Hem and Haw had low-change capacities, slowly (or not) adjusting to the fact that the old cheese was gone.

"In my experience," the coach said, "the SCOR approach has as much to do with culture as with engineering techniques. When it's used well, it can transform the way a company behaves."

The Roles of Change

Academia suggests that there are four common roles critical to the change process. The first, a *sponsor*, has the power to authorize or legitimize change; this role creates the environment (pain) that enables change. The second, an *agent*, is responsible for making the change—the planning and execution to ease the pain. The third, a *target*, is the individual or group that must change; meaningful involvement by the target is essential for sustained change. Fourth, an *advocate*, helps achieve a change but lacks the power to sanction it.

The SCOR project roadmap uniquely offers a formal structure that effectively utilizes these four roles and provides education to support them in their efforts.

Consider what you just learned about Fowlers. A core team of suitably motivated executives was identified to sponsor the effort; they held eight steering team meetings over sixteen weeks to review and approve key SCOR deliverables (see Figure 1-2, SCOR Project Roadmap).

The design team held the role of agent. It conducted thirty-two formal and informal meetings over sixteen weeks, producing key SCOR deliverables.

The extended team held the role of target. There were many formal and informal meetings over the sixteen weeks. Each meeting helped to validate and refine SCOR deliverables and to demonstrate to each member of the target group why all of this was important.

David Able was the advocate. He participated as a design team member and provided the communication link to the rest of the teams.

That leaves one final role—sponsor, which is a little bit more complex because it is so closely linked to the pain of changing the environment.

There are three phases of change: present state, transition state, and desired state. Change is only possible when the pain of the present exceeds the cost of the transition. By clearly analyzing competitive position with standard metrics, identifying disconnects and gaining consensus around the TO BE design, a SCOR project helps people see the AS IS as unacceptable and the TO BE as desirable.

Prior to the Fowlers project, pain was not obvious. The business was growing, profitable, and considered a market-share leader. The key was the transition in strategy from operational excellence (SOURCE and MAKE) to customer intimacy (PLAN and DELIVER). Looking at the SCORcard from the customer's perspective was a revealing exercise. The design team articulated gaps in delivery performance, fulfillment lead-time, and total-delivered cost as they related to the *new* strategy. Each of these gaps became a source of pain.

■ Focus

There is a limit to the amount of change that anyone can handle at one time. Individual changes, organizational changes, and more macro or global changes can fill up capacity. By integrating supply chain changes into operational strategy, material flow, and work and information flow, a SCOR process results in fewer but deeper projects that ultimately produce bigger and faster returns—in other words, a manageable amount of change designed to be measurable and meaningful.

That's why the best part of a project is often the final review, where the design team presents its TO BE design, project list, and associated assumptions. To watch each team member speak to both strategy and tactics in the same conversation and understand the thread that ties it all together is worth the pain of the previous weeks.

SCOR's disconnect analysis—the process of identifying, grouping, quantifying, and prioritizing issues or barriers inhibiting performance—is a self-discovery process that helps design and extended teams through the stages of resistance. When the design team sees problems that have existed for years and makes decisions to close those disconnects, resistance is replaced with a clear motivation to embrace still more change. As design team members lead the discussion based on what they think is wrong, denial is replaced with a shared vision. By this stage, there's a personal investment in solving the problem and finding a solution that works. The roadmap helps guide out of the box thinking via trial and error.

In a slightly more roundabout way, that's where the lunchtime conversation ended at Fowlers as members of the design team started to think again about the work waiting for them at their desks. It was already mid-afternoon, and the day was winding down. The coach had a plane to catch. But even as team members started folding their napkins and pushing back from the table, there was a sense that the celebratory meal had not been the end of the project. It was merely the end of planning and design.

Brian Dowell picked up the check, but David Able had the last word. As he stood up from the table, he announced to nobody and everybody, "I've got to get back. There are a couple of projects waiting to get started."

Appendix A

SCOR Model Overview

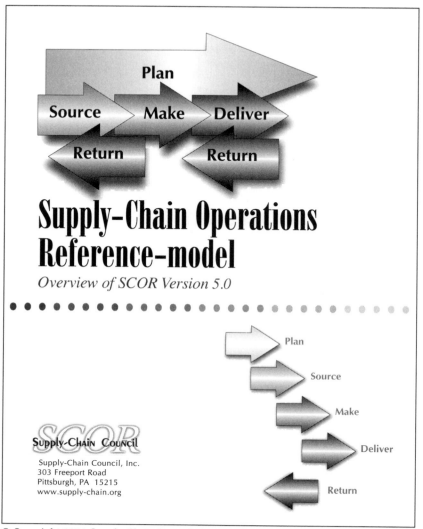

Supply-Chain Operations Reference-model

Overview Version 5.0

CONTENTS

The Supply Chain Operations Reference-model (SCOR) has been developed and endorsed by the Supply-Chain Council (SCC), an independent not-for-profit corporation, as the cross-industry standard for supply-chain management. The SCC was organized in 1996 by Pittiglio Rabin Todd & McGrath (PRTM) and AMR Research, and initially included sixty-nine voluntary member companies. Council membership is now open to all companies and organizations interested in applying and advancing state-of-the-art supply-chain management systems and practices.

Member companies pay a modest annual fee to support Council activities.
All who use the SCOR-model are asked to acknowledge the SCC in all documents describing or depicting the SCOR-model and its use.

All who use SCOR are encouraged to join the SCC, both to further model development and to obtain the full benefits of membership. Further information regarding the Council and SCOR can be found at the Council's web site, www.supply-chain.org.

What Is a Process Reference Model?

Process reference models integrate the well-known concepts of business process reengineering, benchmarking, and process measurement into a cross-functional framework.

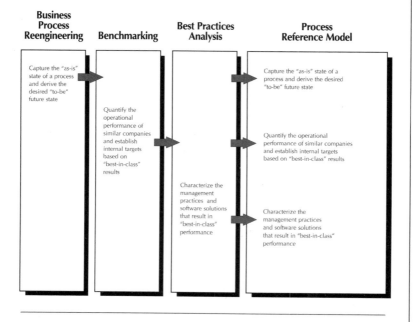

A Process Reference Model Contains:

- Standard descriptions of management processes
- A framework of relationships among the standard processes
- Standard metrics to measure process performance
- Management practices that produce best-in-class performance
- Standard alignment to features and functionality

Once a Complex Management Process is Captured in Standard Process Reference Model Form, It can Be:

- Implemented purposefully to achieve competitive advantage
- Described unambiguously and communicated
- Measured, managed, and controlled
- Tuned and re-tuned to a specific purpose

► **A Process Reference Model Becomes a Powerful Tool in the Hands of Management**

The Boundaries of Any Model Must Be Carefully Defined

"From your supplier's supplier to your customer's customer"

SCOR spans:
- All customer interactions, from order entry through paid invoice
- All product (physical material, and service) transactions, from your supplier's supplier to your customer's customer, including equipment, supplies, spare parts, bulk product, software, etc.
- All market interactions, from the understanding of aggregate demand to the fulfillment of each order

SCOR does not attempt to describe every business process or activity, including:
- Sales and marketing (demand generation)
- Research and technology development
- Product development
- Some elements of post-delivery customer support

Links can be made to processes not included within the model's scope, such as product development, and some are noted in SCOR.

SCOR assumes but does not explicitly address:
- Training
- Quality
- Information Technology (IT)
- Administration (non SCM)

SCOR is Based on Five Distinct Management Processes

Scope of SCOR Processes

Plan

Demand/Supply Planning and Management

▷ Balance resources with requirements and establish/communicate plans for the whole supply chain, including Return, and the execution processes of Source, Make, and Deliver.

▷ Management of business rules, supply chain performance, data collection, inventory, capital assets, transportation, planning configuration, and regulatory requirements and compliance.

▷ Align the supply chain unit plan with the financial plan.

Source

Sourcing Stocked, Make-to-Order, and Engineer-to-Order Product

▶ Schedule deliveries; receive, verify, and transfer product; and authorize supplier payments.

▶ Identify and select supply sources when not predetermined, as for engineer-to-order product.

▶ Manage business rules, assess supplier performance, and maintain data.

▶ Manage inventory, capital assets, incoming product, supplier network, import/export requirements, and supplier agreements.

Make

Make-to-Stock, Make-to-Order, and Engineer-to-Order Production Execution

▶ Schedule production activities, issue product, produce and test, package, stage product, and release product to deliver.

▶ Finalize engineering for engineer-to-order product.

▶ Manage rules, performance, data, in-process products (WIP), equipment and facilities, transportation, production network, and regulatory compliance for production.

Deliver

Order, Warehouse, Transportation, and Installation Management for Stocked, Make-to-Order, and Engineer-to-Order Product

▶ All order management steps from processing customer inquiries and quotes to routing shipments and selecting carriers.

▶ Warehouse management from receiving and picking product to load and ship product.

▶ Receive and verify product at customer site and install, if necessary.

▶ Invoicing customer.

▶ Manage Deliver business rules, performance, information, finished product inventories, capital assets, transportation, product life cycle, and import/export requirements.

Return

Return of Raw Materials (to Supplier) and Receipt of Returns of Finished Goods (from Customer), including Defective Products, MRO Products, and Excess Products

▶ All return defective product steps from authorizing return; scheduling product return; receiving, verifying, and disposition of defective product; and return replacement or credit.

▶ Return MRO product steps from authorizing and scheduling return, determining product condition, transferring product, verifying product condition, disposition, and request return authorization.

▶ Return excess product steps including identifying excess inventory, scheduling shipment, receiving returns, approving request authorization, receiving excess product return in Source, verifying excess, and recover and disposition of excess product.

▶ Manage Return business rules, performance, data collection, return inventory, capital assets, transportation, network configuration, and regulatory requirements and compliance.

A Process Reference Model Differs from Classic Process Decomposition Models

SCOR is a process reference model that provides a language for communicating among supply-chain partners

▶ Process decomposition models are developed to address one specific configuration of process elements

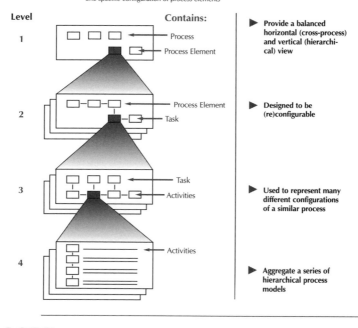

Level	Contains:	
1	Process Process Element	▶ Provide a balanced horizontal (cross-process) and vertical (hierarchical) view
2	Process Element Task	▶ Designed to be (re)configurable
3	Task Activities	▶ Used to represent many different configurations of a similar process
4	Activities	▶ Aggregate a series of hierarchical process models

SCOR Contains Three Levels of Process Detail

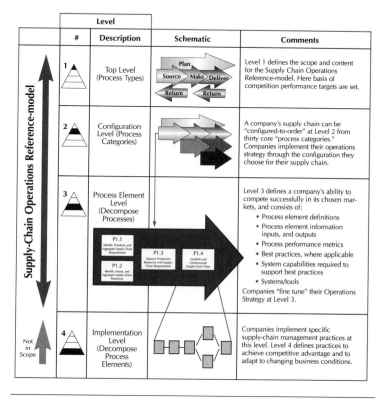

	Level			
	#	**Description**	**Schematic**	**Comments**
Supply-Chain Operations Reference-model	**1**	Top Level (Process Types)	Plan / Source / Make / Deliver / Return / Return	Level 1 defines the scope and content for the Supply Chain Operations Reference-model. Here basis of competition performance targets are set.
	2	Configuration Level (Process Categories)		A company's supply chain can be "configured-to-order" at Level 2 from thirty core "process categories." Companies implement their operations strategy through the configuration they choose for their supply chain.
	3	Process Element Level (Decompose Processes)	P1.1 Identify, Prioritize, and Aggregate Supply-Chain Requirements / P1.2 Identify, Assess, and Aggregate Supply-Chain Resources / P1.3 Balance Production Resources with Supply-Chain Requirements / P1.4 Establish and Communicate Supply-Chain Plans	Level 3 defines a company's ability to compete successfully in its chosen markets, and consists of: • Process element definitions • Process element information inputs, and outputs • Process performance metrics • Best practices, where applicable • System capabilities required to support best practices • Systems/tools Companies "fine tune" their Operations Strategy at Level 3.
Not in Scope	**4**	Implementation Level (Decompose Process Elements)		Companies implement specific supply-chain management practices at this level. Level 4 defines practices to achieve competitive advantage and to adapt to changing business conditions.

SCOR
Supply-Chain Council

Process Categories
Defined by the Relationship Between a SCOR Process and a Process Type

"SCOR Configuration Toolkit"

		SCOR Process					
		Plan	Source	Make	Deliver	Return	
Process Type	Planning	P1	P2	P3	P4	P5	
	Execution		S1- S3	M1- M3	D1 - D3	R1-R3	Process Category
	Enable	EP	ES	EM	ED	ER	

Practitioners select appropriate process categories from the SCOR configuration toolkit to represent their supply-chain configuration(s).

Level 1 Process Definitions
SCOR Is Based on Five Core Management Processes

SCOR Process	Definitions
Plan	Processes that balance aggregate demand and supply to develop a course of action which best meets sourcing, production and delivery requirements
Source	Processes that procure goods and services to meet planned or actual demand
Make	Processes that transform product to a finished state to meet planned or actual demand
Deliver	Processes that provide finished goods and services to meet planned or actual demand, typically including order management, transportation management, and distribution management
Return	Processes associated with returning or receiving returned products for any reason. These processes extend into post-delivery customer support

Level 1 Performance Metrics

Performance Attribute	Customer-Facing			Internal-Facing	
	Reliabilty	Responsiveness	Flexibility	Cost	Assets
Delivery performance	✔				
Fill Rate	✔				
Perfect order fulfillment	✔				
Order fulfillment lead time		✔			
Supply-chain response time			✔		
Production flexibility			✔		
Supply chain management cost				✔	
Cost of goods sold				✔	
Value-added productivity				✔	
Warranty cost or returns processing cost				✔	
Cash-to-cash cycle time					✔
Inventory days of supply					✔
Asset turns					✔

At Level 2, Each SCOR Process Can Be Further Described by Process Type

SCOR Process Type	Characteristics
Planning	A process that aligns expected resources to meet expected demand requirements. Planning processes: • Balance aggregated demand and supply • Consider consistent planning horizon • (Generally) occur at regular, periodic intervals • Can contribute to supply-chain response time

Execution	A process triggered by planned or actual demand that changes the state of material goods. Execution processes:
	 • Generally involve -
	   1. Scheduling/sequencing
	   2. Transforming product, and/or
	   3. Moving product to the next process
	 • Can contribute to the order fulfillment cycle time

Enable	A process that prepares, maintains, or manages information or relationships on which planning and execution processes rely

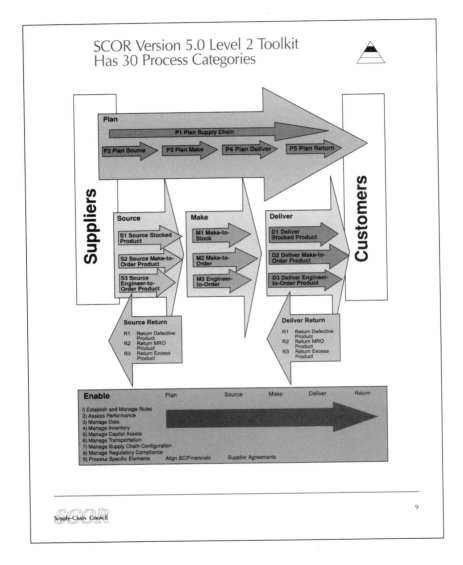

SCOR Level 3

Presents Detailed Process Element Information for Each
Level 2 Process Category

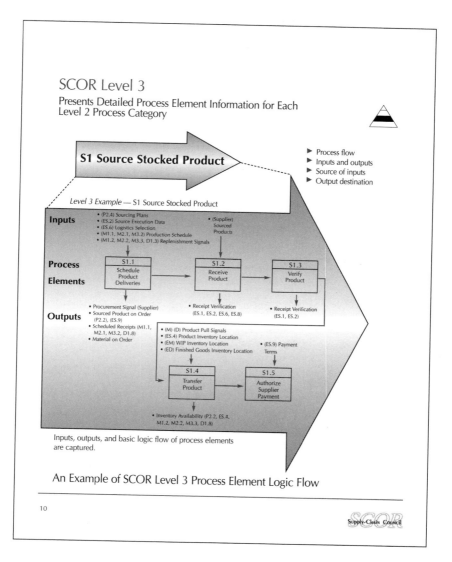

S1 Source Stocked Product

► Process flow
► Inputs and outputs
► Source of inputs
► Output destination

Level 3 Example — S1 Source Stocked Product

Inputs
- (P2.4) Sourcing Plans
- (ES.2) Source Execution Data
- (ES.6) Logistics Selection
- (M1.1, M2.1, M3.2) Production Schedule
- (M1.2, M2.2, M3.3, D1.3) Replenishment Signals

- (Supplier) Sourced Products

Process

Elements

S1.1	S1.2	S1.3
Schedule Product Deliveries	Receive Product	Verify Product

Outputs
- Procurement Signal (Supplier)
- Sourced Product on Order (P2.2), (ES.9)
- Scheduled Receipts (M1.1, M2.1, M3.2, D1.8)
- Material on Order

- Receipt Verification (ES.1, ES.2, ES.6, ES.8)

- Receipt Verification (ES.1, ES.2)

- (M) (D) Product Pull Signals
- (ES.4) Product Inventory Location
- (EM) WIP Inventory Location
- (ED) Finished Goods Inventory Location

- (ES.9) Payment Terms

S1.4	S1.5
Transfer Product	Authorize Supplier Payment

- Inventory Availability (P2.2, ES.4, M1.2, M2.2, M3.3, D1.8)

Inputs, outputs, and basic logic flow of process elements
are captured.

An Example of SCOR Level 3 Process Element Logic Flow

Examples:

SCOR Level 3 Standard Process
Element Definition, Performance Attributes, and Accompanying Metrics

Process Element: **Schedule Product Deliveries**	Process Number: S1.1

Process Element Definition

Scheduling and managing the execution of the individual deliveries of product against an existing contract or purchase order. The requirements for product releases are determined based on the detailed sourcing plan or other types of product pull signals.

Performance Attributes	Metric
Reliability	% Schedules Generated within Supplier's Lead Time
	% Schedules Changed within Supplier's Lead Time
Responsiveness	Average Release Cycle of Changes
Flexibilty	Average Days per Schedule Change
	Average Days per Engineering Change
Cost	Product Management and Planning Costs as a % of Product Acquisitions Costs
Assets	None Identified

SCOR Level 3 Best Practices and Features

Process Element: **Schedule Product Deliveries**	Process Number: S1.1

Best Practices	Features
Utilize EDI transactions to reduce cycle time and costs	EDI interface for 830, 850, 856, and 862 transactions
VMI agreements allow suppliers to manage (replenish) inventory	Supplier managed inventories with scheduling interfaces to external supplier systems
Mechanical (Kanban) pull signals are used to notify suppliers of the need to deliver product	Electronic Kanban support
Consignment agreements are used to reduce assets and cycle time while increasing the availability of critical items	Consignment inventory management
Advanced ship notices allow for tight synchronization between SOURCE and MAKE processes	Blanket order support with scheduling interfaces to external supplier systems

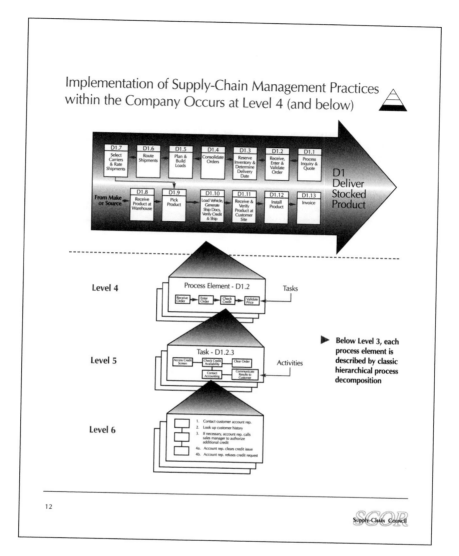

Implementation of Supply-Chain Management Practices within the Company Occurs at Level 4 (and below)

D1 Deliver Stocked Product

| D1.7 Select Carriers & Rate Shipments | D1.6 Route Shipments | D1.5 Plan & Build Loads | D1.4 Consolidate Orders | D1.3 Reserve Inventory & Determine Delivery Date | D1.2 Receive, Enter & Validate Order | D1.1 Process Inquiry & Quote |

From Make or Source | D1.8 Receive Product at Warehouse | D1.9 Pick Product | D1.10 Load Vehicle, Generate Ship Docs, Verify Credit & Ship | D1.11 Receive & Verify Product at Customer Site | D1.12 Install Product | D1.13 Invoice |

Level 4   Process Element - D1.2   Tasks
Receive Order → Enter Order → Check Credit → Validate Price

Level 5   Task - D1.2.3   Activities
Access Credit Screen   Check Credit Availability   Clear Order   Contact Accounting   Communicate Results to Customer

▶ Below Level 3, each process element is described by classic hierarchical process decomposition

Level 6
1. Contact customer account rep.
2. Look up customer history
3. If necessary, account rep. calls sales manager to authorize additional credit
4a. Account rep. clears credit issue
4b. Account rep. refuses credit request

12

Supply-Chain Council

The Concept of "Configurability"

A supply-chain configuration is driven by:

- ▶ Plan levels of aggregation and information sources
- ▶ Source locations and products
- ▶ Make production sites and methods
- ▶ Deliver channels, inventory deployment and products
- ▶ Return locations and methods

SCOR must accurately reflect how a supply-chain's configuration impacts management processes and practices.

Each Basic Supply-Chain is a "Chain" of Source, Make, and Deliver Execution Processes

Configurability

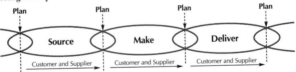

Each intersection of two execution processes (Source-Make-Deliver) is a "link" in the supply chain

- ▶ Execution processes transform or transport materials and/or products
- ▶ Each process is a customer of the previous process and a supplier to the next

Planning processes manage these customer-supplier links

- ▶ Planning processes thus "balance" the supply chain
- ▶ Every link *requires* an occurrence of a plan process category

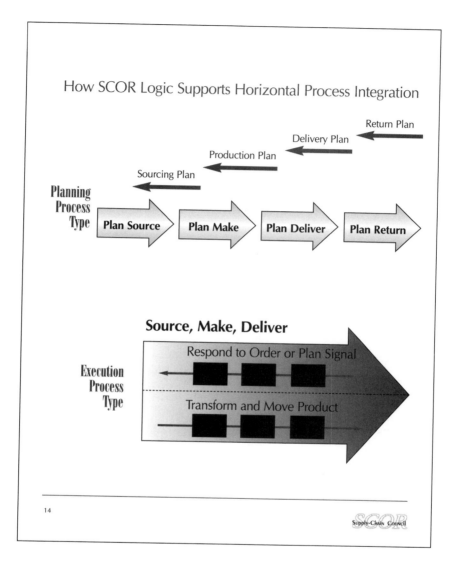

How SCOR Describes One SCM Trade-off
Make-to-Stock Configuration

Common SCM objective — achieve "market-winning" fulfillment time with the least inventory risk. *Example:* "pure" make-to-stock configuration. Plan Deliver and Deliver activities are taken upon receipt of Customer Order.

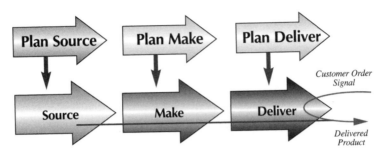

Common SCM objective — achieve "market-winning" fulfillment time with the least inventory risk. *Example:* Replenish-to-order Deliver network. Plan Deliver activities are already in place and ready to be executed when Customer Order Signal is received.

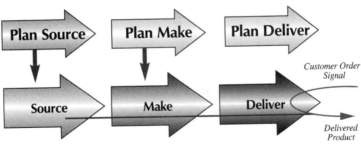

15

How SCOR Describes One SCM Trade-off
Make-to-Order Configuration

Common SCM objective — achieve "market-winning" fulfillment time with the least inventory risk. *Example:* make-to-order configuration. Plan Make and Plan Deliver activities are already in place and ready to be executed when Customer Order Signal is received.

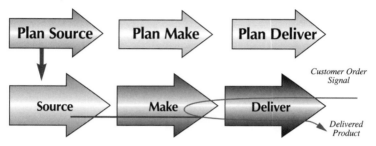

Common SCM objective — achieve "market-winning" fulfillment time with the least inventory risk. *Example:* make-to-order configuration that extends through the Source process. All interenterprise planning functions are already in place and ready to be executed when Customer Order Signal is received. This scheme requires some degree of intraenterprise P1 Planning.

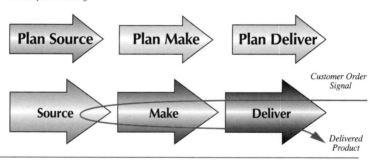

16

Configuring Supply-Chain Threads

Configuring a supply-chain "thread" illustrates how SCOR configurations are done. Each thread can be used to describe, measure, and evaluate supply-chain configurations.

1. Select the business entity to be modeled (geography, product set, organization)

2. Illustrate the physical locations of:

   ► Production facilities (Make)

   ► Distribution activities (Deliver)

   ► Sourcing activities (Source)

3. Illustrate primary point-to-point material flows using "solid line" arrows

4. Place the most appropriate Level 2 execution process categories to describe activities at each location

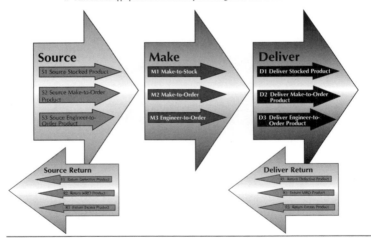

Supply Chain Threads are Developed from the Geographic Product Flow

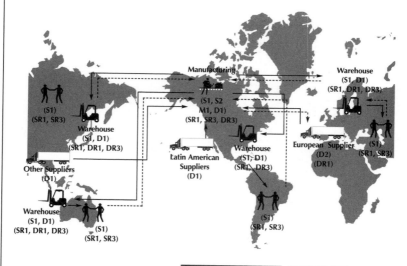

Manufacturing

Warehouse
(S1, D1)
(SR1, DR1, DR3)

(S1)
(SR1, SR3)

Warehouse
(S1, D1)
(SR1, DR1, DR3)

(S1, S2
M1, D1)
(SR1, SR3, DR3)

Latin American
Suppliers
(D1)

Warehouse
(S1, D1)
(SR1, DR3)

European Supplier
(D2)
(DR1)

(S1)
(SR1, SR3)

Other Suppliers
(D1)

Warehouse
(S1, D1)
(SR1, DR1, DR3)

(S1)
(SR1, SR3)

(S1)
(SR1, SR3)

	Consumers		Production Site
	Suppliers		Return
	Warehouse		Execution Process

SCOR Process Maps are Used as a Basis for Evaluating/Understanding the Supply Chain

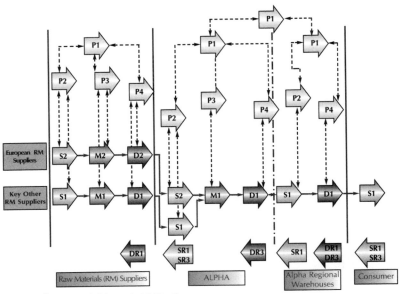

5. Describe each distinct supply-chain "thread"

    - A supply-chain thread ties together the set of Source-Make-Deliver supply-chain processes that a given product family flows through

    - Develop each thread separately to understand common, and distinct, execution and return process categories

    - Consider end-to-end threads in the inter-company case

6. Place planning process categories, using dashed lines to show links with execution processes

7. Place P1, if appropriate

    - P1 - Plan Supply Chain aggregates outputs from P2, P3, and P4

SCOR
Supply-Chain Council

19

In a Classic Logistics World

A change in a supply chain often "ripples" through each linkage, affecting other areas.

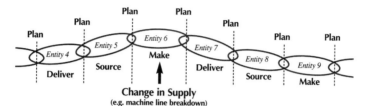

Change in Supply
(e.g. machine line breakdown)

The impact of a change can be felt both up and down the supply chain

► A change in supply caused by a "production planner" may impact a "materials planner" and an "inventory planner"

► Further, such a change may impact both your customer's and supplier's supply-chain planning

Effective Supply-Chain Management
Requires Balancing Multiple Links Concurrently

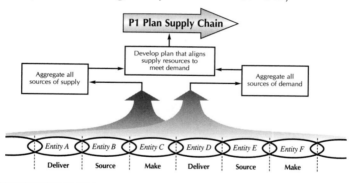

20

SCOR Overview: Summary

SCOR is a process reference model designed for effective communication among supply-chain partners.

- A standard *language* helps management to focus on management issues
- As an industry *standard*, SCOR helps management focus across inter-company supply chains

SCOR is used to *describe, measure* and *evaluate* Supply-Chain configurations

- **Describe:** Standard SCOR process definitions allow virtually any supply-chain to be configured.
- **Measure:** Standard SCOR metrics enable measurement and benchmarking of supply-chain performance.
- **Evaluate:** Supply-chain configurations may be evaluated to support continuous improvement and strategic planning.

Appendix B

Fowlers' Business Context Summary

■ Strategic Profile

Business Description

Fowlers Inc., is a billion-dollar conglomerate with worldwide leadership in three businesses: food processing (food products group), optical technology products (technology products group), and business services (durable products group). Fundamental to the success is the Fowlers mission to continually exceed customer expectations. The company and its employees believe that if they go beyond what customers require, those customers will return again and again.

Food Products Group

Fowlers is a leading North American supplier of premium fresh and frozen meat products and management services to the food service, retail, online retail, and government sectors. Customers include SuperValu, Walmart, Aramark, Simon Delivers, and thousands of independent groceries and specialty restaurants.

Technology Products Group

Fowlers is one of the world's largest independent suppliers of optical storage products and services such as CD-ROM replication; CD-R and CD-W media; title fulfillment and distribution services; and optical drives. Customers include retail leaders like Wal-Mart and Target as well as category leaders like Best Buy, Circuit City, Office Max, and CompUSA. Fowlers is also a major supplier to the North American original equipment manufacturers for the personal computer market. Customers include HP, Dell, and Apple Computer.

Durable Products Group

Fowlers acquired one of the United States' fastest growing suppliers of business services providing personalized apparel, office supplies, and promotional products to over 14,000 companies and 1 million individual wearers. Using a dealer franchise as the route delivery mechanism, Fowlers has gained a competitive edge as being both knowledgeable and responsive to individual customers in the markets it serves.

■ SWOT Analysis Summary

Strengths

- ❑ Product quality in both the food products group and technical products group is superior.
- ❑ Fowlers had achieved low-cost manufacturer status in the technical products group prior to outsourcing several key items in the product line.

❑ The durable products group is perceived to be the most responsive in its chosen geographic markets, often delivering products and services on the same day as the request.

❑ The food products group has earned the reputation for superior delivery performance, mitigating criticism of premium prices in a commodity marketplace.

❑ Growth in durable products exceeds expectations.

Weaknesses

❑ Organizational assimilation of the new Tier One enterprise resource planning system.

❑ Delivery performance is inconsistent, especially in the technical products group; customer complaints in this market are especially high. Because the market visibility is so high, Fowlers is developing a reputation in the customer's eyes as being "tough to do business with" (hard to place an order, incomplete and incorrect product shipments, inaccurate pricing, poor order status capability, etc.). This is negatively impacting overall satisfaction ratings.

❑ Erosion of operating income in the food and technical product groups due to price pressure.

❑ Costs to purchase increasing despite lower cost of sales.

❑ Rate of cost increase for customer service cost centers are substantially outpacing sales.

❑ In spite of sales growth, Fowlers' stock price has taken a hit due to five quarters of poor profit-after-tax results and a bloating cash-to-cash cycle; analyst criticism focused on Fowlers' inability to effectively manage return on assets and integrate profit potential of the business services acquisition.

Opportunities

❑ Leverage commodity buys across all Fowlers product groups to improve gross profit.

❑ Improve effectiveness and efficiency of order fulfillment to improve customer satisfaction and indirect spend.
❑ Develop more advanced knowledge management capability to add financial value to customers beyond pure price decrease.
❑ Accelerate market share in the durable products group by introducing an online catalogue for end customers.
❑ Leverage cost-to-manufacture leadership in the technical products group to increase profits.

Threats

❑ Key competitors in the food products group are buying their way into the marketplace using a "lowest list price" strategy.
❑ Technical products group market share is declining faster than the market overall; customer satisfaction scores put it in the lowest quartile of performance.
❑ Price point in the technical products group is getting too low to meet profit targets with the current cost structure.
❑ Established catalogue apparel companies are potential competitors to the online sales channel being introduced this quarter by the durable products group.

■ Value Proposition

Fowlers will grow profitably as the preferred supplier of customers in our targeted markets, driven by exceeding customer requirements.

Critical Success Factors

❑ Maintain revenue contribution by increasing share of food products group product line in existing markets preserving OI (operating income) return.

❑ Drive revenue growth by introducing durable products in the direct-to-consumer market and capturing targeted share.
❑ Achieve overall revenue growth for current year, targeted at 10 percent and after-tax profit of 7 percent.
❑ Maintain image as technical leader in technical products group and food products group product lines while improving overall return on assets.
❑ Rapidly optimize newly implemented Tier One enterprise resource planning system.
❑ Effectively integrate assets of new acquisition.

Critical Business Issues

❑ Customer satisfaction from all channels in the technical products group is negatively impacting sales.
❑ Profits are disappearing from the technology and food products group products based on higher direct and indirect costs.
❑ Revenue forecast to grow to $1.018 billion; actual projection after nine months is $1.000 billion.
❑ Durable products group integration of online capability is behind schedule.
❑ Inventory and receivables are expanding seemingly uncontrollably.
❑ Key customers in food products group are leaving based on price-only criteria.

Fowlers Financial Information

Fowlers 2000, 2001 Consolidated Income Statement (in millions)

	2001	2000	Change
Revenue	1,000	925	8%
Cost of Revenue (Sales) Expense	860	750	15%
Gross Profit	140	175	-20%
%	14%	19%	
Selling, General, Administrative Expenses	70	65	8%

Research and Development Expense	0	0	0%
Total Operating Expenses	930	815	14%
Operating Income	70	110	−36%
%	7%	12%	
Interest Expense	(10)	(11)	−9%
Income Before Tax	60	99	−39%
%	6%	11%	
Income Tax Expense	23	38	−39%
Income After Tax	37	61	−39%
%	4%	7%	
Extra Item Expense	(2)	(3)	−33%
Net Income	35	58	−40%
%	4%	6%	

Fowlers 2000, 2001 Consolidated Balance Sheet (in millions)

	2001	2000	Change
Cash and Short-Term Investments	20	15	26%
Total Receivables	371	370	0%
Total Inventory	215	175	19%
Other Current Assets	50	58	−17%
Total Current Assets	656	618	6%
Property/Plant Equipment Gross	269	248	8%
Accumulated Depreciation	(140)	(123)	12%
Goodwill	122	116	5%
Long-Term Investments	16	14	15%
Other Long-Term Assets	24	25	−4%
Total Net Assets	291	279	4%
Accounts Payables	72	62	14%
Accrued Expenses	31	32	−3%
Short-Term Debt	21	26	−24%
Leases	2	2	20%
Other Current Liabilities	62	60	4%
Total Current Liabilities	188	181	4%
Long-Term Debt	76	71	6%
Minority Interest	11	13	−14%
Other Liabilities	40	43	−6%
Total Liabilities	127	127	0%

Total Employees	6,200	5,700
$/Employee expressed in real $	$161,290	$162,281

Fowlers Product Group Revenue and Operating Income Performance

	Food Products			Technology Products			Durable Products		
	2001	2000	Change	2001	2000	Change	2001	2000	Change
Revenue	250	278	−10%	450	463	−3%	300	185	62%
Cost of Revenue (Sales) Expense	215	225	−4%	390	375	4%	255	150	70%
Gross Profit	35	53	−33%	60	88	−31%	45	35	29%
%	14%	19%		13%	19%		10%	8%	
Selling, General, Administrative Expenses	18	20	−10%	35	33	8%	18	13	35%
Research and Development Expense	0	0		0	0		0	0	
Total Operating Expenses	233	245	−5%	425	408	4%	273	163	67%
Operating Income	18	33	−47%	25	55	−55%	28	22	25%
%	7%	12%		6%	12%		6%	5%	

◼ Financial Performance–Key Points

- ❑ Based on 2000 and 2001 actual costs and revenues as reported in the annual reports.
- ❑ Cost-of-revenue ratio of direct to indirect expense
  Food products group—80 percent to 20 percent
  Technology products group—65 percent to 35 percent
  Durable products group—35 percent to 65 percent
- ❑ Cost of capital (money) for Fowlers is 10 percent

Internal Profile

Organization

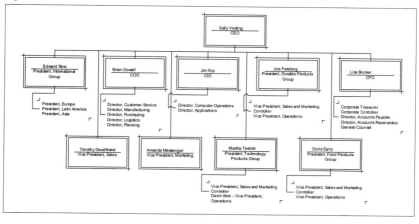

■ Manufacturing Locations

- ❑ Food products group has three plants: Des Moines, IA; Madison, WI; and Minneapolis, MN.
- ❑ Technical products group has four plants: San Jose, CA; Chicago, IL; St. Paul, MN; and Memphis, TN.
- ❑ Durable products group has four plants: Houston, TX; Dallas, TX; New Orleans, LA; and Atlanta, GA.

■ Distribution Locations

Fowlers owns and operates four regional distribution centers: Portland, OR; Atlanta, GA; Harrisburg, PA; and Santa Fe, NM. Durable products group has one additional distribution center in Kansas City, MO, and twelve branch sales locations supporting plant capacity and servicing customer routes in the southeast.

■ Key Performance Indicators (Bold is bad, plain text is good)

Unit Cost
Line Item Fillrate
Operating Income
Revenue (Growth)
Backorders

■ External Profile

Market Channel/Customer

- ❑ Retail markets including mass merchant and category killer

- ❑ Distributor/wholesaler markets
- ❑ Direct-to-consumer markets
- ❑ OEM/key account customers
- ❑ Home delivery/route sales markets

Suppliers

- ❑ Main raw material commodity types include resins, packaging, electronic components, live produce, hard goods, and apparel.
- ❑ There are several contract manufacturers that supply apparel, optical media, precooked food, and computer hardware.

Appendix C

Fowlers' Supply Chain Improvement Project Charter

Project Sponsor: Brian Dowell, chief operating officer
Department: Operations
Project Manager: David Able, vice president operations—technology products
Start Date: Aug. 5, 2002
Approval Date: Targeted for Sept. 2, 2002
Revision Date:

1. Introduction

Purpose of the Project Charter

The project charter is created during the initiation phase of a project to ensure that a complete understanding of the project

The source for Appendix C is Pragmatek Consulting Group © 2000. Used with permission.

scope and objectives is established. The document allows confirmation of assumptions and expectations with the executive team, project sponsors, stakeholders, project managers, program manager project, and validation and resource team members. During the course of the project, change requests may be generated and approved that vary the scope, schedule, or cost of the project. These changes should be documented through the change management process and updates reflected through revisions of the project charter.

Project Charter Contents

The project charter documents the background and business need for the project as well as expectations for the project moving forward. The project overview provides the project scope, business and project objectives, and any assumptions. The project approach outlines the methodology to be used in completing the project along with the schedule, milestones, deliverables, and any project dependencies. A budget for the project is presented and the organization of the project team is discussed. Project expectations will be discussed and how project success will be measured. A plan for communication on the project will also be presented.

Maintenance of the Project Charter

After the initial approval by project sponsor, the project charter will be updated with approved change requests and noted with a revision date on the cover page.

■ 11. Project Overview

Scope—Summary

Supply Chain Definition Matrix		Geography—Customer or Market Channel						
		U.S. Retail Markets	U.S. Distributor Markets	U.S. Direct-to-Consumer Markets	U.S. OEM—Key Accounts	U.S. Government	U.S. Home Delivery	International
Product	Food Products	X	X	X		X		
	Technology Products	X			X			
	Durable Products							

In Scope—White Areas

In addition to the product lines and channels summarized in the supply chain definition matrix, other organizational, process, people, and technology performance drivers considered in scope include:

1. Relevant supply chain functions at corporate level and in business units
2. SCOR Level One metrics and specified shareholder metrics for profitability, effectiveness of return, and share performance estimated in Three SCORcards.
3. SCOR Level One, Two, and Three process types including PLAN, SOURCE, MAKE, DELIVER, and RETURN.
4. Technology architecture mapped to SCOR Level Three process types.
5. Physical locations for the U.S. food and technology products group supply chains, including four domestic regional distribution centers, four manufacturing plants that "MAKE" for the technology products group, three manufacturing plants that "MAKE" for the Food Products Group, raw material suppliers of resin, packaging, and live produce, and contract manufacturers for optical media, precooked food, and optical drives.

6. Specific product lines in scope for the U.S. technology products group supply chain are CD-ROM replication, fulfillment, and life cycle management; optical drives; and optical media. Specific product lines in scope for the U.S. food products group supply chain are fresh, frozen, and precooked.

7. Detailed market/customer channels in scope for the U.S. technology products group supply chain are all retail, including mass merchants/category killer, OEM, and distributor. Detailed market/customer channels in scope for the U.S. food products group supply chain are retail/mass merchant grocery; retail/independent grocery; retail/online grocery; and food service distributor.

Out of Scope—Gray Area

The product lines and channels are summarized in the supply chain definition matrix. Other organizational, process, people, and technology performance drivers considered out of scope of this project include durable products group, market/customer channels, and sales represented in international and current or planned acquisitions.

Business Objectives

Aligned with the Fowlers Critical Success Factors and Key Performance Indicator improvements for 2002:

1. Improve cash-to-cash.
2. Improve delivery performance.
3. Improve operating margin.
4. Develop effective supply chain knowledge management capability.
5. Improve utilization of Tier One ERP system to leverage capital investment.

Project Objectives

1. Set competitive performance requirements by supply chain. Create a SCORcard for each supply chain, as well as a consolidated enterprise SCORcard.
2. Identify gaps between current and desired performance.
3. Define the current material, work, and information flow for each supply chain, identify the disconnects/inefficiencies in the flows, and quantify the internal and external impacts of the disconnects.
4. Create TO BE material, work, and information flows for each supply chain, incorporating the high-level supply chain strategy and appropriate leading practices; addressing identified disconnects and closing or narrowing the identified SCORcard gaps.
5. Create and communicate a prioritized list of supply chain change recommendations to support a multiyear project portfolio of improvements.
6. Develop internal Fowlers competence in implementing SCOR projects in the future.

▓ III. Project Approach

Methodology

SCOR (Supply Chain Operations Reference) model version 5.0 will be used to analyze basis of competition, configure material, work, and information flows, identify disconnects, align processes and systems, and define processes to meet internal and external performance standards. SCOR has a set of tools and templates that will guide us through reviewing Fowlers' worldwide performance in the areas of PLAN, SOURCE, MAKE, DELIVER, and RETURN.

Project Schedule

MILESTONE	START	FINISH
Project Initiation and Management	8/5/02	8/23/02
Phase 1—Discover the Opportunity Project Charter, Scope Review/Approval, Project Kickoff	8/26/02	8/30/02
Phase 2—Analyze Basis of Competition Supply Chain SCORcard and Gap Analysis	9/2/02	9/27/02
Phase 3—Material Flow Analysis and Design	9/30/02	11/1/02
Phase 4—Work & Information Flow Analysis and Design	11/4/02	12/13/02
Implementation Planning	12/16/02	12/20/02

Design Team Meetings, Two Days Per Week Face-to-Face

Week Tasks
1. Planning and organizing
2. Project kickoff and SCOR metrics
3. Benchmarks, competitive requirements, steering team review number one
4. SCORcards
5. SCORcard gap analysis, initiate AS IS material flow, steering team review number two
6. AS IS material flow performance summary
7. Material flow disconnect analysis, steering team review number three

8. Disconnect and opportunity analysis
9. Opportunity summaries, initiate TO BE material flow, steering team review number four
10. TO BE material flow
11. Quick-hit plans, steering team review number five, initiate work and information flow analysis
12. Staple yourself analysis
13. AS IS swim diagram, steering team review number six
14. AS IS productivity summary
15. TO BE work and information flow blueprint, steering team review number seven
16. TO BE summary, project portfolio
17. Implementation planning, steering team review number eight

Steering Team Meetings

MTG. #	FOCUS	DATE
1	Supply chain metric definitions, competitive requirements	9/13/02
2	Supply chain SCORcard and gap analysis; approve supply chain design recommendations	9/27/02
3	Material flow disconnect analysis	10/11/02
4	Opportunity summary and leading practices	10/25/02
5	TO BE material flow	11/8/02
6	AS IS swim diagram	11/22/02
7	Work and information flow productivity opportunity summary	12/6/02
8	Project portfolio, projected ROI, preliminary implementation plans	12/20/02

Project Deliverables

1. Business context document
2. Project charter

3. Customized SCOR education material
4. Supply chain definition matrix
5. Industry competitive summary
6. SCORcard, competitive requirements, gap analysis
7. Material flow performance assessment
8. Material flow SCOR level two configuration, leading practice summary
9. Staple yourself analysis interview list by transaction type
10. SCOR level three quick reference guide
11. Transactional analysis summary for all appropriate SCOR level three elements
12. AS IS swim diagrams
13. Transaction productivity summaries for purchase order, work order, sales order, return authorization, forecast, and replenishment order
14. TO BE SCOR level three work and information flow blueprints
15. Logical test—business scenarios
16. Gross opportunity summary—disconnect grid
17. Project portfolio and estimated return on investment schedule

Risks and Dependencies

1. Executive sponsorship from Fowlers' business units
2. A Fowlers financial analyst will be available for performance requirements and benchmarking phase of the project.
3. Availability of in-scope worldwide Fowlers raw historical data to collect and calculate actual performance against SCOR methodology
4. Consistent availability of steering committee and design team members

Project Budget

Coach	50 Days @ $2,000 per day	$100K
Expense	SCC Membership	$2K
	PMG Competitive Benchmarking	2K
Total		$104K

Project Organization Chart

Steering Team
Joe Farelong, President—Durable Products Groups Martha Tekitch, President—Technology Products Group Doris Early, President—Food Products Group Lisa Booker, CFO Tim Goodfriend, Vice President—Sales Amanda Messenger, Vice President—Marketing Jim Erp, CIO Brian Dowell, COO—**Project Sponsor**

Design Team
Director, Logistics Director, Customer Service Director, Manufacturing Director, Purchasing Director, Planning VP Sales and Marketing—Food Products Group Corporate Controller Director, Applications VP Operations, Technology Products Group—**Project Manager** SCOR Coach

Roles and Responsibilities—Fowlers Steering Team

1. Ensure organizational commitment.
2. Resolve cross-functional issues.
3. Provide resources in support of program as needed.
4. Support change management cross-functionally.
5. Prioritize projects within the program and enterprise.

Fowlers Project Sponsor

1. Endorse and communicate changes.
2. Communicate and represent the business vision and objectives of the initiative.
3. Measure team progress against deliverables.
4. Initiate and champion projects.
5. Provide resource support to the design team.
6. Review and approve deliverables at project milestones.
7. Resolve escalated issues.
8. Initiate and champion projects identified.
9. Approve and manage budget and schedule.
10. Ensures availability of key resources.
11. Provide final approval for all changes within defined scope.

Fowlers Project Manager

1. Staff project team.
2. Facilitate design team and business interactions.
3. Serve as liaison between project team and executive sponsors.
4. Define, communicate, and facilitate necessary changes to policies and standards.
5. Measure team progress against deliverables.
6. Ensure that project staff and vendor communications, morale, and quality of work-life is conducive to the successful attainment of project objectives.
7. Manage all external resources assigned to the project to contractual commitment.
8. Manage all aspects of the project in a manner consistent with Fowlers' business requirements, policies, project management methodology, and budget procedures.
9. Define and plan the project. Responsible for establishing quality standards and acceptance criteria in the statement of work.
10. Manage project budget and timeline.
11. Escalate the resolution of critical issues.
12. Identify, manage, and communicate project constraints.
13. Ensure that project staff and vendors complete all deliverables as defined in the statement of work, according to

the terms and conditions of the statement of work or subsequent change orders.

14. Obtain necessary deliverable approvals.
15. Define required staffing.
16. Create and recommend change orders to the statement of work where required for the successful attainment of the business vision and objectives.

Fowlers Design Team

1. Expected to be available for twenty hours per week for team meetings and other blocks of time as required.
2. Complete any assigned work on time including all project deliverables.
3. Identify competitive requirements and put together SCORcard.
4. Identify current material, work, and information flows.
5. Identify material, work, and information disconnects.
6. Define and document desired material, work, and information flows.
7. Prioritize supply chain improvements and the supply chain improvement plan.
8. Provide subject matter expertise as requested.
9. Review and validate design team deliverables.

Fowlers Extended Team

1. Expect to be available by appointment with advance notice.
2. Participate in team meetings, as required.
3. Contribute to all activities of the design team as requested.

Coach

1. Provide training to the Fowlers project team in the understanding and utilization of the SCOR model.
2. Participate in the modeling and disconnect analysis of Fowlers' supply chains.

3. Facilitate leading-practices discussion and analysis.
4. Provide supply chain content expertise

Benefits and Measures of Success—Stakeholder Expectations

Based on stakeholder interviews, the following key points represent a summary of expectations:

1. Improve corporate inventory turns
2. Cross-functional process changes, ownership
3. Superior delivery
4. Purchased finished goods (merchandise) turns from five to ten
5. Improve transaction process with suppliers
6. Complete metrics for each area of the supply chain
7. Clearly identify supply chain performance gaps
8. Drive 2002 and 2003 profit after-tax performance
9. Expand supply chain knowledge of the team
10. Develop a repeatable process for future SCOR initiatives

Benchmarks

1. Supply-Chain Council—Performance Measurement Group (PMG) for SCOR level one metrics
2. Existing internal benchmarking data from operational business units
3. Hoovers.com industry comparison for general 10K income statement and balance sheet financial measures

Benefit Analysis

Supply chain improvement project portfolio and projected return on investment is the final deliverable for "analyze and design." Based on experience, the average size of project portfolios is 3 percent operating income improvement. The project portfolio will be sequenced to yield a minimum of $208,000, based on 2X return-on-investment of the green-dollar cost of this project.

Project Communication

A formal communication plan will be established for each group of stakeholders in this project including the steering team, project manager, design team, extended team, and Fowlers at large.

Project Name: *Fowlers Supply Chain Improvement Project*				
Project Manager: *David Able*				
Stakeholders	**Communication Need**	**Communication Method**	**Communication Contents**	**Frequency**
Steering Team	• Create awareness • Establish commitment • Monitor and evaluate progress • Issue escalation and resolution	• Meetings • One on one • Team • Updates from Project and/or Program Managers & Quality Assurance • Project Status Reports	• Schedule and budget updates • Issue management • Change management • Risk management	• Biweekly and as needed by project phase
Project Manager	• Milestone management • Create awareness • Establish commitment • Coordinate dependent activities • Issue escalation and resolution	• Team Status Reports (Meeting Minutes) • Deliverable Review	• Schedule and budget updates • Issue management • Change management • Risk management • Resource management • Procurement management	• Weekly as needed
Design Team	• Activity coordination • Work prioritization • Issue escalation and resolution • One-on-one meetings with executive and validation team members	• Updates from project manager • Project Plan • Team Status Meetings	• Activities and dates	• Weekly and as needed by project phase
Extended Team	• Activity coordination • Work prioritization • Issue escalation and resolution	• Updates from project manager and/or design team • Project Plan	• Activities and dates	• As needed

Appendix D

Partial List of SCOR Model Leading Practices, Sorted by Business Area

Business Planning

Activity-based accounting
Advanced planning optimization
Asset optimization
Attribute-based process planning
Collaborative planning, forecast, and replenishment
Constraint-based planning
Demand-driven production
Make/buy decision process
Multiplant supply synchronization
Operations and network analysis
Sales and operations planning
Service/inventory balancing
Strategic sourcing

The source for Appendix D is Streamline ECM © 2002. Used with permission.

Customer Service

Automated order validation
Automatic documentation generation
Available-to-promise
Cost-to-serve price structure
Customer data validation
Customer profitability review
Customer relationship management
Customer service measurement
Customer team empowerment
Delinquent account resolution
Dynamic order scheduling and allocation
Efficient consumer response
Integrated credit checking
Integrated order editing
Order segmentation
Quote generation without resource allocation
Remote order entry

Delivery

Compliance labeling
Exact delivery scheduling
Factory direct shipment
Integrated customs processing
Integrated load management
Load balancing
Pay on receipt

Demand Management

Demand planning, demand flow leadership
Dynamic restock prioritization
Instantaneous supply synchronization
Integrated sales promotions

Item level demand planning
Point of sale demand integration
Pull production systems
Real-time consumption data

■ E-Commerce

Electronic conformance documentation
Electronic data interchange
Electronic invoicing
Electronic manifesting
Electronic order management
Electronic product transfer
Electronic sourcing
Electronic sourcing rules
Online business rules
Online catalogues
Online documentation
Online marketplaces
Online order tracking
Online ordering
Online production status
Online request for quote
Online resource management
Online rule management
Online schedule integration
Online scheduling
Online shipment tracking
Online source data
Online spend data
Online supplier evaluation
Online transaction services
Partner trading network
XML or EDI data transfer

■ Information Management

Advance ship notices
Advanced planning/ERP integration

Automated data entry, barcode
Automatic Identification, RFID
Business intelligence
Business rules repository
Cross-organizational data visibility
DRP/ERP integration
Electronic batch recording/configuration
Enterprise data visibility
Enterprise information systems
Integrated logistics systems
Material backflush
Mode-specific data capture
Process data integration
Production data integration
Real-time production data
Regulatory requirements repository
Single customer data source
VMI system integration

Inventory Control

ABC classification
Consigned inventory
Date-based part management
Dynamic location assignment
Dynamic pick simulation
First in/first out inventory
Genealogy tracking
Inventory, cycle counting
Inventory disposition rules
Inventory lot reporting
Inventory ownership rules
Item profile analysis
Item segmentation and disposition
Item traceability
Kanban replenishment systems
Lot traceability
On-hand inventory visibility

Point of use delivery
Point of use replacement
Real-time inventory control
Removal of obsolete stock
Speed racks
Strategic safety stock
Vendor-managed inventory
WIP handling rules
WIP inventory optimization

Return Product Management

Advance planning systems, return
Automated ROA management
Dynamic return restocking
Historical return analysis
Rapid reconfigurable return capacity
Real-time return anticipation
Return product data visibility
Return product forecasting

Supplier Management

Automated supplier performance updates
Blanket purchase orders
Cost of nonconformance analysis
Enterprise level spend analysis
Enterprise spend consolidation
Inventory program, Kanban
Inventory programs, consignment
Inventory programs, vendor managed
Joint service agreements
Just-in-time agreements
Long-term supplier agreements
Performance-based sourcing
Postponed inventory agreements

Purchase contract sharing
Strategic spend groupings
Supplier certification programs
Supplier development programs
Supplier performance rating
Supplier qualification systems

Transportation management

Back-haul trading exchanges
Carrier performance analysis
Carriers consolidation
Freight consolidation
Load optimization
Load sequencing
Route optimization
Route scheduling
Transportation modeling and rate analysis

Appendix E

SCOR Version 5.0 Quick Reference Guide

The source for Appendix E is Pragmatek Consul~~~~~~~~~~ ~00. Used
with permission.

ENABLE

EP Enable Plan	ES Enable Source	EM Enable Make	ED Enable Deliver	ER Enable Return
EP.1 Manage Business Rules for PLAN Processes	ES.1 Manage Sourcing Business Rules	EM.1 Manage Production Rules	ED.1 Manage Deliver Business Rules	ER.1 Manage Business Rules for Return Processes
EP.2 Manage Performance of Supply Chain	ES.2 Assess Supplier Performance	EM.2 Manage Production Performance	ED.2 Assess Delivery Performance	ER.2 Manage Performance of Return Processes
EP.3 Manage PLAN Data Collection	ES.3 Maintain Source Data	EM.3 Manage Production Data	ED.3 Manage Deliver Information	ER.3 Manage Return Data Collection
EP.4 Manage Integrated Supply Chain Inventory	ES.4 Manage Product Inventory	EM.4 Manage In-Process Products (WIP)	ED.4 Manage Finished Product Inventories	ER.4 Manage Return Inventory

PLAN

P1 Plan Supply Chain	P2 Plan Source	P3 Plan Make	P4 Plan Deliver	P5 Plan Return
P1.1 Identify, Prioritize, and Aggregate Supply Chain Requirements	P2.1 Identify, Prioritize, and Aggregate Product Requirements	P3.1 Identify, Prioritize, and Aggregate Production Requirements	P4.1 Identify, Prioritize, and Aggregate Delivery Requirements	P5.1 Identify, Prioritize, and Aggregate Return Requirements
P1.2 Identify, Assess, and Aggregate Supply Chain Resources	P2.2 Identify, Assess, and Aggregate Product Resources	P3.2 Identify, Assess, and Aggregate Production Resources	P4.2 Identify, Assess, and Aggregate Delivery Resources	P5.2 Identify, Assess, and Aggregate Return Resources
P1.3 Balance Supply Chain Resources with Supply Chain Requirements	P2.3 Balance Product Resources with Product Requirements	P3.3 Balance Production Resources with Production Requirements	P4.3 Balance Delivery Resources with Delivery Requirements	P5.3 Balance Return Resources with Return Requirements
P1.4 Establish and Communicate Supply Chain Plans	P2.4 Establish Sourcing Plans	P3.4 Establish Production Plans	P4.4 Establish Delivery Plans	P5.4 Establish and Communicate Delivery Plans

EP.5 Manage Integrated Supply Chain Capital Assets	ES.5 Manage Capital Assets	EM.5 Manage Equipment and Facilities	ED.5 Manage Deliver Capital Assets	ER.5 Manage Return Capital Assets
EP.6 Manage Integrated Supply Chain Transportation	ES.6 Manage Incoming Product	EM.6 Manage Transportation	ED.6 Manage Transportation	ER.6 Manage Return Transportation
EP.7 Manage Planning Configuration	ES.7 Manage Supplier Network	EM.7 Manage Production Network	ED.7 Manage Product Life Cycle	ER.7 Manage Return Network Configuration
EP.8 Manage PLAN Regulatory Requirements and Compliance	ES.8 Manage Import/Export Requirements	EM.8 Manage Production Regulatory Compliance	ED.8 Manage Import/Export Requirements	ER.8 Manage Return Regulatory Requirements and Compliance
EP.9 Align Supply Chain Unit Plan with Financial Plan	ES.9 Manage Supplier Agreements			

	SOURCE			MAKE			DELIVER			RETURN		
	S1 Source Stocked Product	S2 Source Make-To-Order Product	S3 Source Engineer-to-Order Product	M1 Make-to-Stock	M2 Make-to-Order	M3 Engineer-to-Order	D1 Deliver Stocked Product	D2 Deliver Make-to-Order Product	D3 Deliver Engineer-to-Order Product	R1 Return Defective Product	R2 Return MRO Product	R3 Return Excess Product
.1	S1.1 Schedule Product Deliveries	S2.1 Schedule Product Deliveries	S3.1 Identify Sources of Supply	M1.1 Schedule Production Activities	M2.1 Schedule Production Activities	M3.1 Finalize Engineering	D1.1 Process Inquiry & Quote	D2.1 Process Inquiry & Quote	D3.1 Obtain and Respond to RFP/RFQ	DR1.1 Authorize Return	DR2.1 Authorize Return	DR3.1 Identify Excess Inventory
.2	S1.2 Receive Product	S2.2 Receive Product	S3.2 Select Final Supplier(s) and Negotiate	M1.2 Issue Product	M2.2 Issue Product	M3.2 Schedule Production Activities	D1.2 Receive, Enter, & Validate Order	D2.2 Receive, Configure, Enter and Validate Order	D3.2 Negotiate and Receive Contract	DR1.2 Schedule Product Return	DR2.2 Schedule MRO Product Return	DR3.2 Schedule Product Shipment
.3	S1.3 Verify Product	S2.3 Verify Product	S3.3 Schedule Product Deliveries	M1.3 Produce and Test	M2.3 Produce and Test	M3.3 Issue Product	D1.3 Reserve Inventory and Determine Delivery Date	D2.3 Reserve Resources and Determine Delivery Date	D3.3 Enter Order, Commit Resources and Launch Program	DR1.3 Receive Defective Product	DR2.3 Determine Product Condition	DR3.3 Receive Product Return
.4	S1.4 Transfer Product	S2.4 Transfer Product	S3.4 Receive Product	M1.4 Package	M2.4 Package	M3.4 Produce and Test	D1.4 Consolidate Orders	D2.4 Consolidate Orders	D3.4 Schedule Installation	SR1.4 Verify Defective Product	DR2.4 Transfer MRO Product	SR3.4 Approve Request Authorization

S1.5	S2.5	S3.5	M1.5	M2.5	M3.5	D1.5	D2.5	D3.5	SR1.5	SR2.5	SR3.5
Authorize Supplier Payment	Authorize Supplier Payment	Verify Product	Stage Product	Stage Product	Package	Plan and Build Loads	Plan and Build Loads	Plan and Build Loads and Shipments	Disposition Defective Product	Verify MRO Product Condition	Receive Excess Product Return
		S3.6 Transfer Product	**M1.6** Release Product to Deliver	**M2.6** Release Product to Deliver	**M3.6** Stage Product	**D1.6** Route Shipments	**D2.6** Route Shipments	**D3.6** Route Shipments, Select Carrier	**SR1.6** Return Replacement or Credit	**SR2.6** Disposition MRO Product	**SR3.6** Verify Excess Product
		S3.7 Authorize Supplier Payment			**M3.7** Release Product to Deliver	**D1.7** Select Carriers and Rate Shipments	**D2.7** Select Carriers and Rate Shipments	**D3.7** Pick Staged Product		**SR2.7** Request MRO Return Authorization	**SR3.7** Recover & Disposition Excess Product
						D1.8 Receive Product at Warehouse	**D2.8** Pick Staged Product	**D3.8** Load Vehicle, Generate Ship Docs & Ship Product			
						D1.9 Pick Product	**D2.9** Load Vehicle, Generate Ship Docs & Ship Product	**D3.9** Receive and Verify Product at Customer Site			
						D1.10 Load Vehicle, Generate Ship Docs, Verify Credit & Ship Product	**D2.10** Receive and Verify Product at Customer Site	**D3.10** Test and Install Product			
						D1.11 Receive & Verify Product at Customer Site	**D2.11** Test and Install Product	**D3.11** Invoice & Receive Payment			
						D1.12 Install Product	**D2.12** Invoice				
						D1.13 Invoice					

**DR=Deliver Return
SR=Source Return

Appendix F

SCOR and Six Sigma DMAIC Comparison

DMAIC	SCOR
Define	Analyze Basis of Competition
Measure	
Analyze	Configure Supply Chain
Improve	Align Performance Levels, Practices, and Systems
Control	Implement Supply Chain Changes

The source for Appendix F is Pragmatek Consulting Group, Ltd. © 2002. Used with permission.

DMAIC	SCOR
Define	Analyze Basis of Competition
DMAIC Project Charter	SCOR Project Charter Template Supply Chain Definition Matrix
Identify Customer Requirements: Kano Analysis; Voice of the Customer Analysis	Chip Exercise
Idenfity and Document the Process: SIPOC	Thread Diagram

DMAIC	SCOR
Measure	Analyze Basis of Competition
Appropriate Measures: CTQ; Stratification	SCOR Metrics Template SCORcard Baseline and Gap Analysis
Operational Definitions	
Data Sources, Data Collection, and Sampling	
Sigma Calculation: Unit, Defect, Defect Opportunities	SCOR Level 2 and 3 Measures for Material Flow Efficiency and Transactional Productivity
Yield	
Cost of Poor Quality	

DMAIC	SCOR
Analyze	Configure Supply Chain; Align Performance, Practices, and Systems
Data Analysis Pareto Chart, Run Chart, Histogram, Scatter Plot, and Fishbone Analysis	AS IS Material Flow: Geographic Map; Transportation, Inventory, Warehouse, and Returns Expense Summary; Delivery Performance and Order Fulfillment Lead Time Summary
Process Analysis: Detailed Process Maps, Cross-Functional Process Maps, Process Value and Time	AS IS Work and Information Flow: Staple Yourself Analysis; Swim Diagram; Transactional Productivity for purchase, work, replenishment, and sales orders; forecasts; and return authorizations

DMAIC	SCOR
Improve	Configure Supply Chain; Align Performance, Practices, and Systems Implement Supply Chain Changes
Generate Creative Solutions "Cook the Solutions"	TO BE Material Flow: SCOR Level 2 Configuration Strategy and Thread Diagram; Appropriate Leading Practices
	TO BE Work and Information Flow: SCOR Business Blueprint; Application Architecture—Use Case; Organizational Design—Swim Lane Efficiency
Select and Solution: Impact—Effort Matrix; Decision Matrix; Force Field Analysis	TO BE Work and Information Flow: SCOR Business Blueprint; Application Architecture—Use Case; Organizational Design—Swim Lane Efficiency
Pilot the Solution Full Scale Roll Out	Implement Supply Chain Changes: Detailed Solution Design; Pilot and Evaluation Roll Out Solution

DMAIC	SCOR
Control	Implement Supply Chain Changes
Discipline	Supply Chain Program Management Office
Documenting the Improvement	TO BE Business Blueprint, associated Material Flow Thread Diagrams, Supply Chain Definition Matrix
Keeping Score	SCORcard
Process Management Plan	Organizational Responsibility Matrix

DMAIC	SCOR
Six Sigma	SCOR
Leadership Council	Potential Core Planning Team and Steering Team Candidates
Champion—Sponsor	Active Executive Sponsor
Implementation Leader	Potential Evangelist
Master Black Belt—Coach	Potential Evangelist
Black Belt—Project Leader	Project Manager Candidate and Potential Evangelist
Green Belt—Team Members	Project Manager Candidate
Process Owner	Potential Core Planning Team and Steering Team Candidates

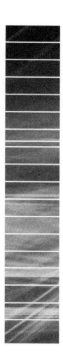

Index